THE POLITICS OF PREJUDICE

THE POLITICS OF PREJUDICE

*The Anti-Japanese Movement in California
and the Struggle for Japanese Exclusion*

ROGER DANIELS

University of California Publications in History Volume LXXI

NEW YORK ATHENEUM 1968

PREFACE

LOCAL AND regional history is all too often perverted into mere self-congratulation and other forms of civic boosterism. This study, by its very nature, falls toward the opposite extreme. Few contemporary Californians can be proud of the events narrated here; no monuments, commemorative plaques, or festivals may be expected to celebrate their anniversaries. Yet, less than a generation ago, the accomplishments of the anti-Japanese movement were viewed as great deeds; its leaders held the highest place in the commonwealth. Today the last legal vestiges of anti-Orientalism have been wiped from the state's statute books, although *de facto* discrimination lingers on. This revolutionary change in the climate of opinion will not be otherwise noted in these pages, nor will the many factors contributing to that change be analyzed. I cannot, however, forego the opportunity to express my firm conviction that the largest single causal component of that change was the undeniable fact that the vast bulk of California's Issei and their descendants were, despite almost continuous abuse and provocation, superlatively good citizens.

Some further stipulations are necessary lest this work be misunderstood. With the overwhelming majority of my contemporaries, I have little sympathy with the basic assumptions of the California exclusionists whose chronicler I have chosen to become. I have tried to understand them. To a very great degree, I have let them tell their own story; its unfolding must tarnish several reputations. Yet in no sense have I attempted to evaluate the total careers of the leaders involved. Almost all these men played many roles, and this study inspects only one facet—some would say flaw—of their public characters. To cite a conspicuous example, it would be foolhardy to attempt any sort of over-all evaluation of the public services (and disservices) of Hiram Johnson on the basis of the evidence presented here. Johnson was a leading actor in state and national life for almost four decades; his anti-Japanese role, crucial as it was, comprised only a small scene in a long public performance.

In the course of preparing this study, I traveled throughout the state and talked to hundreds of its citizens. Many of them expressed both surprise and regret that such a disagreeable set of events should be plucked from the dustbin of history. No historian really needs a justification for resifting the ashes of the past; he does it because they are there and because he must. Yet, in this case, as in perhaps most others, "ulterior" motives governed the selection of the particular heap of ashes to be sifted. I am persuaded that not nearly enough attention has been paid to the antidemocratic threads that make up a goodly part of the fabric of our national heritage, and that by careful studies of these threads we may discover hitherto unnoticed patterns. The main task here was to present in some detail the essentials of California's more than quarter-century struggle for Japanese exclusion; at the same time I made a consistent effort to make the data uncovered meaningful in a larger frame of reference.

In the process I think I have discerned two such patterns worthy of mention. Because of the problem of Oriental immigration, which dates from the 1850's, many Californians developed a frontier psychology more akin to that prevailing in the border marches of Europe than to the one hypothesized by Frederick Jackson Turner and his followers. The Californian often felt that his rocky coastline should serve as a bulwark or dike against the human sea of Asian immigrants which seemed to threaten his very way of life. If this is a valid observation, at least some of the more mechanical applications of the frontier thesis to California history should be reconsidered.

The study also clearly reveals that the generators of much of California's antidemocratic energy were those very groups supposedly dedicated to democracy: the labor unions, the progressives, and other left groups. Conversely, conservative forces—businessmen, educators, and clergymen—were often on the democratic side, or to be more precise, generally less antidemocratic. This is not to suggest that historians have mislabeled our political battery, but to point out that the opposition was a good deal less than polar. Perhaps the valid generalization to make here is that, so far as immigration matters were concerned, conservatives did less violence to the traditional American concepts of democracy than did their opponents.

Before turning to the task at hand, I would like to acknowledge at least the most pressing of the obligations I have acquired in the course of this study. My mentor, Professor Theodore Saloutos, provided guidance and friendship throughout the project. Many other members of the faculty of the University of California, Los Angeles, offered criticisms and suggestions: Professors Eugene N. Anderson, Keith Berwick, Harold Hyman, Blake Nevius, Lynn White, Jr., Robert Winter, and Robert Wilson were particularly helpful. A major part of the research was conducted at the Bancroft Library during 1959 and 1960; the entire staff was knowing and helpful, but special mention must be made of Mrs. Julia Macloud and Miss Estelle Rebec, who patiently and skillfully guided a neophyte through the intricacies of manuscript collections. Other thanks must go to the Library of the University of California, Los Angeles, the California State Library at Sacramento, and the public libraries of Los Angeles, San Francisco, and Berkeley. The morgues of the San Francisco *Chronicle* and the Los Angeles *Times* were opened to me. The University of California, Los Angeles, supported a year of research and writing with a university fellowship. Fellow graduate students—Richard Levensky, F. Thomas Foley, John Dizikes, Robert Hennings, Masakasu Iwata, Francis Schruben, and Hugh Walker—helped sharpen my ideas and were generous with their time. My wife, Judith Daniels, a historian herself, performed the drudgery of proofreading and editing with skill and good humor. Despite the help of these many accomplices, the final responsibility is my own.

ROGER DANIELS

CONTENTS

Chapter I

THE ISSEI GENERATION

"Of sea and the first plantings and the men,
And how they came in the ships, and to what end."
—S. V. Benét, *Western Star*

THIS STUDY will tell the story of California's anti-Japanese movement through its first major triumph, the Japanese exclusion provisions of the Immigration Act of 1924. The emphasis will thus be on the excluders rather than the excluded. But before our narrative can begin we must take an all too brief look at the real focus of the movement: the Issei in California and how they came there.[1]

In comparison with the vast stream of more than thirty million immigrants who came from Europe in the years between the end of the Civil War and 1924, the modest flow from Japan seems an insignificant trickle. Immigration from Japan may be conveniently divided into five periods:[2]

1. 1861–1890 Unrestricted and scattered............................... 3,000
2. 1891–1900 Unrestricted and growing 27,000
3. 1901–1908 Peak, unrestricted immigration 127,000
4. 1909–1924 Gentlemen's Agreement in effect........................ 118,000
5. 1925–1952 Exclusion; no immigration ....

Grand total (about) 275,000

Less than 300,000 souls, then, are what all the agitation was about. But even this is a misleading figure. Many of the immigrants were birds of passage who returned to Japan or went elsewhere; some made more than one trip, while of course others died. The census figures for Japanese immigrants and native-born give a much more accurate picture:

	United States	*California*
1880	148	86
1890	2,039	1,147
1900	24,326	10,151
1910	72,157	41,356
1920	111,010	71,952
1930	138,834	97,456

When compared with the total populations of California and the United States, the figures show that at the time of their highest incidence in the population, Japanese immigrants and native-born comprised two and one-tenth per cent (.021) of the population of California and one tenth of one per cent (.001) of the population of the continental

United States. The reader will do well to keep these figures in mind, for he will encounter some strange statistical manipulations thereof.

As the tables show, large numbers of Japanese did not begin to migrate to the United States until late in the nineteenth century. Their failure to do so earlier was not owing to ignorance, for Japanese had been in the New World exactly a decade before the Pilgrim Fathers; in 1610 and 1613 Japanese diplomatic missions visited Mexico.³ Their passage had been made relatively simple by nature. The Japanese Current will, almost automatically, bring eastbound ships from northern Japan to the Puget Sound area and on down the coast. This was the route of the fabled Manila Galleon.⁴ A hypothetical geographic determinist in the early seventeenth century could have concluded that while Europeans were destined to settle the eastern half of the North American continent, Japanese and other Orientals might well colonize its western slopes. This, of course, was not to be. After almost a century of intercourse with the Occident, the human beings who controlled the destinies of Japan decided, in 1638, that their country would be better off without such exotic influences. In that year Japan embarked on a policy of isolation which lasted for more than two centuries until its forcible rupture by Perry in 1853. Emigration did not become legal until 1886.

This does not mean that all contact was broken; curtains, whether of iron or bamboo, have never been a hundred per cent effective. Stranded and castaway Japanese seamen were frequently brought into contact with Americans. In the period from 1782 to 1856 at least thirteen Japanese vessels were shipwrecked on the Pacific Coast and a number of Japanese seamen were picked up at sea, with more than a few of the latter being brought to the United States.⁵ These contacts were largely ephemeral and have little significance for our story, although at least two such sailors received an American education and, upon their return to Japan, exerted some influence.⁶ After Perry and his black ships reopened Japan to the West, this hitherto accidental intercourse became regularized. Direct shipping between San Francisco and Japan was begun in 1855, and reciprocal diplomatic relations date from 1860.⁷

It is impossible to pinpoint the date of the earliest immigration from Japan to the United States, but it seems to have begun in the 1860's. Starting with a lone traveler in 1861, the statistics record that 185 Japanese entered the country in that decade, but it is not certain that all of them were immigrants.⁸ As we have seen, the census could find only 55 in 1870. The earliest group of Japanese settlers that I have been able to discover settled in Alameda County sometime in 1868. According to a local newspaper report they were educated men—there is no mention of any women—who spoke "English and French" and were "gentlemen of refinement and culture in their own country." They seem to have been political refugees.[9] The following year saw the founding of the celebrated but short-lived agricultural colony at Gold Hill, Eldorado County, which has been regarded as the first Japanese colony in the state. The settlers were led by J. H. Schnell, a German who had a Japanese wife and who claimed that he had been the consular representative of "Germany" in Japan. Encouraged by reports of the success of the earlier group, he tried to establish a large-scale agricultural colony which would produce commodities exotic to California—tea and silk. Schnell had a flair for publicity, but lacked talent for or experience in farming. He acquired 600 acres and probably invested at least $10,000 in his experiment, but the dry California summers proved too much for the tender tea bushes and mulberry trees; the colony failed and dispersed after two or three years.[10]

Despite the fact that California was, by the end of the 1860's, already violently anti-Chinese, it is interesting to note that these early colonists from Japan were received with great favor. A typical newspaper editorial pointed out that "the objections raised against the Chinese ... cannot be alleged against the Japanese.... They have brought their wives, children and ... new industries among us."[11] If there was a single word of protest raised against these early immigrants, I have failed to find record of it. This, then, was the early pattern of Japanese immigration—isolated colonies and educated individuals who were accepted and even absorbed with very little ado.[12] This early immigration was minuscular; the total Japanese population of the United States was only 148 persons according to the census of 1880, and in all probability the majority of these were students rather than immigrants.

In the next decade the whole pattern of Japanese immigration was to change. The reasons for that change were several: the socioeconomic dislocations brought about within Japan by the Westernization embarked upon during the Meiji restoration, the need of Hawaiian sugar planters for cheap labor, and the passage of the Chinese Exclusion Act by the United States Congress.

Almost everyone is aware of the rapid transformation which industrialization on the Occidental model wrought in nineteenth-century Japan. In 1850 she was isolated, her warriors crudely armed; by the turn of the century she was, militarily, a first-class power, although this did not become evident until 1905, when she defeated Russia. The measures necessary to bring about so striking a change naturally caused serious dislocations on all levels of Japanese life, and, as is usually the case, the heaviest burdens fell upon those least able to bear them—in this instance, the small farmers. By 1884 the leading English-language Japanese weekly could say:

> The depression . . . has increased month by month and year by year. . . . Most of the farmers have been unable to pay their taxes. . . . In more than one case self-destruction has been resorted to. . . . If any other territory can [support them] then we should say that it would be a judicious step to get them there as fast as possible.[13]

There was such a territory—the kingdom of Hawaii—and it had been trying to get Japanese laborers for its booming sugar plantations for several years, but the Japanese government had been unwilling to have its citizens emigrate as contract laborers because it rightly concluded that this would, in the long run, lower the prestige of Japan as a nation. The Chinese coolie trade had long been a stench in the nostrils of most of enlightened mankind, and Japan's one previous experience with the Hawaiian plantations had not been good. In 1868 (the year 1 of the Meiji era) one shipload of Japanese—141 men, 6 women, and 1 child—had been brought to Hawaii as contract laborers by the Hawaiian Board of Immigration. The terms of their contract called for the Japanese to perform thirty-six months of actual labor in Hawaii at the rate of $4 per man per month, half of which was to be withheld until the contract had been completed. Labor contracts were enforceable in Hawaii under the provisions of the Masters' and Servants' Act of 1850, which was modeled after the current laws governing merchant seamen. In Hawaii a worker could be sent to jail for breach of contract, i.e., quitting his job. To those who suggested, after the American Civil War, that such contracts smacked of slavery, the planters insisted that the law merely required that "a man do what he has contracted to do," and liked to argue that "the right to *break* a voluntarily made contract with impunity [did not constitute] any part of the system of free labor."[14]

Evidently the Japanese newspapers were aware of the conditions in Hawaii, for a loud roar of protest arose. A Yokohama newspaper compared the recruiting methods in Japan to "stealing Negroes" and pointed out that because of the revolution then in progress "even the government does not have time to deal with things of this sort," but it assured its readers that as soon as peaceful conditions were restored the government would put a stop to such practices. Actually, labor emigration was illegal under Japanese law (and remained so until 1886), but the government did issue the passports. These *Gannen Mono* ("First Year People"), as they are known in Japanese, were not a great success as plantation workers, probably because, having been recruited on the streets of Yokohama during a period of civil war, "very few, if any, were farmers."[15] Nevertheless, the Hawaiian planters wanted more.

The planters could not afford to be particular. They were faced with the converse of most modern population problems, in that the native Hawaiians were dying faster than they were being born. When, in 1778, Captain Cook chanced upon what he named the Sandwich Islands, the Hawaiian population was perhaps 200,000 thriving pagans. By 1853, thanks to the progress of the white man's civilization and concomitant diseases, there were about 70,000, and their number continued to decline.[16] With a booming sugar industry—Hawaii produced 4,286 pounds of sugar in 1837 and 17,127,161 pounds in 1868—the American planters who dominated Hawaii knew that they would have to import labor. They would have preferred white labor, but, as a committee ruefully reported, such labor could only be had under "onerous conditions which would result in the complete demoralization of labor in these islands."[17] Forced to make a choice between maintaining a low wage scale and their desire to make Hawaii a white man's country, the planters chose the former. In 1851 they began to import Chinese laborers under five-year contracts.[18] By 1884 there were almost 18,000 Chinese in the islands, comprising more than 22 per cent of the population.[19] Many of these had worked out their contracts and, instead of continuing to work on the plantations or returning to China, had chosen to remain in Hawaii and set up their own businesses. Exhibiting that genius for commerce which has characterized Chinese communities throughout Asia, they became what Professor Conroy has aptly called "troublesome elements in a class society." To counterbalance the economic power of the Chinese, the planters continued to search for other sources of labor. After 1868 Japan had refused all further requests for laborers. But in April, 1884, the economic realities noted above caused the Japanese government to compromise its principles. The Hawaiian envoy in Japan was informed that the government was "not inclined to interpose any obstacle" to large-scale contract labor immigration.[20] Once the green light had been given, the immigration—the first large-scale migration from Japan in history—poured forth in an ever-broadening stream. In the nine years that the contract immigration continued, 1885–94, more than 30,000 Japanese were brought to the Hawaiian Islands.[21] Since the patterns of this immigration were to influence, in more ways than one, the immigration to the United States, it will be worthwhile to examine it in some detail. Fortunately, very complete statistics are available for this period.

It has been noted by almost every student of Japanese immigration, both to Hawaii and to the United States, that a surprisingly high per-

centage of the immigrants came from four prefectures in one small area
of southwestern Japan. The territory around the then obscure city of
Hiroshima sent forth more than any other.[22] One of the earliest studies
of Japanese immigration pointed out that all four of the prefectures
were among the poorest in Japan, although there were other poor districts which did not contribute many immigrants.[23] There the matter
rested until Professor Conroy's researches into the Hawaiian archives
revealed a hitherto unknown human factor. The agent in Japan for the
Hawaiian Board of Immigration, Robert W. Irwin, was determined to
avoid the error of his predecessor. He deliberately selected his laborers
from a rural backwater "about 1000 miles from Tokyo."[24] Thus all the
contract immigration came from one general area. This influenced the
later immigration to the United States in two ways. First, a very large
percentage of California's Issei came by way of Hawaii. Second, since
these areas were the only part of Japan whose people had had experience with transpacific migration, it naturally followed when the period
of heavy free immigration ensued that this area furnished a dispro-
portionate share of the migrants. In the five years from 1899 to 1903
more than 60 per cent of the non-Asian passports issued by the Japanese government went to residents of the four prefectures, and in 1908
a survey conducted by the semiofficial Japanese Association of America
showed that the same group controlled almost half of the acreage tilled
by Issei in California.[25]

The origins of the Hawaii-California transmigration, like that of the
Japan-California migration, are shrouded in obscurity. When the first
group of contract laborers arrived in Hawaii in 1868, they "found three
Japanese in Honolulu, two of whom left immediately for the United
States!"[26] These two unknown travelers may well have been the first
Japanese to make the Hawaii-California trip, but we cannot even be
sure that they arrived safely. By the end of the contract labor period
(1894), at which time, unfortunately, the keeping of accurate statistics
lapsed, 771 laborers whose contracts had expired were listed as having
"left for America."[27]

Wages on the highly unionized Pacific Coast of the United States,
where employers chronically complained of a "labor shortage" (usually
they meant a shortage of labor willing to work at close-to-subsistence
levels), were substantially higher than in Hawaii, where unions were
almost unknown until after American annexation annulled the contract
labor laws. From that time (June, 1900, was the effective date) until
the Gentlemen's Agreement went into effect (1908), more than 40,000
Issei made their way to the Pacific Coast, most of them to California.[28]

The passage of the Chinese Exclusion Act of 1882 had barred Chinese from the United States, and, after their numbers began to diminish, the so-called shortage of cheap and reliable agricultural labor in California acted as an inducement to prospective Japanese immigrants. Had Chinese immigration continued, the total number of Japanese immigrants would certainly have been smaller.

It must have taken a good deal of courage to make the trip from Hawaii. Although the immigrants from Japan to California or Hawaii did not travel under conditions that could be called luxurious by any stretch of the imagination, the Japanese government, always solicitous for the welfare of its subjects, insisted upon at least a minimum standard of decency. On the Hawaii-California trip, before 1900, these standards sometimes completely disappeared. A San Francisco newspaper described one such immigrant ship as loaded with a cargo of 24,494 sacks of sugar and an unspecified number of Japanese, who were packed aboard the *Potter* "much in the fashion cattle are imported, only with less regard to the health and comfort of the Japs," and added that "A sheep or a cow costs money [but] a Jap more or less does not count." The master of the *Potter*, a vessel of 1,803 tons, merely stowed the "passengers" in on top of the sacks without even the pretense of bunks. For several days, during a storm, they had been enclosed under battened-down hatches in "Cimmerian darkness," without water, since "water in a cargo of sugar is like fire in a cargo of gunpowder." Somehow, according to the amazed shipping reporter of the *Call*, all the immigrants survived conditions that "would have killed a waterfront tough outright."[29]

Having survived such a voyage, or a more pleasant one, what did the newly arrived immigrant do? If he had come from Hawaii, he would know at least a little of Western ways, but in the course of a short term on a sugar plantation, surrounded by fellow Japanese, he might acquire only a very limited English vocabulary. Immigrants from Japan often could not boast even that. How did they get their bearings in an alien world? They did so exactly as non-English-speaking Europeans were doing in New York and other Eastern centers. They were assisted, and exploited, by fellow immigrants who were often themselves "just off the boat." There rapidly developed, along the Pacific slope, clusters of boardinghouses run by Issei who doubled as small-scale labor contractors. Although most of the officials who commented on this system regarded it as a unique product of "Asiatic cunning," similar institutions had developed spontaneously in the East. There, supplying unskilled industrial employment, it became known as the padrone system.

In the West an agricultural proletariat was needed. Both systems had a common basis: a need for varying amounts of unskilled labor, a mass of newly arrived immigrants unfamiliar with the language and customs of the country, and a group of small-scale entrepreneurs—"padrones" in the East, "boardinghouse keepers" in the West—who served as convenient and perhaps necessary middlemen. It was the constant complaint of officials in the West, state and federal, that they could never prove that these Issei entrepreneurs were violating the contract labor laws. Since these officials, who, as a body, were zealously anti-Japanese, could never prove a single violation against resident Issei, the historian must assume their innocence.[30]

We can get a glimpse into the far-flung activities of these contractors from advertisements that frequently appeared in the Japanese-language press of Hawaii. A typical example, from the *Hawaiian-Japanese Chronicle* of March 22, 1905, proclaimed:

GREAT RECRUITING TO AMERICA

Through an arrangement made with Yasuwaza, of San Francisco we are able to recruit laborers to the mainland and offer them work. The laborers will be subjected to no delay upon arriving in San Francisco, but can get work immediately through Yasuwaza. Employment offered in picking strawberries and tomatoes, planting beets, mining and domestic service. Now is the time to go! Wages $1.50 a day. Tokujiro-Inaya-Niigata Kejin—care of the Nishimura Hotel. Apply to the Honolulu agencies for further particulars, giving the name of your plantation.[31]

The contractors thus served as an adjunct to California agriculture, which, in contrast with the usual American pattern of family-sized farms, has always been dependent upon large numbers of seasonal workers. As a recent authority put it: "Many localities [in California] are dependent for their farm operations on a mobile labor supply which has neither stability in employment nor in domicile."[32] In the decades after the Civil War this transient labor supply was, in the main, Chinese. After the passage of the Chinese Exclusion Act of 1882, it is often asserted, a vacuum was created by the ensuing shortage of cheap agricultural labor, and this vacuum attracted the Japanese to America.[33] This is an oversimplification. California, like the rest of the nation in the curiously named "gay nineties," was in the throes of the most prolonged panic of the century. The earliest Japanese labor gangs were in direct competition with the remaining Chinese, and had to resort to wage cutting to get employment. In 1894, in Santa Clara County, Japanese were working for 50 cents a day and boarding themselves. The normal scale for Chinese had long been established at a dollar a day. Similarly, in 1896, Japanese reduced the sugar beet harvest price from $1.20 to 70 cents per ton.[34]

Naturally, employers welcomed these early Issei recruits to the ranks of American agriculture, particularly since the Chinese, abetted by their rapidly diminishing number, were trying to raise wages. Within a few years the growers were singing a different tune. Around the turn of the century business conditions improved, both in California and the nation, and the decline in number of the Chinese laborers became even more noticeable. At the same time, as a group, Japanese labor began to serve notice that it would not be long content with the lowest rung of the economic ladder. Although the earliest recorded strike of Japanese agricultural laborers occurred in 1891, strikes do not seem to have become a frequent tactic until 1903. A standard device was to wait until the fruit was ripe on the trees and then insist upon renegotiating the contract. The growers protested that this was unethical, since a contract was a contract, and remembered that the Chinese, to their credit, had never done such things. But, as there were no longer enough Chinese to go around, in many instances the Japanese demands had to be met. From about this date, 1903, we begin to hear invidious comparisons of the two races from agriculturalists, almost always to the detriment of the Japanese. One grower even complained about the "saucy, debonair Jap, who would like to do all his work in a white starched shirt with cuffs and white collar accompaniments." That is, of course, hyperbole, but it can be taken as a symptom of something quite tangible; the intense desire of many Issei to move up the social and economic ladder.[35] From 1910 on, despite the prewar slump, the earnings of Japanese in agriculture were generally equal to, and sometimes above, those of other groups. This latter condition was particularly true when piecework rates were in force.[36]

But a seasonal farm laborer, no matter how well paid, could never climb very high. Many, perhaps most, Issei had their eyes fixed on the same goal; they wanted to work their own land. Because of lack of capital, it often took many years of toil before this goal could be realized. In many instances the individual would first sharecrop, then rent or lease, and finally, if possible, buy land. The statistics of Japanese land tenure in California dramatically illustrate the upward climb of thousands of Issei. In 1900 the holdings of thirty-nine Issei farmers, unspecified as to tenure, aggregated 4,698 acres. From 1904 on, the statistics are more detailed:[37]

	Owned (in acres)	Leased (in acres)	Shared crop (in acres)
1904	2,422	35,258½	19,572½
1909	16,449½	80,232	59,001½
1919	74,769	383,287[a]	. . . . .

[a] Lease figure includes cropping contracts.

In 1919 the market value of crops produced by the Issei was over $67 million, a bit more than 10 per cent of the total value of California crops.[35] At this time agriculture occupied about half of the 70,000 Japanese in California. One of them, George Shima, an emigrant from Fukuoka Prefecture, was undoubtedly the best-known Issei. Although his career is certainly not typical, it is surely worth considering, since he probably symbolized the aspirations of many of the first generation.

Shima, who was born in 1863 in pre-Meiji Japan, came to this country in 1889 with less than a thousand dollars in capital.[36] After working first as a common laborer and then as a labor contractor, he formed a partnership with several other Issei and leased 15 acres of reclaimed land. By use of the latest techniques, both agricultural and managerial, Shima and his associates created an agricultural empire on the virgin "drowned islands" of the San Joaquin delta and were among the first to raise potatoes successfully for the market in California. As early as 1909 Shima was referred to as the "Potato King," and each year the press speculated as to his net income. By 1920 it was alleged that he controlled 85 per cent of the crop, whose total value was over $18 million. Thanks to a graduate student at the University of California, who visited the Shima holdings in 1913 as part of his research, we can get an accurate picture of his operations at that time. In that year Shima controlled 28,800 acres actually in production and, by means of marketing agreements, handled the produce of thousands more. His working force numbered over five hundred, from engineers and boat captains (the islands were then accessible only by water) to common laborers, and included Japanese, East Indians, and Caucasians, both native and foreign born. At his death, in 1926, a newspaper estimated his estate at $15 million; his pallbearers included David Starr Jordan, the chancellor of Stanford University, and James Rolph, Jr., the mayor of San Francisco. Shima's was surely a Horatio Alger story without any trace of kind benefactor or boss's daughter; but when the real-life hero was a California Issei there was bound to be a bitter twist not found in dime novels. Shima, despite his millions, was still an "alien ineligible to citizenship"; and when, in 1909, he bought a house in one of the better residential neighborhoods of Berkeley, a cry of protest went up from the citizens of that quiet university town. Although obviously embarrassed, Shima stayed. He informed the protestants, who included a University of California professor, that they need not worry, since he was putting up "a high . . . fence to keep the other children from playing with his."[40] If even a millionaire had problems finding a home, what must it have been like for his less prosperous compatriots?

Those in the cities, when they became numerous enough, were crowded into a ghetto which soon became a "Little Tokyo" or "Little Osaka" to its residents and "Japtown" to most outsiders. Although they practiced many occupations (a group of shoemakers had been among the first to come), the vast majority fell into two groups: domestics—house servants and gardeners—and small businessmen. Most of the latter catered to the growing Japanese community; a few, but ever increasing in number, dealt primarily with Caucasians.

The servant problem—for the well to do, at least—seemed quite important in an earlier America. In California, first Chinese and then Japanese immigrants offered temporarily successful solutions. After the 1882 exclusion act, Chinese servants, a traditional leisure-class symbol in San Francisco (as even television has discovered), became increasingly scarce. As in the case of agricultural laborers, the Japanese substitutes were only a stopgap, for their ambition would not permit many Issei to remain domestics. Thus arose the phenomenon of the "Japanese schoolboy," usually a very recent immigrant and often not at all involved in higher education, although many students from Japan did work their way through college in domestic service. The "schoolboy," however, wanted to learn English and the "ropes," then move on to greener pastures. To get a foothold, he accepted what seem almost token wages—in 1900 $1.50 per week, plus board (by 1907 this had gone up to $2, while a trained servant earned from $15 to $40 per month, plus board). The classified sections of the San Francisco newspapers during the height of immigration (1904–1907) give striking evidence of the situation. Ads such as "Good Japanese boy wants situation as schoolboy," or "Japanese nice boy wants position as school boy in small family," dominated the "situations wanted" column. By 1909 their number had decreased. In that year there were an estimated 2,000 Japanese domestics in San Francisco; a few years earlier there had been more than twice as many." Another, but more permanent, upper-class symbol was the Issei gardener, whose green thumb made California lawns and shrubs bloom as never before. Since anything connected with the soil had status in the Japanese culture, the gardeners are a continuing feature of California life; the indoor domestics have almost completely disappeared.

What did the "schoolboy" do when he left domestic service? Because of the high degree of unionization in northern California and the anti-Oriental agitation which had been prevalent since the 1860's, no significant number of Issei were ever hired by white firms for factory or office work. The "schoolboy," if he stayed in town, had to go into busi-

ness for himself, or, more probably, go to work for an already established Issei.[42] Commenting on the relatively large number of businesses
owned by Orientals in America ("In 1929 they owned one-and-a-half
times as many [businesses] per 1,000 population as other residents of
the United States") and contrasting this with the proportionately
fewer establishments owned by Negroes, Gunnar Myrdal seemed not to
realize that he was comparing two different kinds of phenomena. Most
Oriental businesses (restaurants, laundries, and curio shops were, to a
degree, exceptions) catered primarily to Orientals.[43] This practice was
not just the result of clannishness; unlike the Negroes, whose wants and
needs were purely American, the Issei, bringing their own language
and culture with them, had special requirements. Patronizing Mr.
Watanabe's grocery store was not only a convenience (the store was
closer and he spoke the language even if his prices were a little higher
than those of the A & P)—if one wanted Aji-no-moto Sauce, or some
other Japanese delicacy, it was a necessity. The basic function of most
Issei businesses can be summed up in a phrase—"they took in each
other's washing."[44]

The United States Immigration Commission's 1909 survey located
and categorized 1,380 Japanese businesses in California; thirteen years
later Matsui found the total had grown to 2,176. Both agreed that these
were essentially family businesses, having small capital and serving
primarily their own community. Both studies found that when Issei
businessmen competed with Caucasians price cutting was apt to be used
as an entering wedge, but that after a time price agreements would be
made with Caucasian trade associations, which Issei were rarely able
to join. Within the Japanese community, however, wages were generally
lower and hours longer than in other businesses. All these generalizations would apply almost equally well to most first-generation immigrant businesses in the United States irrespective of the origin of the
proprietors.[45]

Whether they lived on farms or in cities (for the period under consideration the rural-urban division was roughly equal) the Issei and
their descendants tended to cluster in certain areas, thereby heighten-
ing what the sociologists like to call their "high social visibility." Although the distribution pattern within the state was to change, the
tendency to congregate became, if anything, more pronounced. Even
without the extralegal segregation which existed everywhere, such concentrations would be understandable from both social and economic
points of view. Up to about 1907, the San Francisco Bay area, the area
around Sacramento, and the upper San Joaquin Valley were the major

foci of immigrant population. After that date the population grew
more rapidly in the south. This was owing both to the fact that the anti-
Japanese agitation started in San Francisco and had not yet become
serious in southern California, and that the latter region, particularly
Los Angeles County, was, for all newcomers, much more a land of economic opportunity than the more heavily populated middle part of the
state. By 1910 Los Angeles, which at the previous census had contained
less than one per cent of the state's Japanese population, had more
Japanese than any other county. By 1920 almost 20,000 (18 per cent)
lived there. The other centers of Japanese population were Sacramento,
Fresno, San Francisco, Alameda, and San Joaquin counties, which
together contained more than 50 per cent of the state's Japanese population; another 22 per cent were in ten other counties; the remaining
10 per cent were scattered in thirty-four counties, and in eight counties
the enumerators failed to find a single Japanese.[46]

Demographically, the outstanding feature of the immigration before
1907 was its imbalance. There was an overwhelming preponderance of
young adult males, the majority of whom came from "the agricultural
class." The Immigration Commission, whose agents personally inter-
viewed 12,905 Issei, reported that more than 75 per cent had been less
than thirty years old when they arrived in the United States. Since
many of them had come by way of Hawaii, the median age at the time
of original emigration had been less than twenty-four years.[47] The next
year the census reported that there were almost eight Japanese males
of more than fifteen years of age for each Japanese female in the same
age group. Only 28 per cent of these men were married (more than half
of their wives were still in Japan), while almost half of the comparable
group of native white males were no longer single. For Issei girls and
women, catching a husband was no problem; more than 86 per cent of
the women over fifteen years of age were married, compared to only
57 per cent of their native white sisters. The predominantly female
immigration of the next decade helped equalize the sex ratio, but there
were still several thousand more men than women by the next census,
at which time the "picture bride" immigration was stopped.[48] Some of
these Issei bachelors were able to go to Japan and bring back brides
before the exclusion provisions went into effect (the Japanese steam-
ship lines did a thriving "peace excursion" business in those years);
others later married Nisei women much younger than themselves (these
marriages were often arranged in the old-country manner); but the
majority of these unmarried men was doomed to be the last of their
line, a particularly cruel fate for the strongly family-oriented Japanese.

Those Issei males able to marry generally did so rather late in life, and took wives much younger than themselves. Statistical verification can be found in the data compiled when the West Coast Japanese were incarcerated during the Second World War. At that time most of the Issei males were between fifty and sixty-four years of age, and most of the Issei females were between forty and fifty-four. The major group of the Nisei were between twenty and twenty-four years of age.[49] When these and other data are plotted on a chart, it becomes apparent that there was a "missing"generation of Japanese, i.e., the generation which, under conditions of a normal population-sex ratio, would have been born in the years 1905–1915. The figures also indicate that in a typical Issei family, children were born in the years 1918–1922 to a thirty-five-year-old father and a twenty-five-year-old mother. In the years to come, the absence of this generation would exacerbate the tension between Issei father and Nisei son, although it should be noted that "rejection" of the immigrant parents by the second-generation children is one of the classic motifs of the history of immigrants in America.[50]

The Nisei were born into homes which they made bilingual; most Issei continued to use Japanese among themselves, and some had no alternative. Their homes partook of both cultures. One Nisei remembered that he

sat down to American breakfasts and Japanese lunches. My palate developed a fondness for rice along with corned beef and cabbage. I became equally adept with knife and fork and with chopsticks. I said grace at meal times in Japanese, and recited the Lord's Prayer at night in English. I hung my stocking over the fireplace at Christmas and toasted "mochi" at Japanese New Year. The stories of "Tongue-cut Sparrow" and "Momo-taro" were as well known to me as those of Red Riding Hood and Cinderella. . . . On some nights I was told bedtime stories of how Admiral Togo sent a great Russian fleet down to destruction. Other nights I heard of King Arthur or from *Gulliver's Travels* and *Tom Sawyer*. I was spoken to by both parents in Japanese and English. I answered in whatever was convenient or in a curious mixture of both.[51]

The homes were generally modest, especially in the earlier years, but most Issei were not economically disadvantaged. Matsui concluded, in 1922, that "in general . . . the standard of living of the Japanese is still a little lower than the well established American, although it is not inferior to that of [other] recent immigrants."[52] In general, by the 1920's, the Issei were what in modern parlance might be called "lower-middle class," although it cannot be overemphasized that, for the Issei, associations were ethnically rather than economically determined. They lived in a world modeled on what they had known in Japan, but a world strangely and eccentrically transmuted by the omnipotent American environment. Some Issei were or became Christians, but even Buddhism, the religion of the majority, became Americanized. It was not uncommon, for example, for Protestant hymns to be swallowed almost whole; one of the most popular thus evolved into "Buddha loves me, this I know." Other, more malleable, aspects of life changed even more. Culturally, then, the Issei generation was transitional, neither Japanese nor American; the Nisei, their children, became, in law and fact, Americans.

But the role of the Issei was not unique, except for their peculiar status. Along with other Asians, they were "aliens ineligible to citizenship." The selfsame transitional role has been played out by millions of immigrants from Europe, particularly those of the new immigration whose exodus from southern and eastern Europe occurred at about the same time. Operating in the freer and more expansive California economy, the Issei, as a group, undoubtedly were economically better off than the new immigrants in the East.[53] Their acceptance into American society, however, was greatly retarded by ever-growing fires of social antagonism. The flames were deliberately fanned by the assorted individuals and groups who collectively comprised the anti-Japanese movement.

CHAPTER II

LABOR TAKES THE LEAD

*"The menace of an Asiatic influx is 100 times greater than
the menace of the black race, and God knows that is bad
enough."*

—C. O. Young, Special Representative, A.F. of L.

THE ANTI-JAPANESE movement was in many ways merely a continuation
of the long-standing agitation against the Chinese which began in the
early 1850's.[1] The coming of the Chinese was roughly contemporaneous
with the discovery of gold in 1848, and the first arrivals were welcomed,
as the original Issei were later. By 1852, however, feeling was turning
against them and Governor John Bigler informed the legislature that
"measures must be adopted to check this tide of Asiatic immigration."[2]
Sporadic protests against "Mongolian" immigration continued for the
next fifteen years, but it was only after the Civil War that the anti-
Chinese issue assumed major proportions. By that time there were more
than 60,000 Chinese in the country. They were predominantly adult
males working as laborers and were concentrated in California and, to
a lesser degree, in other Western states. Some ten thousand employed
by Leland Stanford and his associates did most of the manual labor
during the construction of the Central Pacific Railroad. The driving of
the golden spike, in 1869, which symbolized the completion of the trans-
continental railroad, threw most of these Chinese workers, along with
thousands of others, into an already depressed labor market.

Anti-coolie clubs had been organized in San Francisco as early as
1862; by 1867 there was a club in every ward of the city. By 1870, when
Chinese formed about 10 per cent of the state's population, the anti-
Chinese issue had become perhaps the most important in the state. On
the night of July 8, 1870, the first large anti-Oriental mass meeting in
America took place in San Francisco. Held under the aegis of various
labor organizations, it was preceded by a torchlight parade through the
streets of the city. The demonstrators then assembled for an evening of
speechmaking (Henry George was one of the featured orators), which
was followed by the passing of resolutions calling for the end of Chinese
immigration and asking for the support of state and national labor
bodies. Throughout the 1870's San Francisco, along with the rest of the
nation, was in the grip of the long postwar depression, and the local
unemployed were numbered in the thousands. While elsewhere in the
country financial manipulation by Wall Street was blamed for the dis-
tress, in California workingmen tended to attribute all their ills to the
presence of cheap "Mongolian" labor and, consequently, directed their

protests against the Chinese and the men who employed them. This period saw the forging of the San Francisco labor movement, for many years the most advanced in the country. The struggle against the Chinese is generally acknowledged to have "contributed more than any other one factor" to its strength.[3]

The anti-Chinese movement did not confine itself to making speeches and holding torchlight parades. No one will ever know how many Chinese were murdered in California; in the best-known outrage, about twenty Chinese were shot and hanged in the sleepy village of Los Angeles during one night in 1871. For many years Chinese, like slaves in the South, could not under any circumstances testify against white men in a California court. Congressional enactments during Reconstruction unintentionally improved their legal status, but Western juries were usually convinced that all Chinese were "born liars." Incidental brutality and casual assault were "John Chinaman's" daily lot; cutting of his queue was a favorite pastime for the larger bullies, and a shower of rocks was apt to greet him at any time. Little, if any, legal punishment was meted out for any crime against a Chinese, but an occasional tormentor who went too far—according to the shifting standards of the community—might have to answer in turn to the local vigilance committee. Indignity and insult were not reserved for the laborer and the living; when a Chinese professor at Harvard died of pneumonia, the headline in the Los Angeles *Times* was "A GOOD CHINA-MAN." Anti-Chinese sentiment was not restricted to labor unions, ruffians, or the gentlemen of the press. Soon after the agitation became widespread, every political party in California was straining to be the most anti-Chinese.[4]

From 1871 on, both major parties in California adopted and kept anti-Chinese planks in their platforms. Nevertheless, an independent Workingmen's party arose in the 1870's and garnered about a third of the vote in state elections. Much of its strength must be attributed to its uncomprisingly anti-Chinese character. This party's best remembered feature is its colorful leader, Dennis Kearney. A recent arrival from Ireland, Kearney was a stump orator of no mean power, and his slogan "The Chinese Must Go!" soon became the watchword of the movement. Probably too much attention has been focused upon what historians like to call "Kearneyism" and not enough upon the protest movement Kearney came to characterize. Actually, the full program of the Workingmen's party was a well-organized critique of American society in the Gilded Age and reads like a prelude to Populism. But, to adapt Henry Demarest Lloyd's metaphor about the Populists, "anticoolieism" became the "cowbird" of the movement. This single-minded concentration upon a panacea, a frequent failing of American third parties, helped cause the movement's collapse, for when Congress passed the Chinese Exclusion Act of 1882, what had become its chief *raison d'être* temporarily disappeared.[5]

Before that happened, however, the Workingmen and their allies gained control of the 1879 California Constitutional Convention; four provisions they wrote into this document epitomize the whole anti-Chinese movement.

ARTICLE XIX

CHINESE

SECTION 1. The legislature shall prescribe all necessary regulations for the protection of the state, and the counties, cities, and towns thereof, from the burdens and evils arising from the presence of aliens who are and may become ... dangerous or detrimental to the well-being or peace of the state, and to impose conditions upon which such persons may reside in the state, and to provide the means and mode of their removal ...

SECTION 2. No corporation now existing or hereafter formed under the laws of this state shall, after adoption of this Constitution, employ, directly or indirectly, in any capacity, any Chinese or Mongolian...

SECTION 3. No Chinese shall be employed on any state, county, municipal, or other public work, except in punishment for crime.

SECTION 4. The presence of foreigners ineligible to become citizens of the United States is declared to be dangerous to the well-being of the state, and the legislature shall discourage their immigration by all the means within its power. Asiatic coolieism is a form of human slavery, and is forever prohibited in this state.... The legislature shall delegate all necessary power to the incorporated cities and towns of this state for the removal of Chinese without the limits of such cities and towns, or for their location within prescribed portions of those limits, and it shall also provide the necessary legislation to prohibit the introduction into this state of Chinese after the adoption of this Constitution....

These provisions were merely expressions of sentiment and, except for the third section, were not capable of being put into effect. In 1849 the United States Supreme Court had decided in the Passenger Cases that the regulation of immigration was the exclusive domain of Congress and that no state could regulate or impose a tax on immigrants.[6] In the 1850's the California legislature, ignoring this precedent, tried to tax and regulate Chinese immigration, but its laws were quickly voided by the courts.[7] Therefore, if Chinese immigration was to be stopped, Congress had to do it. A Chinese exclusion bill passed Congress, but was vetoed by President Hayes; President Arthur in 1882 negated a similar bill, but signed a compromise measure suspending immigration for ten years, which temporarily halted the long campaign for exclusion. Agitation was twice renewed because the Chinese Exclusion Act of 1882 suspended immigration for only ten years; the law was renewed for another decade in 1892 and then made "permanent" in 1902. Thus, anti-Oriental agitation was a continuing factor in state politics for fifty years before the Issei became a prominent feature of the California landscape.

This agitation, at first, was directed along fairly well-defined lines of economic interest. Employers and their upper-middle-class adherents wanted Chinese as inexpensive laborers and respectful servants "who knew their place," while laboring men and their adherents rigorously opposed all forms of what Californians learned to call "Mongolian labor." But in the later agitation for the renewal of the act the need to preserve "racial purity" and "Western civilization," which had always been an element in anti-Chinese propaganda, was stressed more and more. The increasing emphasis laid on this moral issue both explains the growing support among nonworking-class Californians which the labor movement received in its successive campaigns for renewal and reflects that blurring of class lines which seems to be a continuing process in the United States of the late-nineteenth and twentieth centuries.[9]

With this heritage of opposition to Oriental immigration, it is not surprising to find the spokesmen of organized labor among those who first expressed alarm when Japanese immigration began to increase. The initial two decades of anti-Japanese agitation were conducted largely under the auspices of organized labor, although animus toward the Issei was by no means confined to those within its ranks. Before 1900, anti-Japanese incidents are few and, in themselves, of little import. They are worth recording only in relation to later events.

On July 25, 1888, the *Coast Seaman's Journal*, the most influential labor weekly west of Chicago and spokesman for the San Francisco Federated Trades Council, alerted its readers to what it called a "recently developed phase of the Mongolian issue."[10] American shipowners were employing Japanese seamen aboard American ships. This was to be a long-term minor irritant. The paper's editor, Walter MacArthur, remembered years later that

During the Dunsmuir Coal strike [in British Columbia, 1890–91] a number of Japs were imported as scabs. Later they migrated southward. These are said to be the first of their kind to enter the United States as laborers. Some of them shipped as sailors in the coastwise trade and proved a thorn in the side of the Sailor's Union [of the Pacific]. During this period the schooner Sparrow carried a crew of Jap scabs, being the only vessel on the coast so manned. Every time the Union drove them off they came back on board *over the other side*.[11]

The presidential election year of 1892 saw two brief flurries of anti-

Japanese sentiment. In the spring of that year a series of feature articles appeared in the San Francisco *Morning Call*, the first of many sustained journalistic barrages to be directed against the Issei. The articles, five in number, were not completely unsympathetic; the first managed to find some good things to say about the immigrants. They were "picturesque ... polite, courteous, smiling.... They rarely get into the Police Courts.... But they are taking work away from our boys and girls [and] men and women."[12] The next article dealt with the size of the immigration and, in a flight of statistical fancy, predicted that the tides of Japanese immigration would rise to a yearly level of 120,000 persons at the turn of the century.[13] Two weeks after the first article, in the face of some disbelief by most of the California press (after all, at this early date many Californians had never *seen* a Japanese), the *Call* insisted that it had not turned in "a false alarm" and correctly noted that much of the immigration came from Hawaii, rather than from Japan.[14] But what the paper liked to call its "crusade against Japanese contract labor" was ignored by most Californians; despite the *Call*'s extravagant claim that it had "attracted world-wide notice" (the notice of a few Pacific Coast newspapers and two English-language weeklies in Japan), the campaign attracted so little attention that it has hitherto escaped the notice of historians.[15]

At least one Californian took the warnings seriously. As if in answer to the newspaper's summons, Dennis Kearney returned to the hustings after a decade's absence. In May, 1892, he harangued a crowd in San Francisco about the newly discovered Japanese "menace," and in July a Sacramento shorthand reporter recorded him as berating

the foreign Shylocks [who] are rushing another breed of Asiatic slaves to fill up the gap made vacant by the Chinese who are shut out by our laws.... Japs ... are being brought here now in countless numbers to demoralize and discourage our domestic labor market and to be educated ... at our expense.... We are paying out money [to allow] fully developed men who know no morals but vice to sit beside our ... daughters [and] to debauch [and] demoralize them.

Kearney then complained that neither politicians nor trade-unionists were then willing to listen to him, but insisted that he, and apparently he alone, knew what was causing the current hard times. It was a sinister coalition of "absentee money-lenders and the importation of Japanese slave-laborers." Then, closing his peroration with a slightly revamped echo of the seventies, he proclaimed: "The Japs Must Go!"[16]

But it was merely an echo; neither Kearney nor the *Call* succeeded in enlisting many Californians in their crusades. The newspaper dropped the matter and Kearney slid back into obscurity. The time was not yet ripe. But, thirteen years later, answering the summons of different champions, much of California would harken to an almost identical call.

In 1900 the anti-Japanese campaign was renewed, but it was mainly a tail to the anti-Chinese kite. California was extremely alarmed at that time over reports, widely discussed in the press, that Congress would either allow the expiring Chinese Exclusion Act to lapse, or, as seemed more probable, enact a law providing something less than total exclusion. Conveniently, in March, 1900, the Board of Health "discovered" what it supposed to be a victim of bubonic plague in San Francisco's Chinatown. Mayor James Duval Phelan made a few extravagant statements, declared a quarantine, and variously blamed Chinese and Japanese. When, however, business leaders protested that the scare, widely reported in the nation's press, would act as "an incubus upon our industries," Phelan backed down, and later admitted that the Board's "zeal outruns its discretion." The Board had earlier investigated living conditions among the Japanese, but the puzzled inspector could report only that in one bathhouse he had found "three Japanese in one tub . . . but he knew of no law which compelled Japanese to bathe one in a tub."[17]

Then, in May, in San Francisco, the mecca of the movement, the first large-scale protest against the Japanese in California took place.[18] It was called by various local labor groups, but the fact that Walter Mac-Arthur was in the chair suggests that the Sailor's Union might have been the instigator. It was fitting that the major political speaker was James Duval Phelan, then mayor of San Francisco, who would play a prominent role in the anti-Japanese movement up to the time of his death in 1930. Phelan's basic argument remained the same for thirty years, and the frequent charges of insincerity and demagoguery that have been made against him have little merit. Whatever else he may have been, Phelan was sincere. To the end of his days he believed what he said on May 7, 1900:

> The Japanese are starting the same tide of immigration which we thought we had checked twenty years ago. . . . The Chinese and Japanese are not bona fide citizens. They are not the stuff of which American citizens can be made. . . . Personally we have nothing against Japanese, but as they will not assimilate with us and their social life is so different from ours, let them keep at a respectful distance.[19]

Most of the other speakers argued along economic lines. They included various local labor leaders, Cleveland L. Dam, an attorney and former state official, and Professor E. A. Ross, of Stanford University. Ross was the most conspicuous exception to the general rule, prevailing throughout our period, that California university professors and presidents were opponents of anti-Japanese measures. On this occasion, Ross denied any racism and insisted that his opposition to the Japanese was purely an economic matter. Making an analogy that restrictionists of all kinds were to use for a quarter-century, he compared immigration to the tariff: "We keep out pauper-made goods but let in the pauper.... A restrictive policy devised in the true interest of labor would think first of keeping out the foreigner, and then of keeping out his product."[20]

Later that summer, three national parties showed that they were aware of the renascence of the Oriental issue on the West Coast. The Democratic plank called for a "continuance ... of the Chinese exclusion law" and urged "its application to the same classes of all Asiatic races." The pro-Bryan Populists more specifically demanded a halt to the "importation of Japanese and other laborers under contract" and the "exclusion of Mongolian and Malayan immigrants." The Republicans, under McKinley's cautious direction, favored "a more effective restriction of cheap [foreign] labor"—a plank which Republican orators could interpret any way they chose.[21] In December the American Federation of Labor, meeting in Louisville, Kentucky, declared that "the Pacific Coast and intermountain states are suffering severely from Chinese and Japanese cheap coolie labor" and asked Congress to "re-enact the Chinese exclusion law, including in its provisions all Mongolian labor."[22]

The climax of the drive for renewal of the Chinese Exclusion Act came in the following year. In January Governor Henry T. Gage, a Republican, told the California legislature that for the "protection of American labor" it was "essential" that "Chinese and Japanese laborers" be excluded.[23] Then, in November, just before the new session of Congress was to begin, more than a year and a half of renewed agitation came to a climax with the calling of the Chinese Exclusion Convention, which met in San Francisco and was attended by perhaps a thousand delegates (about eight hundred were trade unionists, most of the rest officials and politicians—Democratic, Republican, and Socialist). The convention debated the advisability of including a plea for the exclusion of Japanese as well as Chinese in its memorial to Congress, but decided, solely on the grounds of expediency, that scattering its fire would weaken the force of the appeal. The memorial to Congress therefore contained no mention of the Japanese, but the accounts of the assembly show a great deal of concern about the growing number of Japanese immigrants. A headline in the San Francisco *Bulletin* caught the convention's mood: "SOME HAVE COME TO MAKE WAR ON THE JAPANESE TOO." The delegates heard two days of speechmaking, endured a

certain amount of political maneuvering, and went home. For some of
them the convention must have served as an introduction to the Japanese question when they were informed that "The Japs . . . were more
dangercus" because they were "more intelligent and civilized . . . than
the Chinaman."

Many of the delegates may have been willing to concede as much
when, on entering the meeting hall, they had to pass through a small
group of Issei who were handing out leaflets protesting against any
move to exclude Japanese. One of the Issei even made an "aggressive
and flamboyant" speech in what must have been fairly good English,
since the *Bulletin* reporter got the gist of it. The burden of the message
on the leaflet was that it was all right to exclude Chinese, but not Japanese, and the Issei speaker, a local Japanese editor, insisted that his
people were the equals of Americans.[24] For the exclusionist delegates
this was a new experience. In half a century of anti-Chinese agitation
no such counterdemonstration had occurred; what advocacy the Chinese
enjoyed was furnished by their Caucasian supporters, mostly missionaries and businessmen. But the Japanese, both immigrants and visitors,
would in the years to come constantly organize demonstrations and
meetings of their own and, with their white backers, make thousands
of speeches and publish dozens of books and pamphlets answering the
exclusionists. In attacking the Chinese (whose comments on the matter,
if any, were not recorded), the Japanese showed that they, too, had
strong race feelings; they showed also a certain political ineptness that
was not to be atypical. This demonstration and others like it were, of
course, the work of a handful of leaders and intellectuals. The bulk of
the Issei was neither capable of nor, perhaps, even interested in molding
American public opinion, except as their mere physical presence did so.

Since there were very few Japanese in California outside of San
Francisco, the agitation against them had not yet attracted much support. It was pitched to a labor audience and had little appeal in the
small towns and rural areas which then made up the rest of the state.
In one of the small towns, however, a highly articulate and intelligent
editor put the problem in middle-class rather than working-class terms.
Chester Harvey Rowell later played an influential part in California
politics, but in 1900 he was only an owner-editor making his Fresno
Republican one of the most respected organs in the state. Late in April,
1900, he took a long and penetrating look at the Japanese issue which
is worth quoting at length.[25]

Japanese who come to this country [are no more objectionable, wrote Rowell]
than the immigrants from Southern Europe [except that] they do not belong to

the white race, but the country is hardly ready to enact the principle "this is a white man's country" into laws.

...Japanese coolie immigration is of the most undesirable class possible, and we are quite right in objecting to it and in demanding that something be done about it. The only question is what we can get done, and in this we must reckon with the cowardice and apathy of the rest of the country. Nothing is going to be done that is worth doing in regard to Japanese immigration unless the country can be aroused to the necessity of doing something in regard to immigration in general....

But, when all is done, there will still remain more Japanese than we want [who are] neither paupers nor contract laborers...and in regard to these there is simply nothing to do but accept the inevitable, until we can arouse the sentiment of the East, not on the Japanese question alone, but on the whole menace of unfit immigration.

Two of Rowell's points merit further comment. The anti-Eastern bias he expressed soon became a constant California complaint. It can only be likened to the similar Southern complaint that Northerners did not properly understand "their" Negroes and the Southern attitudes toward them. His other premise, that all and not just Japanese immigration should be restricted, was not yet generally held; some of the leading figures in the anti-Japanese movement (a Catholic like Phelan, or a German-born Jew like Congressman Julius Kahn) would always favor any European immigration. But most of the California exclusionists eventually came to oppose all immigrants except those from the "nordic homeland" of Northern Europe. Rowell was one of the first to lay down the prerequisites under which Japanese exclusion would be brought about. But this was far in the future. The Chinese Exclusion Act having been renewed in April, 1902, the agitation subsided, and even in San Francisco not much was heard about the "Oriental menace" for several years. The next peak of anti-Orientalism was reached in 1905, a year that saw anti-Japanese agitation put on a permanent basis.

In that year an unsuspecting world was entering the last, uneasy decade of what we now think of as a century of peace. The Victorian Age had ended, the era of global warfare was not yet begun. In the United States, enjoying both prosperity and the presidency of Theodore Roosevelt, things seemed quite bully. Most Americans, if they bothered to take an interest in the struggle then being waged at the eastern edge of Asia, seemed to favor the underdog Japanese against the Russians.[20] California, judging from its press, did likewise.

Then, in early 1905, as the *Call* had done thirteen years before, the San Francisco *Chronicle* launched a crusade against the Japanese; this crusade, however, would have almost immediate results. The opening gun went off suddenly on February 23. Most Americans, as they scanned their front pages that morning, read headlines about the advance of the Japanese army toward Mukden and feature articles about Roosevelt's inauguration, a little over a week away. *Chronicle* readers, however, saw a page-one streamer: "THE JAPANESE INVASION, THE PROBLEM OF THE HOUR." In its "careful and conservative exposition" the newspaper asserted that at least 100,000 of "the little brown men" were here already, that they were "no more assimilable than the Chinese," and that they undercut white labor. In a topical note it warned that, "once the war with Russia is over, the brown stream of Japanese immigration" will become a "raging torrent." The page-one story concluded, without explaining why, that "the class of immigrants is likely to become worse." For months similar stories appeared almost daily under menacing headlines:[27]

CRIME AND POVERTY GO HAND IN HAND WITH ASIATIC LABOR

HOW JAPANESE IMMIGRATION COMPANIES OVERRIDE LAWS

BROWN MEN ARE MADE CITIZENS ILLEGALLY

JAPANESE A MENACE TO AMERICAN WOMEN

BROWN MEN AN EVIL IN THE PUBLIC SCHOOLS

ADULT JAPANESE CROWD OUT CHILDREN

THE YELLOW PERIL—HOW JAPANESE CROWD OUT
THE WHITE RACE

BROWN PERIL ASSUMES NATIONAL PROPORTIONS

BROWN ARTISANS STEAL BRAINS OF WHITES

Had these headlines and the usually exaggerated and often lurid stories beneath them appeared in a labor paper, the effect would probably have been negligible. But the *Chronicle*, owned by M. H. de Young, was Republican and conservative to the core. It was, without doubt, the most influential newspaper on the whole Pacific Coast. Why had the paper initiated the series? Writers have speculated that it was de Young's political ambition or perhaps a desire to wean working-class readers from William Randolph Hearst's rival *Examiner*. Neither explanation is very convincing. De Young did not subsequently run for political office, and the *Chronicle*, since it remained politically orthodox and, for American newspapers of the period, reasonably literate, was obviously not trying to pander to the same tastes that built Hearst's journalistic empire. A recently conducted analysis of the *Chronicle*'s pages for fifteen years *before* 1905 shows that its editor, John P. Young, had long been anxious about the Orient—first China and, then, as her

progress become more and more evident, Japan.[28] Young himself later
stated, as a participant in a widely read symposium, that he had prepared "a monograph on the subject of Japanese competition" nine
years before the series began. In line with a general tendency to dis-
credit the motives of the exclusionists whenever possible, many of the
writers who have treated the anti-Japanese movement have unreason-
ably assumed insincerity on the part of the *Chronicle*. The anti-Japanese
movement in California, however, can never be understood unless it is
realized that the vast majority of the leaders and instigators were as
sincere, say, as the Catholics and Protestants of an earlier day who
cheerfully burned communicants of the opposite persuasion.

Young, for instance, felt that if the "inundation of Japanese" were
not "checked" the result would be a "complete orientalization of the
Pacific Coast."[29] The *Chronicle* was constantly embarrassed by the fact
that most of its fellow Japanophobes at this time were labor leaders
whom the *Chronicle*, as a supporter of the Employers' Association, opposed on almost every other issue. Ideology, as well as politics, often
makes strange bedfellows.

The sustained attacks of the *Chronicle* quickly evoked a response
from the Methodist clergy of San Francisco, who, as a body, denied the
accuracy of the charges against the Japanese. They almost immediately
set up a committee to "study" the Japanese problem in California. The
head of this committee, Dr. H. B. Johnson, was superintendent of the
Pacific Coast Japanese Mission of the Methodist Episcopal Church.
Protestant churches, especially those with missionary interests on both
sides of the Pacific, generally were the most vocal defenders of the Issei.
The *Chronicle* remarked that while it respected the motives of the protesting pastors it felt that their judgment was biased by their missionary zeal.[30] The Japanese themselves were also spurred to action; the
Japanese Association of America, founded during the plague scare of
1900, began to assume importance from this time. While much ink has
been spilled disputing the Association's connection with the Japanese
government, it seems quite clear that this organization did in fact have
very close ties with the Japanese government and should properly be
designated as semiofficial. There was nothing sinister or improper in
its connections with Tokyo; after all, the Issei were, because of their
status as "aliens ineligible to citizenship," still Japanese nationals despite their permanent residence here. They were, therefore, to a certain
extent, the responsibility of the home country—a responsibility that,
through its consuls, Japan shouldered. Had she not done so, the Issei
would have passed into the legal limbo of stateless persons, a category

then almost unknown, but all too familiar today. There is not a scintilla of evidence to suggest that the various Japanese associations were ever used for espionage or other illegal purposes.[31]

Most of the responses, within California at least, were in rapport with the *Chronicle*'s exclusionist spirit. On the first two days of March, by a unanimous vote of both houses, the California legislature passed an anti-Japanese resolution that summarized most of the newspaper's complaints. The resolution called upon Congress to "limit and diminish the further immigration of Japanese," and drew up a ten-point bill of particulars against them:[32]

I. . . . Japanese laborers, by reason of race habits, mode of living, disposition and general characteristics, are undesirable . . .

II. [Japanese] are debarred from naturalization, and cannot, if they desired— which they do not—become citizens.

III. . . . Japanese laborers do not evince any inclination to assimilate with our people, or to become Americans. . . .

. . . .

IX. . . . Japanese laborers . . . are mere transients [who] do not buy land [or] build or buy houses. . . . They contribute nothing to the growth of the State. They add nothing to its wealth, and they are a blight on the prosperity of it, and a great and impending danger to its welfare.

X. . . . Now not less than five hundred [Japanese] each month [are] landed at the port of San Francisco [and] we cannot but regard with the greatest sense of danger and disaster, the prospect that the close of the war between Japan and Russia will surely bring to our shores hordes, to be counted only in thousands, of the discharged soldiers of the Japanese Army, who will crowd the State with immoral, intemperate, quarrelsome men, bound to labor for a pittance, and to subsist on a supply with which a white man can hardly sustain life.

The resolution was not only insulting; it demonstrated that the legislators did not know what was happening in their own state. They would soon discover, to their sorrow, that the ninth point was wholly erroneous. The Issei were buying land and building houses, and later legislatures would spend much time and energy trying to stop them. But the unknowing 1905 legislature adjourned a few days later without introducing any significant anti-Japanese legislation.[33] For the next four decades, without exception, anti-Japanese bills were introduced in every biennial session.

The major locus of anti-Japanese activity that year was not in the capital, but in San Francisco. There, on the second Sunday in May, delegates from sixty-seven local and near-by organizations met to form what became the Asiatic Exclusion League.[34] From the day of the League's formation, May 14, 1905, until after the end of the Second World War, there was in California an organized anti-Japanese movement that would eventually draw support from all segments of the state's population. In the beginning, the organized movement was an extension of the San Francisco labor unions. The most prominent labor leaders attending the initial meeting of the League were Patrick Henry McCarthy, head of the Building Trades Council of San Francisco, and Andrew Furuseth and Walter MacArthur, both of the Sailor's Union. A satellite of McCarthy's, Olaf Tveitmoe, was named president. It is interesting to note that all four of these men were immigrants from Europe.[35]

The League objected to the Japanese on both economic and racial grounds. In its most detailed statement of principles it argued that the Japanese must be excluded because

1. We cannot assimilate them without injury to ourselves.
2. No large community of foreigners, so cocky, with such distinct racial, social and religious prejudices, can abide long in this country without serious friction.
3. We cannot compete with a people having a low standard of civilization, living and wages.
4. It should be against public policy to permit our women to intermarry with Asiatics. . . .
5. We cannot extend citizenship to Asiatics . . .
6. If we permit the Jap to come in, what will . . . become of our Exclusion with [*sic*] China?[36]

The League's immigrant leaders knew from their own experience that Europeans of various nationalities could be assimilated into the American melting pot, but were convinced that assimilation could not cross the color line. As one speaker put it, "an eternal law of nature has decreed that the white cannot assimilate the blood of another without corrupting the very springs of civilization." When confronted with the principles of the Declaration of Independence, the League subscribed to them, of course, but it pointed out that Jefferson had not included the "right of migration" among his inalienable rights.[37] Working with the League in the San Francisco area were two smaller organizations that also drew their strength almost exclusively from the ranks of labor: the Anti-Jap Laundry League, which collected and spent about $400 a month from the laundry drivers and owners in trying to enforce boycotts of Japanese laundries, and the Anti-Japanese League of Alameda County, a largely fictitious organization which shared leadership and office space with the Laundry League.[38]

Most observers, from the 1909 United States Immigration Commission on, have been misled by the Asiatic Exclusion League's inflated membership figures. It was, in fact, mainly a paper organization, with little funds. In 1908 the League asserted that 231 groups were affiliated with it (195 were labor unions) and President Tveitmoe stated that "something like 200,000 members... have rendered... financial support." But the average contribution must have been about two cents per member per year, since an examination of the League's financial statement reveals that it never received as much as $5,000 in any one year. Most of its money seems to have come from P. H. McCarthy's Building Trades Council, an organization whose members, like most trade unionists in California, never faced job competition from the Japanese.[39] But even after these inflated claims are cut down to proper size, the founding and continued existence of the League remains a nodal point in the whole anti-Japanese movement. For the first time there was an organization whose sole purpose was to exclude the Japanese. All the League's efforts were directed toward one goal—exclusion. Its chief weapons were legislation, boycott, and propaganda.

When Congress met in December, 1905, at least two California congressmen were prepared to try to implement the League's program. Duncan E. McKinlay, of Santa Rosa, and Everis A. Hayes, of San Jose, both Republicans, dropped similar exclusion bills into the hopper. As they were no part of the administration's program, Speaker Cannon funneled both bills into the obedient Foreign Affairs Committee, where they were bottled up.[40] Later in the session Hayes made the first congressional speech devoted to Japanese exclusion; he acknowledged that most of his arguments came from the League. The most significant reaction came from Oscar W. Underwood, an influential Alabama Democrat. Hayes stated that the country already had one serious race problem in the South and should try to avoid getting another. Underwood made a friendly interruption to assure the California Republican that "the South has already tried to stay by the Pacific coast on this question."[41] The House then moved on to other business and no action was taken on the Japanese during that session.

A similar fate befell all the League's proposals. During its lifetime no measure it supported ever passed any legislative body. Its boycotts, proclaimed over and over against both Issei shops and Japanese imports, were short-lived, ineffective, and reeking of extortion. The organization and its leadership became almost completely discredited. Yet, despite its low caliber and apparent failure, the League advanced the anti-Japanese cause. Its constant propaganda helped distort further the already twisted image of the Issei; its very existence set the pattern for more efficient successors. While the League lasted, the flames of prejudice were never allowed to go completely out.

The Asiatic Exclusion League represented the conservative forces in the labor-union movement typical of the American Federation of Labor at that time. It is worth noting that a more radical segment of the American left was equally anti-Japanese. The American Socialist party, despite its allegedly international principles and a certain amount of internal opposition, was vehemently opposed to the Issei. The National Executive Committee of the party unanimously resolved, in December, 1907, to oppose Asiatic immigration.[42]

While some Socialists justified their stand on economic grounds alone, others openly put forth racist arguments. A writer in a Socialist journal felt that "our feelings of brotherhood toward the Japanese" must be postponed "until we have no longer reason to look upon them as an inflowing horde of alien scabs."[43] One leading theoretician, Morris Hillquit, wanted to restrict immigration from all "backward races," while another, Victor Berger, insisted more bluntly that the United States and Canada must be kept "White Man's countries" and expressed alarm lest America become "a black-and-yellow country within a few generations." Berger, who was later to oppose United States entry into the First World War, expressed his willingness to "fight for my wife and children . . . for all your wives and children" against the menace of Asiatic immigration.[44] Jack London clearly spoke for most of his comrades when he declared, "I am first of all a white man and only then a Socialist."[45] This attitude perplexed the Japanese Socialist party, which appealed to their American brethren to "be true to the exhortation of Marx—'Workingmen of all countries, unite.' " There is no record of any reply.[46]

These attitudes are, perhaps, startling and difficult to fathom in a day when much of the American labor movement and what there is of the American left usually lead in the fight for racial equality. From the post–Civil War period until the days of the New Deal, however, organized labor in this country was a consistent foe of foreign immigration in general and the immigration of colored laborers in particular. The economic basis for this attitude is obvious. It is comforting to think that ethical principles have achieved dominance over economic motives in shaping organized labor's present-day attitude, but it should be remembered that, on the part of much of organized labor, this change of attitude did not occur until immigration quotas, minimum wage laws, and industry-wide bargaining agreements had made the threat of the immigrant to the American wage standards almost negligible.

Chapter III

SEGREGATION AND DIPLOMACY

"If the Southern States can segregate the races in its
schools, why may not the Californians do so?"
—San Francisco *Argonaut*, Jan. 5, 1907

"The subject of the exclusion of laborers is acquiring a
new interest in my mind. . . . The whole subject of peaceful
invasion by which the people of a country may have their
country taken away from them, and the analogy and contrast between the swarming of peaceful immigration and
business enterprise and the popular invasions of former
times, such, for instance, as those overrunning the Roman
Empire, are most interesting."
—Elihu Root to Oliver Wendell Holmes, Jr., March 6, 1907

BEFORE 1906 the anti-Japanese movement, concentrating on exclusion,
attracted little notice outside of California and the neighboring states.
The event that finally called attention to the racial tension in California
was, curiously enough, considered trivial by those who initiated it. A
routine decision by the San Francisco school board, affecting only a
few score children, catapulted the Japanese problem into the national
and international limelight.

The school board crisis, as it has come to be known, can be understood
only within the framework of local politics. In the years after the turn
of the century San Francisco went through a time of troubles. The
powerful Employers' Association launched a concerted antiunion drive
that culminated in the bitter teamsters' strike of 1901, a qualified defeat
for labor.[1] Stung by what it considered undue police protection given
strikebreakers by the relatively conservative reform administration
headed by Mayor James D. Phelan, resurgent labor formed a Union
Labor party and elected what it felt would be its own city administration. The new mayor was a dapper and personable musician, Eugene E.
Schmitz, but the real power was in the hands of Abraham Ruef, an
intelligent but unscrupulous lawyer. The new administration was
utterly corrupt, although probably not more so than the administrations in many other contemporary American cities.[2]

Animus against both Chinese and Japanese was reflected in the Union
Labor platform from the first—but anti-Orientalism had been a standard plank for all San Francisco parties since the 1870's. Despite the
fact that Schmitz was elected on a platform recommending that "all
Asiatics, both Chinese and Japanese, should be educated separately,"
the Board of Education, which was reconstituted by the new administration in January, 1902, took no steps in this direction for more than

three years.[3] The leading members of the Board were the mayor's personal friends as well as political associates: the superintendent of schools, Alfred Roncovieri, had played the trombone in Schmitz's orchestra (his honor was a bassoonist), and the Board's president, Aaron Altman, was the brother-in-law of Boss Abe Ruef. Until 1905 the members of the Union Labor administration, despite the platform pledge, showed no interest at all in the Japanese; perhaps, as one observer commented, they were too busy enriching themselves at the city's expense.[4]

Only after the *Chronicle*'s crusade was well under way, and just before other Union Labor partisans organized the Asiatic Exclusion League, did the Board take any action. On All Fool's Day, 1905, a budget proposal for the enlargement of the facilities at the one Oriental (Chinese) school was submitted to the supervisors, but it was turned down. On May 6 the Board announced that it would, at some future but unspecified date, remove the Japanese pupils to the Oriental school so that "our children should not be placed in any position where their youthful impressions may be affected by association with pupils of the Mongolian race."[5]

The use of the word "Mongolian" was not an anachronism: it was a legal necessity. The Board intended to act under the authority of an old California law which empowered school boards to "exclude all children of filthy or vicious habits, or children suffering from contagious diseases, and also to establish separate schools for [American] Indian children, and for the children of Mongolian and Chinese descent. When such separate schools are established [these] children must not be admitted into any other schools."[6] Most of the local press cheered the Board's action, and the Asiatic Exclusion League, from its first meeting, sporadically pressed for implementation of the resolution. For more than a year, none came. Schmitz was elected mayor for the third time in November, 1905, despite mounting complaints of corruption from both outside and within the Union Labor party. After his reëlection the administration continued to do nothing. Even among convinced exclusionists the "menace" of the Japanese pupils seemed a relatively unimportant issue; the real concern was exclusion.

Then nature took a hand. On April 18, 1906, San Francisco shuddered and groaned through several successive earthquake shocks of very high magnitude; these were followed by three days of fire which destroyed whole sections of the city. For a short period all thought of politics vanished as San Franciscans tried to restore order and to feed and house the refugees. The nation and the world sent sympathy and assistance; the largest foreign contribution, more than all the rest combined, was $246,000 from the citizens and government of earthquake-conscious Japan.[7] By June, however, the anti-Japanese campaign was again becoming vigorous.

In that month, physical attacks against individual Japanese began to take on serious proportions. These attracted a large amount of local notice, particularly since about a dozen separate incidents involved four Japanese scientists who were inspecting the earthquake and fire damage. Led by Dr. F. Omori, an eminent seismologist from the Imperial University, Tokyo, the scientists were stoned and otherwise molested by groups of boys and young men in various parts of the city. When it developed that one of the culprits was a messenger boy employed by the post office, the postmaster promptly fired him, but the local press made a hero of the young hooligan. The luckless Dr. Omori continued his investigations in northern California and was again assaulted, this time in Eureka. The mayor of that city apologized, and insisted the assault was owing to local "labor troubles," not the professor's race, but it is difficult to understand how a Japanese scientist, whose normal dress in this country would not have been inappropriate at a formal wedding, could have been mistaken for either a strikebreaker or a walking delegate.[8]

Toward the end of June the Asiatic Exclusion League complained that "many wage-earners, laborers, and mechanics patronize Japanese restaurants," and added rather unconvincingly that there were "eating houses" run by whites "as easy of access and more inviting." The League urged all affiliated unions "to enforce the penalties . . . for patronizing Japanese or Chinese" and threatened to have all patrons of Oriental restaurants photographed. The same meeting warned of the danger to health from many of the fruits then on the market, which had been "picked and packed by unclean and unhealthy Asiatics."[9]

A real boycott was begun in October. It lasted about three weeks. Japanese restaurants were picketed, prospective customers were handed matchboxes bearing the slogan "White men and women, patronize your own race," and windows were smashed and a few proprietors beaten. Until protests were lodged by the Japanese consul, the police seem consistently to have looked the other way. The boycott came to a quick end when the Japanese restaurant owners agreed to pay $350 in "protection."[10]

In August and September assaults upon San Francisco Issei came too regularly to have been accidental. As President Roosevelt's special investigator conservatively reported, the assaults were motivated by "racial hostility" and "stirred up possibly by newspaper accounts." He obtained statements from nineteen Issei; none reported serious injury, and all the statements followed the same pattern. One victim related:

> I am proprietor of Sunset City Laundry. Soon after the earthquake the persecutions became intolerable. My drivers were constantly attacked on the highway, my place of business defiled by rotten eggs and fruit; windows were smashed several times.... The miscreants are generally young men, 17 or 18 years old. Whenever newspapers attack the Japanese these roughs renew their misdeeds with redoubled energy.

Japanese pedestrians were not safe either. M. Sugawa, a shoemaker, stated:

> As I was passing on Sutter Street, near Scott, three boys, 21 or 22 years of age, attacked my person. I nearly fainted. Upon rising to my feet they again assaulted me. This time they smashed my nose. I grabbed the coat of one of the trio, and after having my nose dressed at one of the nearby hospitals, I went home. The next day a policeman came, requesting me to give up the coat. I at first refused, but finally, upon his assuring me that it would be deposited at the police station, I gave it up. I reported the matter to the police. When the case came up for trial the youngster was dismissed on the plea of insufficiency of evidence.

There is no record, during this period, of any white person's being convicted for an assault on a Japanese, although several Japanese were arrested for assault and disturbing the peace when they tried to defend themselves.[11] These were minor annoyances and, of course, the local authorities apologized and the more responsible newspapers deplored the breaches of law and order. Discriminations against Japanese in San Francisco were still a local matter. In October, however, they became a *cause célèbre*.

On October 11, 1906, the Board of Education, under mounting pressure from the Exclusion League, ordered all Japanese and Korean pupils to join the Chinese in the Oriental school. This action was little noticed in the San Francisco press, and it seems that the rest of the country was quite ignorant of it. Nine days later, garbled reports of the order were printed in Tokyo newspapers—some said that Japanese were completely excluded—and from these Tokyo reports word of the Board's action reached the United States.[12]

Among those who learned belatedly of this action was Theodore Roosevelt.[13] Although taken by surprise by their latest manifestations of hostility, the President, as his published correspondence now shows, had been keeping a disapproving eye on the Californians for more than a year. The first intimation we have of his interest comes in a letter to George Kennan on May 6, 1905, in which he speaks of the "foolish offensiveness" of the March resolution by the "idiots" of the California legislature. It was not the substance of the resolution that annoyed the President, it was the tone.

The California Legislature would have had an entire right to protest as emphatically as possible against the admission of Japanese laborers, for their very frugality, abstemiousness and clannishness make them formidable to our laboring class, and you may not know that they have begun to offer a serious problem in Hawaii—all the more serious because they keep an entirely distinct alien mass. Moreover, I understand that the Japanese themselves do not permit any foreigners to own land in Japan, and where they draw one kind of sharp line against us they have no right whatever to object to our drawing another kind of line against them. . . . I would not have objected at all to the California Legislature passing a resolution, courteous and proper in its terms, which would really have achieved the object they were after.[14]

Thus, there was little real difference between the views of the California exclusionists and those of the President.[15] Had Roosevelt written this letter to one of them, or had someone communicated his views, the Californians doubtless would have adjusted their language. But Roosevelt kept his views within his own circle. In July, 1905, he wrote to the United States Minister to Japan and told him to inform the mikado's government that "the American Government and the American people at large have not the slightest sympathy with the outrageous agitation against the Japanese. . . . While I am President the Japanese will be treated just exactly like . . . other civilized peoples."[16]

The first public hint of the President's attitude came in his annual message in December, 1905, which seemed to serve notice that he would not acquiesce in extending the bar against Chinese to immigrants from Japan:

it is unwise [the President's message read] to depart from the old American tradition and to discriminate for or against any man who desired to come here as a citizen, save on the ground of that man's fitness for citizenship. . . . We cannot afford to consider whether he is Catholic or Protestant, Jew or Gentile; whether he is Englishman or Irishman, Frenchman or German, Japanese, Italian, Scandinavian, Slav, or Magyar.

In the next paragraph, however, came a qualification to this catholic generalization:

the entire Chinese coolie class, that is, the class of Chinese laborers, skilled and unskilled, legitimately come under the head of undesirable immigrants to this country, because of their numbers, the low wages for which they work, and their low standard of living.[17]

The distinction would have puzzled exclusionists had they noticed the insertion of the Japanese in what was an otherwise stock Rooseveltian platitude. They insisted, not without logic, that the Japanese and Chinese presented exactly the same kind of threat, and Roosevelt, as we have seen, secretly agreed with them. But of course there was another factor, which Roosevelt chose not to mention. Japan, by her stunning annihilation of two Russian fleets and the severe mauling she had given Russian armies, had just vaulted into the first rank of world powers. To the power-conscious President, reason of state made the distinction both logical and necessary.[18]

What were Roosevelt's real views on Japan and the Japanese? It seems clear—if anything about the first Roosevelt is clear—that despite his frequent protests to the contrary he was, along with the overwhelming majority of his contemporaries, a convinced racist. He was, however, willing to treat certain individuals of any race as equals. Although he had been pro-Japanese from the outset of the war, he was stunned by the completeness of Admiral Togo's victory in Tsushima Strait. He had rather hoped "that the two powers will fight until both are fairly well exhausted and that then peace will come on terms which will not mean the creation of either a yellow peril or a Slav peril." He could blurt out to Spring-Rice that "the Japs interest me and I like them," but not far beneath the surface there was always a deep-seated distrust of the Orient, the one part of the globe Roosevelt never visited. Despite the fact that Japan's "diplomatic statements had been made good," he reminded his ambassador to Russia that "Japan is an Oriental nation, and the individual standard of truthfulness in Japan is low." He had "no doubt" that the Japanese people disliked "all white men" and believed "their own yellow civilization to be better."[19]

But his distrust did not blind him to the realities of power. He was one of the few Occidentals who, from the beginning, had expected the Japanese to win the war, although even he was surprised at the one-sidedness of their naval victory. Nor did he share Wilhelm II's "yellow peril" phobias. He explained, rather imaginatively, to a Japanese who had been his classmate at Harvard, that some of his "own ancestors in the 10th century had been part of the 'white terror' of the Northmen," and he pointed out to John Hay that the descendants of Genghis Khan were serving "under the banners of Russia . . . not Japan."[20] He wanted the Japanese treated courteously and with the respect that he felt their military prowess demanded. But he also felt very strongly that the Japanese, and all colored peoples generally, should be willing to take fatherly advice, particularly his fatherly advice. Roosevelt, a confirmed believer in the white man's burden, wanted to be a father to the whole world. At the risk of being thought fanciful, I am going to close this discussion of Roosevelt's racial assumptions with a letter which, although completely unrelated to the Orient, seems to show his basic attitude toward peoples of non-European origin. To an American Indian, appropriately named No Shirt, the President wrote that

the earth is occupied by the white people and the red people.... If the red people would prosper, they must follow the mode of life which has made the white people so strong; and that it is only right that the white people should show the red people what to do and how to live right.... I wish to be a father to the red people as to the white.... Now my friend, I hope you will lay what I have said to heart. Try to set your people a good example of upright and industrious life, patience under difficulties, and respect for the authority of the officers I have appointed.... If you try as hard to help them as you do to find something in their conduct to censure, you will be surprised to find how much real satisfaction life holds in store for you.[21]

This paternal admonition had been evoked by Chief No Shirt's unauthorized trip to Washington to complain to the President; when Roosevelt found that the Indian had not gone through the proper channels, he refused to see him, and he wrote the letter only when the presumably chastened chief had returned to the reservation.

That, from Roosevelt's point of view, was one of the troubles with the world: people and nations were always going "off the reservation." In October, 1906, the offenders were the San Francisco school board and the "labor agitators." By the twenty-sixth of the month, Roosevelt had decided upon his course of action. On that day he wrote to his friend Baron Kentaro Kaneko ("A good fellow, but he is a fox, and a Japanese Fox at that") that the situation was causing the "gravest concern" and that he would do everything possible to "protect the rights of the Japanese who are here." He added that he was sending a cabinet member to the scene.[22]

The next day, which happened to be his forty-eighth birthday, Roosevelt had a conference with his Secretary of Commerce and Labor, Victor H. Metcalf, who then left to make an on-the-spot investigation of what had already become the school crisis. On October 29, in view of his forthcoming inspection trip to Panama, Roosevelt gave formal authorization to his Secretary of State, Elihu Root, to "use the armed forces of the United States to protect the Japanese in any portion of this country if they are menaced by mobs." On the day of his departure for Panama the President saw the Japanese ambassador, Viscount Siuzo Aoki, and read to him the passages on this topic in his forthcoming annual message to Congress, which he believed pleased Aoki very much. Roosevelt, of course, had not yet seen Metcalf's report, as the investigation was still in progress.[23]

Metcalf arrived in the San Francisco area on October 31. As the only Californian in the cabinet, he was the obvious choice for the assignment.

A resident of Oakland, he had been a Republican congressman from 1899 until his elevation to the cabinet in 1904. His work there must have been satisfactory, because the White House had already announced that he would soon become Secretary of the Navy, an assignment which, given Roosevelt's scale of values, could only be regarded as a promotion. The Secretary spent two weeks in the San Francisco area and left without giving a hint of his findings. Californians expected that they would receive favorable treatment from one of their own, and no one seems to have remembered, then or later, that Metcalf had already aired his views on the Japanese question. In May, 1905, he had told San Francisco reporters that he was not concerned about Japanese immigration and that he thought the root of the trouble lay with white men who were not willing to work in the fruit districts.[24]

Roosevelt returned to the capital late in November and had a conference with Metcalf and Benjamin Ide Wheeler, president of the University of California, on November 30. Three days later, his annual message was sent to Congress; it contained the President's first important public statement on the Japanese question; it was also the most advanced position he ever took. The part which concerns us—and which presumably had been read to Aoki in early November—followed a paragraph in which the President wrote of the necessity of treating all nations and immigrants fairly. Then Roosevelt became specific:

I am prompted to say this by the attitude of hostility here and there assumed toward the Japanese in this country. This hostility is sporadic and is limited to a very few places. Nevertheless, it is most discreditable to us as a people, and it may be filled with the gravest consequences to the nation.

The President went on to discuss the more than half century of friendly relations between the United States and Japan, and dwelt at some length in the most complimentary terms on the splendid achievements of Japan, military and otherwise, and declared that the "overwhelming mass of our people cherish a lively regard and respect for the people of Japan," and that "in almost every quarter of the Union" Japanese were treated just "as the stranger from any part of civilized Europe."

But here and there a most unworthy feeling has manifested itself toward the Japanese [such as] shutting them out of the common schools of San Francisco [and] mutterings against them in one or two other places, because of their efficiency as workers. To shut them out from the public schools is a wicked absurdity.... I recommend to the Congress that an act be past (*sic*—T. R.'s simplified spelling) specifically providing for the naturalization of Japanese who come here intending to become American citizens.

He went on to complain that the federal government could not properly protect the rights of aliens here and asked Congress to enable the
President to do so. He made it evident that no abstract concept of
justice inspired this request. His stated motivation was reason of state.
He thought it preposterous that

the mob of a single city may at any time perform acts of lawless violence which
would plunge us into war.... It is unthinkable that we should continue a policy
under which a given locality may be allowed to commit a crime against a friendly
nation.[25]

Roosevelt never again publicly proposed naturalization for the Japanese. It may be that, as in the case of the celebrated dinner invitation
to Booker T. Washington, the President's racial views were in advance
of public opinion and that the ensuing reaction forced him to compromise his principles.[26] This is the most favorable interpretation possible,
and the one most often advanced. Yet it is not convincing. Roosevelt
knew well that anti-Japanese feeling was not limited to San Francisco
and "one or two other places"; he knew also that Southern opinion
would support the West on any racial matter. Since there is no evidence
that he ever made the slightest effort to have this proposal imple-
mented—and certainly there were men in Congress who would have
introduced such a bill had the President so requested—it is reasonable
to assume that Roosevelt made it chiefly for Japanese consumption and
in order to have an advanced position from which to retreat in his
dealings with California.[27] Two months later, during diplomatic negotiations, the Japanese government proposed a trade—naturalization
for exclusion. Secretary of State Root informed the American negoti-
ator: "It is wholly useless to discuss the subject of naturalization at the
present time [because] no statute could be passed or treaty ratified
now" which granted naturalization.[28]

The message may have been for Japanese consumption, but Californians felt that the President's views were being forced down their
throats. Their protests were loud, long, and nearly unanimous; every
prominent newspaper in the state except Harrison Gray Otis' Los
Angeles *Times* denounced Roosevelt. Southerners, in and out of Congress, raised the question of state rights, as they are wont to do on any
racial question, and William Jennings Bryan, flexing his vocal cords
for 1908, sided with them.[29] Then, on December 18, 1906, Metcalf's
report and a concurring letter of transmittal by the President went to
the Congress. The report showed that, rather than the hundreds and
even thousands of pupils the San Francisco papers had written about,
there had been at the time of the segregation order a grand total of

93 Japanese students in all the twenty-three public schools of San Francisco, and that 25 of these students were native-born American citizens.
The press had complained of young men in the primary grades, and
Metcalf agreed that this was, to a degree, true. There were 27 alien
teen-agers, who, for one reason or another, were well above the normal
age limits for their grades. For example, 2 nineteen-year-olds were in
the fourth grade. Metcalf recommended that age limits be set, and even
the local Japanese consul had agreed, before the segregation order, that
there could be no objection to the segregation or even removal of such
overage pupils from the system. Metcalf's report concluded:[30]

All the considerations which may move a nation, every consideration of duty in
the preservation of our treaty obligations, every consideration prompted by fifty
years of more or less close friendship with the Empire of Japan, would unite in
demanding, it seems to me, of the United States Government and all its people, the
fullest protection and the highest considerations for the subjects of Japan.

Metcalf, of course, received an even worse pummeling from the California press than did his chief. As a Californian—the *Argonaut* put it,
"Mr. Metcalf was a Californian"—his report was viewed as an act of
treachery toward his adopted state.[31] Most of the country east of the
Rockies, aside from the South, generally supported the President and
his agent, especially when they found out the ridiculous details.

Public opinion, however, would not get the pupils back into school or
solve what might become a very sticky international problem. The one
thing the federal government could do was institute legal proceedings
in both state and federal courts to try to annul the local action and the
state law on which it was based. With the "separate but equal" doctrine
as law of the land, no appeal could be made for the Nisei children, who
were, after all, American citizens and in no way a diplomatic problem;
but the rights of the alien Japanese children might be protected by the
terms of the 1894 treaty with Japan which granted reciprocal "most
favored nation" rights of residence to the nationals of both countries.
As early as November, Root, working through the Department of
Justice, was setting up a test case and was ready to appeal to the United
States Supreme Court if necessary.[32] At the same time Roosevelt and
Root realized that the school board crisis was merely a surface mani-
festation of a deeper problem.[33] By November, they had decided that
they would try to get at the heart of the matter by restricting Japanese
immigration. But, unlike the California exclusionists, they wanted, if
possible, to do this without the deliberate affront of a Japanese exclusion law, which the administration could have put through Congress
at any time.

Even before he left for Panama, the President began to work for the restriction of Japanese immigration. At the same interview in which he showed the draft of his annual message to Viscount Aoki, Roosevelt told the Japanese ambassador that he thought the "only way to prevent constant friction" between the two nations was to "prevent all immigration of Japanese laboring men . . . into the United States." This is the first intimation of what became known as the Gentlemen's Agreement. But first it was necessary to quell the agitation in California and reduce the racial tension there. Roosevelt understood that the "great difficulty in getting the Japanese" to limit immigration themselves was the "irritation" caused by the segregation order. The President hoped that his message would smooth things over, but, as often was the case, his expectations were unduly sanguine.[34]

When Roosevelt found that he had underestimated the temper of the Californians, and that his message was resulting in more rather than less agitation in California, he and Root revamped their plans. Three things had to be accomplished before the restriction of Japanese immigration could be effected: the San Francisco segregation order had to be revoked by one means or another; the California legislature had to be restrained from passing further discriminatory legislation; and a bill had to be passed by Congress giving the President power to restrict Japanese immigration from intermediate points such as Hawaii, Mexico, and Canada.[35] All these preconditions were related; the executive order limiting intermediary immigration was to be offered to the Californians as a sort of prize for good behavior, and it would not be proclaimed until the segregation order was revoked and all anti-Japanese measures in the California legislature were killed.

At the opening session of the legislature early in January, 1907, the outgoing governor, George C. Pardee, gently chastised Roosevelt's position on the Japanese in the state, attributing his position to the fact that "in common with . . . the people of the Eastern States" the President did not really understand the Japanese question. The governor affirmed the right of California to segregate Orientals "until the courts of this country" should rule otherwise.[36] Within a few days, anti-Japanese bills and resolutions were introduced and discussed in both houses of the legislature and some of these seemed certain to pass. On January 30, 1907, Roosevelt called the entire California congressional delegation to the White House; after the meeting the delegation wired the governor:

Delegation has just had important conference with President and Secretary of State. At their request we have wired Superintendent of Schools and President of

Board of Education of San Francisco to come here immediately for conference.
Entire delegation joins in request that you send for leaders in both houses in Legislature, and ask that all legislative action concerning Japanese matters be deferred
for a short time. We consider this most important.[37]

The new governor, James N. Gillett, a conservative Republican,
added his endorsement to this message and transmitted it to the legislature; both houses immediately complied and either tabled or sent back
to committee the pending anti-Japanese measures.[38] For the moment,
legislative action had been checked, but getting the San Franciscans
to Washington was not so easy.

The San Francisco situation was complicated by the fact that the
peculations of Boss Ruef and Mayor Schmitz had finally stirred reform
elements to action. The pair had been indicted by the grand jury, but
had not yet been brought to trial. The President's invitation had been
extended to the Board of Education only, but the wily mayor, perhaps
thinking to cover himself with glory, had his henchmen on the Board
insist on his accompanying them. After three days of dickering, the
invitation was broadened to include Schmitz; the San Franciscans
arrived in Washington on February 8. After a week of parleys with
Roosevelt and Root an agreement was reached along the lines indicated
in Metcalf's report; overage pupils and those who did not have facility
in English might be placed in separate schools, and, to ease Japanese
sensitivities, the new regulations were to apply to all alien children,
although there was never any intention to segregate Caucasians. In San
Francisco and the rest of California, all other Japanese children, aliens
and citizens, would continue to attend the regular public schools. In
return, the federal government withdrew its suits, and Roosevelt and
Root promised to limit Japanese immigration.

Whatever his motives may have been, Schmitz, an engaging rogue
of the same cut as the later Mayor Jimmy Walker of New York, performed, under pressure, the only statesmanlike act of his political
career, and this, it will be distressing for the moralist to note, brought
him more abuse from his constituents than five years of theft and fraud.
His crimes disturbed only the reform element in San Francisco, and
even after his indictment he seems to have remained a popular figure.
But after his "surrender" to the President, Schmitz, who was soon to
go to jail, received from all sides the same sort of excoriation that had
been showered on Roosevelt and Metcalf.

Almost as soon as the San Franciscans had knuckled under, the legislature seemed again about to pass anti-Japanese legislation. This time
Roosevelt corresponded directly with Governor Gillett, pointing out

that the "attitude of the violent extremists" was the only thing standing in the way of a settlement of the immigration problem by direct
negotiation with Japan. Gillett again did the President's bidding, and
the legislature, heeding the governor's advice, adjourned on March 12
without passing any anti-Japanese measures.[39]

It should be noted, however, that each house of the legislature at one
time or another during the 1907 session passed anti-Japanese bills and
resolutions, although no one measure was passed by both houses. In the
senate three measures were passed unanimously; the one recorded vote
in the assembly was 53 for to 8 against. Few members of the legislature
were willing to vote against anti-Japanese measures, but with the political amorality so typical of legislators most were quite willing to take
no effective action. It should also be noted that not all the measures
were sponsored by men who represented constituencies where there
were large numbers of Japanese. In this and subsequent legislatures,
two Democrats, John B. Sanford and Anthony Caminetti, were among
the leading instigators of discriminatory proposals; in the four small
counties represented by Sanford there were a total of 125 Japanese,
and only 51 were found in the five counties which comprised Caminetti's
bailiwick. Once the agitation had assumed major proportions—that is,
any time after December, 1906—there was no constant relationship
between the number of Japanese in a given area of the state and the
amount of anti-Japanese feeling there.

As soon as the Californians fell into line the President carried out
his part of the bargain. Conveniently, there was an immigration bill
already in Congress, and, having previously gained the acquiescence of
the Japanese government, Root himself drafted an amendment designed
specifically to check secondary Japanese immigration, but very pointedly did not specifically say so. The key passage of Root's handiwork
read:

... whenever the President shall be satisfied that passports issued by any foreign
government to its citizens to go to any country other than the United States or to
any insular possession of the United States or to the Canal Zone are being used for
the purpose of enabling holders to come to the continental territory of the United
States to the detriment of labor conditions therein, the President may refuse to
permit such citizens of the country issuing such passports to enter the continental
territory of the United States.[40]

The secretary explained to Henry Cabot Lodge, the administration's
chief foreign policy spokesman in the upper house, that

from the Japanese point of view all that the President will be doing under such
a provision will be to enforce the limitations that Japan herself puts into her pass-

ports, while, from our point of view, the provision will enable the President to keep Japanese laborers out unless Japan undertakes to force them upon us directly, which she is apparently far from wishing to do.[41]

The bill passed Congress on February 18; Roosevelt, waiting for the Californians to demonstrate their good faith, debarred further Japanese immigration from Hawaii, Mexico, and Canada by an executive order on March 14, 1907.[42]

The executive order blocked off several major sources of immigration without giving undue offense to Japan. The stage was now set for the implementation of the final phase of the Roosevelt-Root plan: getting the Japanese to agree to halt the direct immigration of laborers. What has become known as the Gentlemen's Agreement was the result of more than a year and a half of detailed negotiation; its substance may be found in six notes exchanged between the two governments in late 1907 and early 1908.[43] The Japanese agreed not to issue passports good for the continental United States to laborers, skilled or unskilled, but passports would be issued to "laborers who have already been in America and to the parents, wives and children of laborers already resident there."[44] All the evidence indicates that the Japanese government scrupulously kept the agreement. It has been hailed by most historians as a great achievement of honest and patient negotiation. Yet it actually served to irritate further the already raw nerves of the Californians and by its very nature was almost bound to do so.

What the President and his Secretary of State did not envisage was that under this agreement thousands of Japanese men resident in the United States would bring over wives, who in many cases had been selected for them in the traditional manner by their families and other go-betweens in their native villages. Many of these marriages were by proxy, but they were perfectly legal under Japanese law. The steady advent of these "picture brides" for twelve years seemed to Californians to be another example of Oriental treachery.

The Gentlemen's Agreement was represented to the Californians as exclusion. Had Roosevelt and Root realized that under its terms thousands of Japanese women would come to the United States, they might never have sought it; having done so, they made a blunder of the first magnitude by failing to foresee its consequences. The State Department, hypnotized by statistics which began to show more Japanese emigration than immigration, refused for many years to recognize what Californians quickly discovered: Japanese women were joining their husbands and having babies. That these babies were citizens of the United States made no difference to the Californians, most of whom insisted that "a Jap was a Jap," no matter where he was born. Had Washington understood what would happen in California from the first and made it clear to the Californians that they might expect a limited influx of Japanese women, it is within the realm of possibility that much of the future agitation could have been avoided. As it happened, the combination of ignorance in Washington and prejudice in California inevitably caused anti-Japanese agitation to wax rather than wane. It soon became an article of faith with the exclusionists that they had been betrayed by their own diplomats, who, in turn, were held to be mere dupes of the perfidious Japanese.

Even before it became apparent that the Gentlemen's Agreement was not producing the intended results, the anti-Japanese movement continued to show signs of life. A flurry of physical assaults on Japanese and some minor cases of municipal discrimination occurred in the summer of 1907.⁴⁵ The Exclusion League and its allies continued their agitation and propaganda. The San Francisco *Chronicle,* however, began to take a moderate line after Roosevelt's assurances that Japanese immigration would be limited. This was a position that the *Chronicle* and other California newspapers which spoke for the business and commercial interests would continue to hold. Thus ended the bizarre spectacle of the conservative *Chronicle* and the labor-dominated Exclusion League marching side by side at the head of the anti-Japanese parade. The anti-Japanese torch dropped by de Young's paper was soon taken up by those newspapers belonging to William Randolph Hearst. In this, as everything else, Hearst was a follower, not an innovator; he excelled only in the extremes to which he carried every cause he espoused, from the war with Spain to antivivisectionism. Hearst's peculiar contributions to the anti-Japanese movement will be discussed in detail later; let it be noted here that from 1907 on his papers were second to none in their abuse of both Japan and the Japanese.⁴⁶

After 1908, although anti-Japanese feeling continued to run high by the Golden Gate, San Francisco was no longer the vital center of the movement. The shift of Japanese population from urban to rural areas, noted earlier, becomes apparent from about this time. Correspondingly, anti-Japanese feeling began to grow rapidly in the rural areas of the state, particularly in the central valley. The symptoms of this feeling can be best seen in the growing anti-Japanese activity shown in successive biennial sessions of the California legislature, culminating in the passage of the Alien Land Law of 1913.

CHAPTER IV

THE PROGRESSIVES DRAW THE COLOR LINE

"The fear-laden anti-Japanese emotion of the people [of California] is a sleeping lion."

—Japanese Consul General Nagai,
November 29, 1912

"Ill fares the land,
    to hastening ills a prey,
Where Japs accumulate,
    day by day."

Elk Grove *Citizen*,
January 18, 1913

BEFORE THEODORE ROOSEVELT'S intervention during the winter of 1906–1907, the Japanese question had not been a campaign issue, but from that time until 1914 the crusade to "keep California white" can be understood only in partisan political terms. This is not to say that there was no genuine anti-Japanese feeling; it was ever present and, from all the evidence, constantly increasing. The "California position" was still nationally unpopular, however, and most California politicians were very susceptible to advice from their national party leaders. Had California been an independent republic, or had there been no contrary pressures from Washington, most of the anti-Japanese bills introduced in its legislature would have passed without difficulty. In reality, no significant anti-Japanese legislation was passed until 1913. The Alien Land Law of that year must be viewed against the background of the three election campaigns and the convolutions of the two fruitless legislative sessions which came before.

The Democratic party—which did not elect a governor in California between 1894 and 1938—began in 1908 to make the Japanese issue its own. In that year it adopted a plank deprecating "the recommendation of the republican president in his message to Congress in December, 1906, wherein he recommended . . . that 'an act be passed specifically providing for the naturalization of Japanese' " and adding that "we are unalterably opposed to the naturalization of any Asiatics."[1]

Similarly, during the presidential campaign, some Democrats argued that "Labor's choice [is] Bryan—Japs' choice [is] Taft."[2] One important Democratic campaigner made this argument a key point: to James D. Phelan must go whatever honor there is in having originated this tactic. Little realizing that it would be a major issue in California politics for almost two decades, the few editors who noticed Phelan's last-minute effort were amused. One writer felt that a "novelty in the way of campaign arguments" had been furnished when Phelan gave as a "reason why people should vote for Bryan" the warning that only the Great Commoner could prevent "the Pacific slope [from] being overrun by Hordes of Japanese."[3] Despite this effort, the Democrats lost California by a large margin.

As soon as the next legislature assembled, in January, 1909, it became clear that the anti-Japanese issue was no laughing matter. On the first day for submitting bills, five discriminatory measures were introduced and seemed to have broad support from the legislators. The most important were: an alien land act which would allow aliens five years to become citizens or forfeit their lands and also would limit leases to aliens to one year's duration; a school segregation bill which specifically mentioned Japanese; and a municipal segregation ordinance which would give cities the power to confine Japanese and other Orientals in ghettos.[4] Roosevelt and Root, when they learned of the renewal of the agitation, called upon Governor Gillett to prevent the passage of any invidious legislation and pointed out that under the Gentlemen's Agreement more Japanese were leaving the country than were coming in.[5] Once the coöperation of the governor and his lieutenants had been achieved, there was no likelihood of passage of any important anti-Oriental legislation. By February 13 Roosevelt was able to notify President-elect Taft that "the Republican machine finally came to my help" and to assure him that everything was under control.[6]

As a face-saving measure, the legislature passed a resolution asking that Congress extend the Chinese Exclusion Act to "include all Asiatics" and also, at the governor's suggestion, passed a bill ordering the State Labor Commissioner to investigate and report on "the Japanese of the State."[7] Despite its negative statutory results, the sitting produced its share of anti-Japanese oratory. Most attention was centered on school segregation; the bill providing this was actually passed by the assembly, but, under the administration's pressure, it was reconsidered by that body and defeated. The leading anti-Japanese orator of 1909 was Grove Johnson, the father and political opponent of the rising reformer, Hiram Johnson. In a typical passage he denounced executive interference:[8]

I know more about the Japanese than Governor Gillett and President Roosevelt put together. I am not responsible to either of them. I am responsible to the mothers and fathers of Sacramento County who have their little daughters sitting side by side in the school rooms with matured Japs, with their base minds, their lascivious thoughts, multiplied by their race and strengthened by their mode of life. . . . I have seen Japanese twenty-five years old sitting in the seats next to the pure maids of California. . . . I shudder . . . to think of such a condition.

In the upper house Senator Marc Anthony was equally indignant about the "invasion ... of coolie laborers from the empire of Japan," the encroachments of "the executive branch of the Federal Government," and the "commercialism of New England." He asserted that "in twenty years Japanese in the United States have shipped $200,-000,000 in gold from the United States to Japan, accentuating the late financial stringency."[9]

Neither the assemblyman's shuddering nor the senator's indignation touched upon what was to be the real issue. School segregation was never again the paramount issue, although it remained a talking point, and Anthony's self-contradictory arguments (if they controlled that much money, the Japanese certainly were not coolies) were soon forgotten. After 1909 the main issue become the successive attempts to check the acquisition of agricultural land by the Issei.

Reactions to the legislature's failure to act on the Japanese question in 1909 were varied. As might have been expected, some Democrats and the Asiatic Exclusion League were outraged. League president Tvietmoe berated Roosevelt, Gillett, and the assemblymen who had "betrayed California and voted for the Japs."[10] On the other hand, there were, for the first time, influential California voices calling for moderation. Added to the protests of a few religious groups were the authoritative tones of the spokesmen for the business community. The Chambers of Commerce of both San Francisco and Los Angeles petitioned the legislature not to pass anti-Japanese legislation, because the "Oriental trade passing through the ports of this State has assumed large proportions and is likely to be seriously crippled by such ... action."[11] The San Francisco *Chronicle,* the chief instigator of anti-Japanese agitation in 1905, now felt that further action was unnecessary, because the immigration had "virtually ceased" and the Japanese government would "in good faith ... prevent" additional immigration.[12] Also in opposition were a few large-scale farmers like Lee A. Phillips, whose California Delta Farms, Inc., controlled 65,000 acres and had profitable relations with Japanese laborers and tenants. As Chester Rowell noted, the holders of such views were a "minority ... in California, but those who hold [them] own a great deal of California."[13]

Business and labor were now again in their usual polar positions. Their attitudes were dictated by what they believed to be enlightened self-interest. But California, like much of the country during what is called the Progressive Era, was entering into a period of essentially middle-class political leadership. The 1909 legislature was the last to be dominated by the conservative Republicans and the Southern Pacific

Railroad. In the next election, the California Progressives, still nom-
inally Republicans, captured the state and made Hiram Johnson chief
executive. The historian of California progressivism has pointed out
that, while one of their cardinal objectives was to restore competition,
the progressives felt that there were limits to competition. "To the progressive mind, one of these limits should be the color line."[4] The middle-
class progressive liked to think of himself as enlightened and free of
prejudice; yet at the same time he insisted that separate races could
not mix. As one of the chief progressive spokesmen put it:[15]

"[Racial discrimination] is blind and uncontrollable prejudice . . .
yet social separateness seems to be imposed by the very law of nature."
"Race . . . counts more than anything else in the world. It is the mark
God placed on those whom he put asunder. It is grounded in the in-
stincts of man, and is not amenable to reason." "[An educated Jap-
anese] would not be a welcomed suitor for the hand of any American's
daughter [but] an Italian of the commonest standing and qualities
would be a more welcomed suitor than the finest gentleman of Japan.
So the line is biological, and we draw it at the biological point—at the
propagation of the species." "[Intermarriage between a Japanese and a
White would be] a sort of international adultery. . . . The instinct of
self-preservation of our race demands that its future members shall be
members of our race. . . . Personally, I think this instinct is wise and
beneficial." "If we deal with this race question now, our descendants will
have no race questions to deal with. If Californians do not deal with it
now, they, like ante-bellum South Carolinians, will leave a race question
which their descendants will have to deal with, and against which they
will be helpless." "The only time to solve a race problem is before it
begins." "It is for the white peoples to resolve and the brown peoples
to accept the permanent physical separation of their races. But as to
those who are already over the border, it is for Californians to treat
them justly, and for Easterners to be sympathetic and Japanese fore-
bearing if occasionally they fail to do so."

Such were the assumptions which motivated most of the progressives.
As a rule, the progressives did not initiate anti-Japanese agitation, and
were scornful of those who made it their chief stock-in-trade. Most
progressives would have been satisfied to leave the matter in the hands
of the federal government. After the Japanese question had been used
successfully by their opponents, however, the progressives were determined to break the Democratic monopoly. During the 1910 campaign, in
which the governorship was at stake, the Democrats and their allies
continued to monopolize the anti-Oriental issue. Theodore Bell, Hiram

Johnson's Democratic opponent, frankly courted the Asiatic Exclusion League, while Johnson did everything but openly insult it.[16] State Senator J. B. Sanford, the "Grey Eagle of Ukiah," promised his constituents that "if reëlected" he would "use every legitimate effort in his power to secure passage" of an anti-Asiatic land bill: "The Democratic platform endorses [this] bill, and Theodore A. Bell says, that if elected Governor, he will sign such a measure."[17] The Republicans, progressive and conservative, generally ignored this issue. Hiram Johnson's early political success was in no wise owing, as has been alleged, to manipulation of the Japanese question. If anything, his failure to use it cost him votes.[18] As long as a friend was in the White House and that friend urged moderation, Johnson and his supporters "sat upon the lid" and prevented any legislation.[19] This, in essence, is what happened in the 1911 legislature.

In his inaugural address, Governor Johnson pointedly ignored the Japanese problem, but from the first working day of the session it was evident that the legislators would not follow his lead. Altogether, twenty-seven anti-Japanese measures were introduced.[20] The campaign to defeat them, however, had been started a month before the legislature met. In early December, 1910, Secretary of State Philander C. Knox informed the Japanese ambassador, Uchida, that Governor-elect Johnson had given Theodore Roosevelt assurances that he would do everything he could to prevent anti-Japanese legislation.[21] When the first bills were introduced Johnson sent copies to Knox and added, "I think I can assure you that the committees of both Houses that will have in charge measures of this character, are wholly sane and trustworthy, and that, doubtless, they will be guided by the wishes of the Federal Administration."[22] As the session wore on, two things soon became apparent: the senate was more insistent upon anti-Japanese legislation than the assembly, and strong efforts were being made to pass some sort of alien land act. The two most important bills were introduced by Senators Larkins and Sanford (senate bills 2 and 24). The first applied sanctions equally to all aliens, while the second only inhibited the rights of "aliens ineligible to citizenship."

This phrase, "aliens ineligible to citizenship," was vital to most anti-Japanese legislative proposals (which rarely specifically mention Japanese) and it merits explanation. In a series of decisions dating from the 1870's, the courts had ruled that since the original naturalization statute had limited naturalization to "free white persons" (this had been broadened to include Africans after the Civil War), Chinese and other Orientals were aliens ineligible to citizenship until Congress should legislate to the contrary. The Supreme Court had not yet ruled on a case involving a Japanese (and would not do so until 1922), but it was correctly assumed that Japanese fell under the same ban.[23] Californians therefore had a convenient excuse for arguing that the laws of the United States discriminated against Orientals, not the laws of California. Any law which restricted land tenure to citizens in California would operate against Japanese, but it was felt by all moderates that a general alien land bill would be less insulting to Japan than one which applied only to aliens ineligible to citizenship. There were alien land bills on the books of several non-Pacific Coast states and the District of Columbia; most of these had been inspired by the general nativist feelings that tinged so much of the Populist revolt, and had been in no way directed against Orientals.[24]

Another argument used to justify action by California was the fact that in Japan no alien could hold land. We have seen that Theodore Roosevelt used this hypothetical justification as early as 1905. It was specious on three counts. First, the Japanese law applied to all foreigners alike and the Japanese naturalization laws were nondiscriminatory; second, in Japan a foreigner could get a nine-hundred-and-ninety-nine-year lease (such leaseholders paid all the taxes on the property),[25] and, third, American legal treatment of resident aliens had almost always been identical, without regard to their national origin, and any invidious departure from that precedent could rightly be regarded as discrimination. But there was nothing in law or treaty to prevent Californians from deliberately discriminating against resident aliens in the matter of agricultural land tenure.[26]

While various anti-Japanese measures were being debated in Sacramento, two different sets of negotiations were under way in Washington. The diplomatic representatives of Japan and the United States were ironing out the details of a new treaty, and delegations from San Francisco and New Orleans were vying for the honor and profit of being host to what became the Panama-Pacific International Exposition of 1915, celebrating the opening of the Panama Canal.[27] Among the leading California lobbyists for the exposition was Patrick Henry McCarthy, whom we met earlier as the chief patron of the Asiatic Exclusion League. He had since fallen heir to the mantle of the convicted Schmitz and Ruef, taken over the Union Labor machine, and was now mayor of San Francisco. In exchange for the support of the national administration for San Francisco's ultimately successful bid, McCarthy agreed to use his influence to halt the anti-Japanese agitation, at least temporarily.[28] The mayor was as good as his word, and on February 13,

1911, the following startling communication was read into the record of the legislature:[29]

... the Asiatic Exclusion League regrets that regardless of the previous communication on the subject we have not been afforded an opportunity to examine the anti-alien Asiatic bills [now pending]. It is the sense of the board that such bills as these at the present time are not conducive to the final enactment of effective and permanent Asiatic exclusion legislation.... We respectfully request that you proceed cautiously in this manner, as pressing measures of this kind would mean irreparable injury to the exclusion cause.

O. A. TVIETMOE, President

This remarkable *volte-face*, whose motivation was not then understood, had little influence on the legislature. The incident is noteworthy on two counts: it marks the end of the effective influence of the labor-dominated Asiatic Exclusion League, which completely disintegrated within two years, and marks the beginning of the influence of the Panama-Pacific International Exposition. The businessmen who ran the exposition tried to check anti-Japanese legislation because they feared that it might prove detrimental to the success of their venture, in which the people of California had a ten-million-dollar stake.[30]

By the end of January, although the anti-Japanese bills were still in committee, Johnson informed the State Department as follows:[31]

... a very strong sentiment exists in California in favor of ... an act which will prevent Japanese from acquiring and holding land.... We believe, therefore, that before the session is closed the legislature will take up and finally adopt some measure upon the subject; and if this becomes apparent, the Lieutenant Governor, the Speaker and myself believe that [the Larkins Bill], general in character, specifically preserving rights under treaties, might be presented to the exclusion of more radical measures. If ... legislation upon the subject is inevitable ... would such a course ... be acceptable to you?

Secretary Knox wired in reply that both he and the President would "strongly deprecate any legislation aimed directly or indirectly at Japanese subjects," but agreed that as a last resort a general bill would be preferred. Knox expressed the "sincere hope that any such situation may be avoided or at least postponed through your good offices."[32]

In late February a garbled report of the contents of the newly signed but as yet unratified treaty with Japan created the belief that the Gentlemen's Agreement had been abandoned. An exchange of telegrams between the President and the governor was sent to the legislature, giving assurance that the exclusion arrangements were being maintained. In addition, Johnson issued a vigorous statement: "I know nothing of the contents of the treaty. The matter in which the people of the State are interested is exclusion. The question therefore is 'Do we get exclusion?' The President of the United States says we do and that ends the matter so far as I am concerned."[33]

After an extremely long delay—more than two months—California's "sane and trustworthy" Senate Judiciary Committee reported out unfavorably a substitute anti-Japanese land bill on March 15. The bill reported was of the "aliens ineligible to citizenship" variety. After six days of delay and parliamentary maneuvering, the bill was passed by a vote of 29 to 3.[34]

Johnson informed Washington of the senate's action and received in reply a long telegram from Acting Secretary of State F. M. Huntington Wilson expressing the hope that passage of the bill might be avoided. Huntington Wilson, in a very undiplomatic manner, went on to "point out how unfortunate it would be if action in the California Legislature should be such as to require [the President] to hesitate to extend ... invitations to participate in the Panama-Pacific International Exposition, an occasion which requires that atmosphere of a settled spirit of good will and considerateness to all nations."[35]

Johnson, who was as jealous of his prerogatives as any Balkan potentate, felt, with some justification, that the tone of this message was "particularly offensive."[36] "Extraordinary care and pains have been taken," he wired Huntington Wilson, "to follow the suggestions and advice of the Federal Government. ... The Governor of California has a veto. ... There shall be no legislation discriminatory in character." He added, however, that

the State of California reserves the right to legislate as it may see fit in reference to its lands. [In addition] the statutes of the United States contain an alien land bill. ... Do you deny to California the right to pass or the propriety of the passage of such an alien land bill? [Nevertheless] no discriminatory measure shall become a law at this time, and I repeat that this is said to you, not because of your telegram or its threat, but because the only design of this administration is to be just and do that which will redound to the peace, the dignity, the advantage and best interests of the state and nation.[37]

The next day Johnson requested permission to publish Huntington Wilson's telegram of March 23. By this time the more tactful Knox had returned to Washington; he suavely denied that there had been any threat, smoothed Johnson's ruffled feathers, and requested no publicity, a wish Johnson respected.[38]

The anti-Japanese land bill was sent to the assembly on March 23 and was quickly referred to its Judiciary Committee, which had been holding several similar assembly measures since the beginning of the session. None of these was reported out until the day of adjournment, March 27.

Under the constitution of California, a bill must have three readings, on
three separate days, before passage. The anti-Japanese bills had had
only one reading. The approval of two thirds of the assemblymen could
have suspended this constitutional provision, but, with the administration and the floor leaders opposed, that was patently impossible, so no
attempt to force passage was made.[39] The anti-Japanese forces had been
frustrated again.

Senator Sanford wrote bitterly to Phelan that "the manner in
which the [anti-Japanese] bill was defeated in the Assembly was most
cowardly.... I am going after this alien land bill [in 1913] in a red hot
way. I shall be pleased to receive any suggestions from you that you
may see fit to give."[40] But Phelan had his attention focused on an event
closer at hand: the presidential election of 1912. By early October,
1911, he had thrown his support behind the reform governor of New
Jersey, Woodrow Wilson, as did State Senator Anthony Caminetti.
Most California Democrats, however, along with William Randolph
Hearst, supported the candidacy of Champ Clark of Missouri.[41]

As soon as it became clear that Wilson was the candidate to beat, his
opponents began scouring his published works to find ammunition for
the "stop Wilson" movement. The five-volume *A History of the American People* (1901–1902) furnished a goodly supply. As his biographer
points out, it was history from a "conservative point of view" which
Wilson "would not have written if he had known he was some day to
become a presidential candidate."[42] Various passages in the work in-
sulted most of the non-Southern voters to whom a liberal Democratic
candidate traditionally appeals. In the East it was Wilson's denuncia-
tion of the new immigrants which most embarrassed his supporters. In
California the Hearst papers seized upon his statements about Orientals.
Professor Wilson had written of the Chinese that they

were more to be desired, as workmen if not as citizens, than most of the coarse
crew that came crowding in every year at the eastern ports. They had, no doubt,
many an unsavory habit, bred unwholesome squalor in the crowded quarters where
they most abounded in the western seaports, and seemed separated by their very
nature from the people among whom they had come to live; but it was their skill,
their intelligence, their hardy power of labor, their knack at succeeding and driving
duller rivals out, rather than their alien habits, that made them feared and hated....
The unlikely fellows who came in at the eastern ports were tolerated because they
usurped no place but the very lowest in the scale of labor.[43]

Soon after the Hearst campaign against Wilson began, Phelan wired
to William F. McCombs, chairman of the Democratic National Committee:

Has governor spoken against oriental coolie immigration? Charged here volume five history he favors same. Should declare against coolies as unassimilable and destructive to republican government and white labor. Answer.[44]

Phelan continued to press McCombs, who finally suggested that Phelan write to Wilson directly.[45] In mid-April Phelan put the whole California case to Wilson in a lengthy letter.

We on the Pacific Coast [Phelan informed the candidate] will be pleased to know your views at this time on the subject of Oriental immigration. Permit me to briefly state the situation.... The Japanese have invaded the Central valleys of California. Take, for example, one highly productive fruit growing valley known as the Vaca Valley. There, the Japanese, refusing to work for wages after the first year or so, bargained for a share of the crop, and finally ousted in many instances the tenant farmers by offering the land owner larger returns, and in some instances acquired ... the property by purchase. The white man is thus driven off the land to move farther away. The village stores, churches and homes suffer and in many instances are left without patronage or occupants. In other words, the Japanese are a blight on our civilization, destructive of the home life of the people, driving the natives to the city for employment.... The Hawaiian Islands are now practically a possession of Japan, as California will be unless the Japanese question is solved....

President Taft last spring surrendered a clause in the Japanese treaty giving us the right to regulate immigration. No protest was raised by our legislature, because Governor Johnson and others were in Washington seeking the President's support for the Panama-Pacific Exposition. I wrote a protest, however, in the *National Monthly*, Buffalo, New York, of April, 1911, to which I beg to refer you. It is vital, I believe, for our civilization [and] for the preservation of our domestic institutions ... that Oriental coolies be excluded from these shores.

In the campaign, this question will be raised and I would like to be able to answer such charges as have been made against your History.... Even where coolies are capable of doing a day's work, as they admittedly are, the question is, should they be allowed, in a fierce competition, to lower the standards of living ... of members of the white race, who stand for home life, Republican Government and Western civilization? [If Japanese immigration continues] California would be a plantation and the white population would for a period of time, possibly, remain as overseers, but, indeed, with my knowledge of the Japanese, that would be for a very short time. The end would soon supervene.[46]

To this last appeal Wilson replied with a telegram tailored to Phelan's specifications; he merely put his name to a statement Phelan had drafted:

In the matter of Chinese and Japanese coolie immigration [the candidate's message read] I stand for the national policy of exclusion. We cannot make a homogeneous population out of a people who do not blend with the Caucasian race. Their lower standard of living as laborers will crowd out the white agriculturist and is, in other fields, a most serious industrial menace. The success of free democratic institutions demands of our people education, intelligence and patriotism and the state should protect them against unjust and impossible competition. Remunerative labor is the basis of contentment. Democracy rests on the equality of the citizen. Oriental coolieism will give us another race problem to solve and surely we have had our lesson.[47]

Phelan wired McCombs: "I received Governor Wilson's wire on Oriental question and put it out at once. It made a good impression and answered Hearst just as he printed his last letter."[48] The impression seems not to have been deep enough, for Wilson lost the California primary decisively six days later. But, after Wilson's nomination and throughout the campaign (which in California was purely Wilson versus Theodore Roosevelt, since Hiram Johnson's Progressives had taken over the Republican party and the national Republican nominee, Taft, was not even on the ballot), Wilson's message was used to telling effect. His statement was printed on a small card with Roosevelt's 1906 statement in favor of naturalizing the Japanese on the reverse. This card was distributed in large numbers. The state Democratic plank called for an alien land act to "prevent any alien not eligible to citizenship from owning land in the State of California."[49] With Roosevelt as their candidate, the Progressives had to bear this in silence.

In the November election in California the Progressives nosed out the Democrats by 174 votes in a canvass of almost 700,000.[50] The significant fact, however, was that the Democrats captured 44 per cent of the vote, by far their best showing since Grover Cleveland carried the state in 1892.[51] In a postelection analysis Phelan reported to McCombs: "The Japanese question gave us in part the farmer's support. We used [Wilson's] views to good advantage by wide spread publicity in the labor districts, more particularly, and also in the rural communities."[52] Hiram Johnson, who was Roosevelt's running mate, later told Roosevelt that the cards on the Japanese question, "distributed literally by the hundreds of thousands," had cost the Bull Moosers "at least ten thousand votes."[53] The Japanese consul general in San Francisco did not need prophetic powers to realize that the "sleeping lion" of anti-Japanese feeling might roar into action in the coming legislature.

The directors of the Panama-Pacific International Exposition were also aware of the danger and acted accordingly. As early as January, 1912, they learned from semiofficial sources that any discriminatory legislation might result in Japan's taking "little, if any interest in the exposition."[54] Since it was generally felt that the Japanese exhibit would be one of the most important features of the fair, the directors were prepared to go to great lengths to prevent anti-Japanese legislation.

At the end of December, 1912, A. C. Baker was assigned by his fellow directors of the Panama-Pacific International Exposition to make contact with Robert J. Hudspeth of Jersey City, a Wilson appointee to the Democratic National Committee. Baker wired Hudspeth that "If [Wilson] would send a confidential telegram to his representative in California suggesting that he prefers no anti-Japanese legislation be enacted ... it would be desirable both [to] the Wilson administration [and] the Exposition.... Could you use your good offices in bringing this to the attention of President-elect Wilson immediately?"[55] If Wilson ever received this message, he chose not to act on it. In fact, at no time between his election in November, 1912, and his inauguration in March, 1913, did the President-elect give any indication that he had the slightest inkling that his California campaigning had helped create a situation that would embarrass his administration from its very outset.

The outgoing administration also refused to take effective action. The Japanese ambassador, Chinda, called on both Taft and Knox in January, 1913, and asked them to try to prevent passage of anti-Japanese measures. Two years earlier, before the breach between the conservative and progressive wings of the Republican party had become serious, the President and his Secretary of State, with Johnson's coöperation, had been able to take effective preventive measures. In 1913, however, discouraged by their own rejection at the polls and by the party split, which Hiram Johnson had abetted, Taft and Knox made no direct attempt to forestall legislation, nor, it would seem, did they alert the President-elect to the imminent danger. Knox did tell Chinda that he had written to influential members of the California Legislature, but probably these were not members of the controlling Progressive faction.[56]

Throughout the 1913 legislative session, the Panama-Pacific International Exposition again made extensive efforts, both direct and indirect, to prevent anti-Japanese legislation. On January 6, at a special meeting of the Exposition board of directors, who were drawn from the financial and commercial leadership of San Francisco, lists of legislators who might introduce such legislation were distributed to the directors, and it was ordered that "any member of the Board having knowledge as to how any of these Legislators could be influenced" should inform the Exposition president, Charles Caldwell Moore.[57]

On the same day a nine-man Exposition delegation visited the state capitol, where the new legislature was organizing itself. They first had a "conference of several hours with the Governor," in which a "plan of campaign was outlined to head off any agitation" for an alien land act. Governor Johnson "displayed warm interest in the entire matter and assured President Moore of his heartiest cooperation." Members of the delegation saw individually almost every senator and assemblyman and tried to get everyone to agree not to introduce any anti-Japanese bills during that session.[58] The Exposition spokesmen agreed that the question of Japanese landownership had to be met sometime, but felt that "there was no pressing need for it [now]."[59] Johnson and most of the legislators indicated to the delegation that so long as no anti-Japanese bills were introduced they themselves would not introduce any, but they refused to commit themselves to oppose anti-Japanese bills actually introduced.[60]

On January 13, the first day for the introduction of bills, anti-Japanese measures were proposed by Democrats and Progressives in both houses.[61] As in 1911, two different kinds of alien land bills were introduced: one set barred all aliens from the ownership of land; the other barred only those aliens who were "ineligible to citizenship." As we have seen, Johnson and his forces had adroitly opposed anti-Japanese legislation in 1911. For the first two and a half months of 1913 there is no evidence that the Johnson forces, as such, threw their weight on one side or the other. Both sets of bills slowly proceeded through the legislative process. Under a new procedure the legislature met for a month, adjourned for a month, and in early March returned to complete the session.

While the legislature took its recess, Woodrow Wilson became President of the United States. On the second day of his administration Japanese Ambassador Chinda called to discuss the pending legislation in California. "The President commented that the constitution did not allow the Federal Government to intervene in matters relating to the rights of the individual states," Chinda informed his chief, Baron Makino. He understood, however, that the administration would "exercise its influence as far as possible in compliance with the desires of the Japanese Government." On March 13 Secretary of State Bryan gave Chinda similar assurances. Between March 15 and April 1 both Wilson and Bryan informed the ambassador that they were writing Californians to drop anti-Japanese measures.[62]

While the ambassador's main concern was with legislation in California, there was also an anti-Japanese measure pending in the state of Washington, where a Democrat, Eugene Lister, was governor. It is instructive to observe the different way in which Wilson handled each situation. Wilson suggested to Bryan that he write to Governor Lister "urging him to use his influence with the state legislature 'to prevent *discrimination*—that is urge that the bill [pending] be so drawn as to make ownership depend upon something other than race.' "[63] With Hiram Johnson, the Progressive governor of California, a different method was used. Wilson told Chinda that "in view of Johnson's emotional character" it would be useless to appeal to him directly."[64] But Wilson was willing to make indirect appeals.

On March 17, Johnson wrote to Chester H. Rowell, one of his closest advisors, that

the situation [relating to the proposed alien land bills] is unique and interesting now, and not only interesting, but one out of which we can get a good deal of satisfaction. [Democratic State Senator Anthony] Caminetti apparently comes authoritatively to ask that we go slow with Japanese legislation. This is confidential. I think before the session adjourns the present administration at Washington may be asking us in exactly the same fashion as previous administrations have asked us, to take no position.[65]

If Wilson hoped to get results from such tactics, he had completely misjudged Johnson's "emotional character."

Although he had not yet taken any public position on the legislation, it is now quite clear that from about the middle of March Johnson was the behind-the-scenes manager of the alien land bill.[66] At the governor's suggestion, the directors of the Panama-Pacific International Exposition came to Sacramento early in April to attempt to stem the anti-Japanese tide.[67] This second Exposition delegation, which went before a joint meeting of the legislature on April 2, served to intensify rather than lessen anti-Japanese feeling. Johnson himself later described the affair:

... I arranged for a public hearing in the Assembly Chamber, when publicly the Exposition people could present their case to the legislators. At tha' hearing the farmers appeared, and the debate between the very plain rugged, untutored and uncultured men from the fields and our astute and educated, plug-hatted brigade who represented the Exposition was most interesting and memorable. When it had ceased the Exposition people retired crestfallen; the audience roared its approval of the farmers and the Committee in charge of the bill immediately and unanimously reported that it "do pass."[68]

It is hard to believe that a man as politically astute as Hiram Johnson could not have foreseen the result; the "spontaneous" demonstration by the "rugged farmers" has all the earmarks of a well-rehearsed performance. The most impressive "farmer" seems to have been one Ralph Newman, a former Congregational minister.[69]

Near my home [Newman declaimed] is an eighty-acre tract of as fine land as there is in California. On that tract lives a Japanese. With that Japanese lives a white woman. In that woman's arms is a baby.

What is that baby? It isn't a Japanese. It isn't white. It is a germ of the mightiest problem that every faced this state; a problem that will make the black problem of the South look white.[70]

James D. Phelan and Paul Scharrenberg, who represented the California State Federation of Labor, also appeared in favor of the anti-

Japanese bill and contributed to what one writer called "the Exposition's Last Stand." Phelan later remembered that he had said:

Gentlemen, the exposition will be in California only a year, while the white race, I hope, will be here forever.... Japan may not exhibit at our fair, but we cannot sell our birth-right for a tea garden. She is impudent and audacious in her position. If she does not exhibit we shall survive.[71]

While the Assembly was still considering the bill, Johnson received two telegrams from Washington, both sent by William Kent, a Progressive California congressman friendly to President Wilson. The first message advised that "Legislation against alien land tenure in order to be void of unnecessary offense should exclude all aliens but should exempt from excluding... those who have been permitted to file satisfactory first papers for naturalization." The second informed the governor: "Message sent is based on highest authority. This is confidential."[72]

Johnson replied by pointing out to Kent that previous administrations had communicated directly with the governor of the state and insisted that Wilson communicate directly with him if he had anything to say.[73] Rowell, who was shown the exchange of messages, scored Wilson's "petty and cowardly attitude" and expressed the hope that Johnson's telegram would "smoke [Wilson] out into saying... officially the things" he has said privately.[74]

Wilson did not "smoke out" easily. The next communication came from Secretary of State Bryan, who requested only the full text of measures pending and asked that Johnson refrain from signing any bill passed until the federal government could present arguments for a possible veto.[75] Johnson replied: ... it is necessary if any feature of the bill is obnoxious to the views of the state department that the legislature be advised at once."[76] Ineffectual telegraphic sparring continued for more than a week. Up until April 17 the Progressive majority in both houses of the legislature was pressing for an antialien bill general in terms, which, despite its obvious intent, would have been less offensive to Japan. Johnson had assured Bryan that the final bill would be couched in those terms.[77] Then there was a change of policy. As Johnson explained to Rowell:

The Senate Bill was carefully prepared, as you know, but since the agitation commenced the pressure has been tremendous upon the members of the legislature from those interested in foreign corporations, to exclude [from the bill] all foreign corporations, except those in which the holders of the majority of the stock were ineligible to citizenship.

Johnson then made an admission he would never make in public statements on the matter: "Of course, this points the bill."[78]

Meanwhile, California discrimination against Japanese had again created an international crisis. Jingoes and extremists in Japan were screaming for war with the United States. On April 17 "a crowd of some 20,000 Japanese in Tokyo cheered wildly as a member of the Diet demanded the sending of the Imperial fleet to California to protect Japanese subjects and maintain the nation's dignity."[79] Wilson and Bryan, despite their obvious reluctance, had to take some sort of positive action. Yet Bryan, probably unwittingly, had already fumbled the only likely chance for an amicable settlement. On April 12 Ambassador Chinda voluntarily offered a concession which might have served to allay the California agitation: he suggested that Japan might be willing to curb the coming of the "picture brides."[80] Bryan ignored this offer. Had he accepted it, he would have had, like Roosevelt in 1907, something to offer California in exchange for coöperation.[81] As it turned out, he came to California empty-handed; he returned without results.

Wilson was finally "smoked out" on April 22. In identical telegrams to Johnson and the legislature the President appealed "with the utmost confidence to the people, the government, and the Legislature of California" and asserted that if they deemed it necessary "to exclude all aliens who have not declared their intention to become citizens from the privileges of landownership" there could be no complaint. He went on to imply, speciously, that the bill under consideration would violate treaty rights of the Japanese, and ended his request with a high-flown reference to "national policy and national honor."[82] Johnson's answer insisted that the bill did not violate the treaty—a position the State Department itself later took in answering the Japanese protests.[83]

Wilson then requested that Johnson receive Secretary of State Bryan "for the purpose of consulting . . . and cooperating with you and [the members of the legislature] in the framing of a law which would meet the views of the people of the State and yet leave untouched the international obligations of the United States." Johnson agreed, and Bryan started the four-day train ride to California.[84]

While Bryan was traveling all formal legislative proceedings on the land bills ceased; but during that time Johnson, together with Ulysses S. Webb, the state attorney general, and Francis J. Heney, a leading Progressive, drafted a substitute bill that explicitly protected all rights under the 1911 treaty with Japan and eliminated the phrase "aliens ineligible to citizenship" by the substitution of the equally offensive phrases "all aliens eligible to citizenship" and "all aliens other than . . ."[85]

Johnson commented soon afterward that

we all thought, of course, that [Bryan] was coming here with something of great
importance to impart, and the gravity of the situation was during this period of
waiting, more keenly felt than at any other time. When Mr. Bryan arrived, immediately we arranged for his consultation with the legislature, and that consultation,
at his suggestion, was made *executive.* The very suggestion aroused to the highest
pitch the interest of the legislators, and the first meeting with Mr. Bryan was held
with the idea prevalent that he would make such disclosures as would render imperative postponement of our measure.[86]

If Johnson and the legislators entertained such expectations, they
were soon disabused. The transcript of Bryan's two executive meetings
with the California legislature runs to 113 typewritten pages and dem-
onstrates clearly that the onetime "Boy Orator of the Platte" had lost
none of his vocal staying power in middle age. Johnson's acid comment
that "Mr. Bryan presented nothing that could not have been transmitted within the limits of a night letter, without using all of the
allotted words," is reasonably accurate.[87] Bryan himself stated: "I came
here with no program. I came simply to confer."[88] Bryan's hands were
tied by the President, who had instructed him not "to sanction particular statutes or forms of legislation."[89] Bryan's unprecedented trip seems
mostly to have been a matter of window dressing; since the proceedings
were secret, the Japanese must have surmised that the administration
was making Herculean, if belated, efforts to avert invidious legislation.[90]
Most of the outnumbered Democrats in the legislature, including Sanford and Caminetti, heretofore ardent proponents of all anti-Japanese
legislation, did indeed vote to postpone consideration of the bill to the
next legislature, but this was a hopeless effort. The Johnson administration's bill was pushed through both houses in less than four days, passing the senate by 35 to 2 and the assembly by 72 to 3.[91] At Wilson's
request, Johnson held the measure for a time; he then signed it on
May 19.

Johnson wrote a long letter to Bryan justifying his action.[92] Organizing his arguments like the trained lawyer he was, the governor, in terms
reminiscent of his tart telegram to Huntington Wilson two years before,
insisted that:

By the law adopted we offer no offense; we make no discrimination. The offense
and discrimination are contained, it is claimed, in the use of the words "eligible to
citizenship.". . . We do not mention the Japanese or any other race. . . . If invidious
discriminations ever were made in this regard, the United States made [them] when
the United States declared who were and who were not eligible for citizenship. . . .
If discrimination it is discrimination against California. We insist that justly no
offense can be taken by any nation to this law. . . . We of California . . . have violated absolutely no treaty rights; we have shown no shadow of discrimination; we
have given no nation the right to be justified in taking offense.[93]

Was Johnson the mover or the moved? Was the long-deferred anti-Japanese legislation inevitable, or could it have been avoided in 1913? Johnson himself claimed credit for the passage of the bill. He wrote to his political mentor, Theodore Roosevelt, that he regarded the passage of the bill as a political triumph:

It was perfectly obvious to me that when we had started upon our course, there was nothing to do but to go through with it and pass our bill. Of course, all of our timid legislators would have liked to recede, and at times I had extraordinary difficulty in making them understand that having started we must finish and I really believe that many of them went through with the matter more in personal loyalty than because they had any stomach for the particular kind of legislation . . . you can pardon, perhaps a little malicious pleasure, that I took out of the attitude of our democratic brethren and the democrats of the national administration.

I think we have laid the ghost. I know that never again in California can the Japanese question be a political question, except as we shall want it to be.[94]

Under Johnson's leadership the California legislature committed a wanton action—wanton because Johnson, at least, knew well that Japanese land tenure in California would not be seriously affected by it. In effect, the Alien Land Law limited leases of agricultural land to Japanese to maximum terms of three years and barred further land purchases by Japanese aliens. It was quite simple for the attorneys who represented Japanese interests in California to evade the intent of this law, as Californians were soon to discover. One of Johnson's chief advisers pointed this out to him before the bill had been drafted. "It will be perfectly easy," wrote Chester Rowell, "to evade the law by transferring to . . . local representatives enough stock to make fifty-one per cent of it ostensibly held by American citizens."[95] For the growing number of Issei who had American-born children, it was even simpler: they merely had the stock or title vested in their citizen children, whose legal guardianship they naturally assumed.[96]

The passage of the Alien Land Law was regarded as a severe affront by the Japanese government, which protested to Washington vigorously. A long exchange of notes came to nothing. Both governments took rather absurd positions: the Japanese claimed that their treaty rights had been violated, while the American contended that there was, in fact, no discrimination intended by California.[97]

The greater part of the nation's press, particularly in the East, opposed the California law.[98] The controversy became a national issue lasting for several months. Between April 4 and the end of May there were stories on the California land law in the New York *Times* on every day but three; twenty-seven times during that period it was deemed front-page news.

Within California there was a certain amount of dissatisfaction with the Alien Land Law of 1913. The Anti-Jap Laundry League insisted later that "the law as it stands means little or nothing."[99] Theodore Bell, leader of the anti-Wilson Democratic faction in the state, argued that the "Johnson machine has made a bad mess"; the law did not, in his opinion, restrict the Japanese enough, and he threatened to invoke the newly enacted initiative to get a stronger law.[100] Harry Chandler, of the Los Angeles *Times,* a prominent conservative spokesman, attacked the law as an "unwise and uncalled for measure."[101] A leading Protestant periodical in the state felt that it was "unfortunate" and inspired by the "rudimentary race hatred and race prejudice" that was "deeply imbedded in the social life of California."[102]

These, however, were minority views; most Californians seemed to believe, as their governor professed to, that they had "laid the ghost of the Japanese question." For a few years it seemed, superficially, that they had. From 1913 until 1919 there was no widespread anti-Japanese agitation. One reason was that during the First World War such agitation would have been inexpedient (and after the American declaration of war perhaps seditious), since the Japanese were also at war with Germany. But the "sleeping lion" of anti-Japanese emotion in California would reawaken, stronger than before, and would do so in a national climate of opinion much more conducive to ultimate success.

CHAPTER V

THE YELLOW PERIL

"Japan is now a world power and is already clutching
for control of the Pacific and this will ultimately bring
her into conflict with the United States."
—James D. Phelan, Nov. 12, 1907

"Are there any radical antagonisms in the modern capital-
ist world that must be utilized?... War is brewing between [Japan and America]. They cannot live in peace on
the shores of the Pacific, although those shores are three
thousand versts apart.... There is a vast literature devoted to the future Japanese-American war. That war is
brewing, that war is inevitable, is beyond doubt."
—V. I. Lenin, Nov. 26, 1920

SOMETIME between 1913 and 1924 a decided change in American public
opinion toward Japan and the Japanese took place. The "California
position," which, as we have seen, did not win national favor in either
1906–1907 or 1913, was written into the statute book in 1924. There is
every reason to believe that this congressional action accurately reflected majority sentiment. Although it is obviously impossible to make
a quantitative analysis of the reasons for this change, it seems quite
clear that three factors were paramount: a racist ideology, a growing
uneasiness about Japanese military prowess and aggression, and the
consistent anti-Japanese propaganda of the California exclusionists.
While all three factors were important, the existence of the first two
was a necessary precondition if the third was to be effective beyond the
Pacific Coast. The adherence to racism, conscious or otherwise, made it
natural for most Americans to look down upon "the lesser breeds without the law" with a curious mixture of contempt and fear.[1] This is not
the place for a full-length portrait of the development of racism in the
United States, nor even of that rather elusive phenomenon, the "yellow
peril." But to sketch the latter at all, the former must at least be outlined.

Racism, as a pervasive doctrine, did not develop in the United States
until after the Civil War. No common assumptions underlay the en-
slavement of the Negro and the attacks made upon the Irish in Boston.
After the early years of Reconstruction, more and more Northerners
began to accept the Southern view of the Negro question; *Plessy* v.
Ferguson (1896), with its "separate but equal" doctrine, took judicial
notice of the national climate of opinion.[2]

By the 1880's a respectable intellectual basis for an American racism was being developed by the curiously interacting labors of workers in various academic disciplines. Historians, political scientists, and eugenists were in the van. Bluntly, it was "discovered" on the one hand that democratic political institutions had been developed by and could thrive only among Anglo-Saxon peoples, while on the other hand, entirely separate researchers "demonstrated" that, of all the many "races," one alone—variously called Anglo-Saxon, Aryan, Teutonic, or Nordic—had superior innate characteristics. Conveniently for the self-esteem of most Americans, these rather vague terms seemed to describe the majority of those who had hitherto come to America.[3]

At about the same time the sources of immigration began to change. Italians, Slavs, East European Jews, and Greeks began to outnumber incoming British, Germans, and Scandinavians. The census of 1890—the same census that triggered Frederick Jackson Turner's classic essay—demonstrated clearly to those in the grip of the Anglo-Saxon complex that immigration was changing, and changing for the worse, the human composition of their country. After 1894, when a group of Harvard men formed what became the highly influential Immigration Restriction League, an ever-growing group of powerful Americans campaigned with increasing vigor for an immigration policy based on ethnic and racial discriminaiton.[4] This growing concern about the "new immigration" was abetted by lurid stories in the infant yellow press about criminals with strange foreign names; such stories helped to make Americans acutely conscious of "racial" differences, real and imagined.

The course of history itself seemed to point up these differences. Just four years after the founding of the brahmin Immigration Restriction League, the United States embarked upon that "great aberration" in its foreign policy, the Spanish-American War, which not only produced the easy defeat of a Latin nation, but also brought under the Stars and Stripes three overseas dependencies having large nonwhite populations. The Supreme Court soon ruled, in the Insular Cases, that the constitution did not follow the flag, and this ruling was taken by some as an endorsement of the Anglo-Saxonist contention that democratic institutions had inherent ethnic limitations. Aided by success in what ought to be called "the sordid little war," jingoism, with racist implications, was trumpeted throughout the land.

These pyramiding factors, which were cumulative in effect, plus a growing stream of immigration, most of it from southern and eastern Europe, made the country more conscious of race than it had ever been

before. The First World War and its aftermath gave fresh arguments
to racist publicists. During the war superpatriotism took charge. Americanism, as a doctrine, began to mean the negation of the foreign. Then,
in the postwar period, racism went over the top.[5] The obvious failure,
for the first time, of American war aims—the world was demonstrably
not safe for democracy—meant for many a disenchantment with all
things foreign. The antiforeign trend gained its most effective stimulus
from the success of the Bolshevik revolution. This disturbing event,
coupled with an alarming upsurge of domestic radicalism—again seemingly perpetrated only by those with strange-sounding names—convinced some doubters that it was high time to seal off America from
foreign contagion.[6]

What seemed to be the great flowering of American racism in the
post–World War I decades—in retrospect this period seems to have been
its Indian summer—was epitomized by the work of two Eastern elitists,
Madison Grant and Lothrop Stoddard.[7] They wrote glowingly of each
other's books, and their views were almost identical. Like their more
celebrated contemporary, Oswald Spengler, they lacked confidence in
the future. The Bolshevik revolution frightened them:

> The backbone of western civilization is racially Nordic, the Alpines and Medi-
> terraneans being effective precisely to the extent to which they have been Nordicized
> and vitalized. If this great race, with its capacity for leadership and fighting, should
> ultimately pass, with it would pass what we call civilization.... Now that Asia, in
> the guise of Bolshevism with Semitic leadership and Chinese executioners, is organiz-
> ing an assault upon western Europe, the new states—Slavic-Alpine in race, with
> little Nordic blood—may prove to be not frontier guards of western Europe but
> vanguards of Asia in central Europe.[8]

They were haunted by "the rising tide of color":

> Colored migration is a *universal* peril, menacing every part of the white world....
> The whole white race is exposed, immediately or ultimately, to the possibility of
> social sterilization and final replacement or absorption by the teeming colored
> races.... There is no immediate danger of the world being swamped by black blood.
> But there is a very immediate danger that the white stocks may be swamped by
> Asiatic blood.... Unless [the white] man erects and maintains artificial barriers
> [he will] *finally perish*.... White civilization is to-day coterminous with the white
> race.[9]

There was, however, some hope, according to Stoddard:

> One element should be fundamental to all the compoundings of the social pharma-
> copoeia. That element is *blood*...clean, virile, genius-bearing blood, streaming
> down the ages through the unerring action of heredity.... What we to-day need
> above all else is...a recognition of the supreme importance of heredity.[10]

After a generation or two of rigid restriction of the immigration of "lower human types," i.e., non-Nordics, Stoddard had a few modest proposals for what he called a "new idealism":

In those better days, we or the next generation will take in hand the problem of race-depreciation, and segregation of defectives and abolition of handicaps penalizing the better stocks will put an end to our present racial decline. . . . Those splendid tasks are probably not ours. They are for our successors in a happier age. But we have our task, and God knows it is a hard one—the salvage of a shipwrecked world![11]

This sort of pseudo science flourished throughout the twenties. Within four years after its publication in the spring of 1920, Stoddard's *Rising Tide of Color* had gone through fourteen editions and Congress had passed the restrictive and discriminatory Immigration Acts of 1921 and 1924.

The whole antiforeign racist movement would surely have proceeded in much the same way regardless of whether a single Japanese immigrant had set foot on California's golden shores. But it is only in this context that the belief, by the nation at large, of the myriad, usually exaggerated, and often irrational charges against Japan and the Japanese, can be understood. If, in those years, the national climate of opinion was such that all manner of sinister myths could be fabricated and believed about the foreigner in general, was it not natural that about the Japanese, the most alien of the alien, there would be special fears?

Most of the charges against the Japanese—their nonassimilation, their low standard of living, their high birth rate, their vile habits— were made also against European immigrants. But only against Orientals was it seriously charged that the peaceful immigrants were but a vanguard of an invading horde to come. Throughout the years under discussion, and beyond, there was a consistent fear, expressed and believed in many quarters, that some named or unnamed Oriental power—usually, but not always, Japan—was on the verge of invading all or part of the continental United States. This fear can be most conveniently described by a catchword: the "yellow peril."[12]

The origin of the term is obscure, but it seems to be a direct translation of Kaiser Wilhelm II's vaporings about a *gelbe gefahr* threatening Europe and all Christendom (he meant a Chinese invasion à la Genghis Khan).[13] First used in English around the turn of the century, it was in wide public use in the United States by 1905. Most of those who used it meant to warn of an imminent invasion by Japan. But even before Japan became a world power some Americans, usually Californians, expressed fears about the Orient. They feared China.

The earliest expression of this sort that I have been able to discover was voiced by Henry George just after the American Civil War. In an impassioned plea for Eastern support in California's struggle against Chinese immigration, and with traces of that Social Darwinism usually associated with conservatives, he warned that:

The 60,000 or 100,000 Mongolians on our Western Coast are the thin edge of the wedge which has for its base the 500,000,000 of Eastern Asia.... The Chinaman can live where stronger than he would starve. Give him fair play and this quality enables him to drive out the stronger races ... [Unless Chinese immigration is checked] the youngest home of the nations must in its early manhood follow the path and meet the doom of Babylon, Nineveh and Rome.... Here plain to the eye of him who chooses to see are dragon's teeth [which will] spring up armed men marshalled for civil war.[14]

Between 1880 and 1882, doubtless inspired by the campaign for a national Chinese exclusion law, three obscure California authors concocted prophetic accounts of hordes of Chinese invading and conquering the United States.[15] They are the earliest American examples of what became a familiar phenomenon: "scare" literature warning of imminent military disaster. According to Alfred Vagts, the first book of this kind was *The Battle of Dorking* (1871) which warned Britain of an imminent German invasion.[16] The three California Cassandras had no noticeable effect on their contemporaries: at that time China was a victim, not a predator.

In the next decade, however, a new force began to disturb the balance of power in the Far East. On September 17, 1894, Japan fought and won her first modern naval battle, defeating the Chinese off the Yalu River. Three years later, Henry Cabot Lodge believed, erroneously, that Japan was "menacing Hawaii." "I am afraid we shall have trouble there," agreed his colleague Cushman K. Davis (Republican from Minnesota and chairman of the Senate Foreign Relations Committee), "though perhaps I express my self more accurately by writing 'for I am afraid we shall not have trouble.' "[17] A few months later Davis publicly said much the same thing:

The present Hawaiian-Japanese controversy [he declared in a Senate committee] is the preliminary skirmish in the great coming struggle between the civilization and the awakening forces of the East and the civilization of the West.

The issue is whether, in that inevitable struggle, Asia or America [shall control Hawaii].[18]

Shortly thereafter, as a sort of gleaning of the territorial harvest acquired in the Spanish-American War, the United States acquired Hawaii without the hint of a struggle, although Japan did file a rather perfunctory protest. The views of Lodge and Davis were not typical of

American sentiment; as noted earlier, most Americans continued to have friendly, if patronizing, feelings toward Japan, despite her growing power.

The Russo-Japanese War of 1904–1905 clearly demonstrated this power. The shots fired at Mukden and in Tsushima Strait were truly shots heard round the world: for the first time in the modern era a colored nation worsted a white one. Even before the war there had been talk of a yellow peril, mostly by Europeans. From 1905 on, however, the talk grew louder and louder in this country, with the vulgar accents of William Randolph Hearst often drowning out the rest.

Hearst is often erroneously credited with having invented the yellow peril.[19] As a matter of fact, his newspapers for a while ignored it and at one time even printed a feature article by a Japanese nobleman denying its existence.[20] By September, 1905, Hearst had begun to show concern over the Japanese menace; in that month the San Francisco *Examiner* printed a cartoon showing a Japanese soldier casting his shadow across the Pacific onto California.[21] There was, however, no concerted anti-Japanese campaign at that time.

As noted earlier, the change in policy came during the San Francisco school board crisis of 1906–1907. On December 20, 1906, the Hearst press began what would be a thirty-five-year "war" with Japan. The front page of the San Francisco *Examiner* that day warned of Japanese spies:[22]

JAPAN SOUNDS OUR COASTS
BROWN MEN HAVE
MAPS AND COULD
LAND EASILY

A few days later the *Examiner* made its first original contribution to the anti-Japanese campaign—the outright fabrication that Japanese immigrants were actually Japanese soldiers in disguise:

> Japanese in companies of forty are having infantry drill after dark [in Hawaii] two or three nights a week [and are] armed with rifles.... The Japanese of Hawaii have secreted enough rice to feed the entire population for seven months. [There have been] recent arrivals of Japanese troops in the guise of coolies [who are] secretly preparing for hostilities.[23]

At about the same time James D. Phelan began to be worried about the military threat of Japan. In a statement for publication he argued that the Pacific Coast "would be an easy prey in case of attack" and asserted that the Japanese immigrants in California were an "enemy within our gates."[24] It should be noted that Phelan was the only anti-Japanese political leader in California before the First World War to subscribe to the yellow peril. The Californians generally belittled such talk, particularly since alarmed Easterners often argued that the California agitation might involve the whole country in war.

The first detailed description of such a war was given by an American naval hero in the fall of 1907. Richmond Pearson Hobson has three claims on the attention of posterity. His heroic but unsuccessful attempt to blockade Admiral Cevera's fleet in the harbor of Santiago de Cuba by sinking a freighter in the channel made him the only untarnished naval hero of the Caribbean theater of the Spanish-American War. This presumably made him an expert in naval strategy. His ensuing coast-to-coast triumphal tour, during which he was kissed by thousands of women, demonstrated that he was a politician and was followed by a successful campaign for a seat in Congress (as a Democratic representative from Alabama). In 1907, while still in Congress, Hobson again began to attract attention, this time as a prophet of militarism and the yellow peril. His new career caused many to regard him as a "national nuisance."[25] In a two-part series for the Hearst chain he made his case against Japan.

Under the headline "JAPAN MAY SEIZE THE PACIFIC SLOPE," Hobson berated Americans for their "indifference" to the threat from the Far East. "The Yellow Peril is here," he declared. "Absolute control of the Pacific Ocean is our only safety." Hobson went on to show that, unless a big navy were built up, Japan by landing an army of exactly "1,207,-700 men could conquer the Pacific Coast." He predicted that Japan, by taking over China, would "soon be able to command the military resources of the whole yellow race." Hobson insisted that the "Japanese are the most secretive people in the world" and that they were "rushing forward with feverish haste stupendous preparations for war.... The war is to be with America."[26]

Hobson continued in this vein for several years, in published articles and during several nationwide lecture tours. In 1908, commenting on the round-the-world cruise of the American battle fleet, Hobson was ecstatic, but also still apprehensive:

Less than a year ago [an] Asiatic power [was] in control of the Pacific, completely prepared for war, [and] challenged American institutions. It was the first time in history that an Anglo-Saxon race was compelled to surrender the right of self-government to the dictation of a foreign power. [If we do not build up our Navy] the Japanese Navy will again secure control of the Pacific Ocean and the high seas will be controlled by a yellow race instead of by white men.[27]

Nor were merely militaristic jingoes the only ones who spread the doctrine of the yellow peril and the coming race war. The English

Fabian, H. G. Wells, sometimes sounded the same note. In his *War in the Air* (1908), Wells penned a lurid tale of death and destruction in which the Japanese replaced the Martians as bogeymen. In the novel the United States, France, and Great Britain are locked in a death struggle with Germany. Without warning, Japan and China indiscriminately attack the white powers, world-wide chaos reigns, and civilization is almost completely destroyed. "The Yellow Peril was a peril after all," was his comment on the Oriental attack.[28] Wells's basic purpose was, of course, different from Hobson's; the English Fabian was trying to point out the futility of war. Appealing to racial hatreds is a rather peculiar way of doing so.

Hobson and Wells both assumed Sino-Japanese coöperation in a coming racial war. Homer Lea, the most celebrated exponent of the yellow peril, thought that Japan could wage the war alone; besides, he was a friend of China. Lea, a hunchback who somehow became a general in the Chinese army and an adviser to Sun Yat-sen, is a romantic figure about whom reams of nonsense have been written. Clare Booth Luce and others have depicted him as a combination of Clausewitz and Napoleon, with a touch of Nostradamus added; even the staid *Dictionary of American Biography* printed gross exaggerations about him.[29] The hawkers of the Lea legend would have us believe that he was a key factor in the overthrow of the Manchu dynasty and the subsequent establishment of the Chinese republic. All the details of Lea's career in China are by no means clear, but it is certain that he played only a minor role. No evidence has been uncovered to show that he ever participated in any military action, and Lea, himself, never claimed that he had. He was in China in the decade before his death in 1912, and he did have the ear of Sun Yat-sen. The rest is either speculation or out right fabrication.

But not all of the Lea legend rests on his putative career in China; the bulk of the claims hinge on his writings, mainly *The Valor of Ignorance,* first published in 1909 and reissued with much fanfare shortly after Pearl Harbor.[30] The book told, in great detail, of a coming Japanese-American war, with Japan seizing the Philippine Islands and then landing forces on the Pacific Coast and overrunning Washington, Oregon, and California. This would be mere child's play, Lea argued, because of the small standing army and the utter worthlessness of American militia. Lea's concluding paragraph painted a gloomy picture of the future:

The inevitable consummation that follows the investment of San Francisco becomes apparent in the utter helplessness of the Republic. In the entire nation is not another regiment of regular troups; no generals, no corporals. Not months, but years, must elapse before armies equal to the Japanese are able to pass in parade. These must then make their way over deserts such as no armies have ever heretofore crossed; scale the entrenched and stupendous heights that form the redoubts of the desert moats; attempting, in the valor of their ignorance, the militarily impossible; turning mountain gorges into the ossuaries of their dead, and burdening the desert winds with the spirits of their slain. The repulsed and distracted forces to scatter, as heretofore, dissension throughout the Union, brood rebellions, class and sectional insurrections, until this heterogeneous Republic, in its principles, shall disintegrate, and again into the palm of re-established monarchy pay the toll of its vanity and its scorn.[31]

Like most other authors of yellow peril fantasies, Lea was a racist, a Social Darwinist, and a thoroughgoing militarist. He believed that the new immigrants had weakened the "primitive Americanism" of the original settlers and that no naturalized American could be a true patriot.[32] According to Lea, a nation had to keep expanding or die: "National existence is ... a part of life itself, governed by the same immutable laws. . . . Only so long as a man or nation continues to grow and expand do they nourish the vitality that wards off disease and decay."[33] Lea insisted that "War is a part of life, and its place in national existence is fixed and predetermined."[34] The only way the United States and the British Empire could survive was to slough off their commercial "opulence and unmartial qualities" and develop large standing armies and even bigger navies. In the coming racial wars, the stronger race would prevail.

Naïve journalists, particularly after the events of December, 1941, hailed Lea as a military genius. He not only predicted the Japanese invasion of the Philippines, but even indicated two of the beaches on which they actually landed.[35] Actually, the same conclusions were reached by all military thinkers who studied the problem of defending the islands. By the end of 1907 American military planners realized that:[36]

There is no avoiding the conclusion that we have not now, and never will have, sufficient troops in the Philippine Islands to defend Subig Bay from the land side against a land attack by the Japanese for any length of time to enable our fleet to reach the Philippine Islands from the Atlantic Ocean.

As a result of this and other studies, American Pacific strategy assumed the probable loss of the Philippines as the first act of any future Japanese-American war.[37] Thus Lea's prophetic foresight was merely an axiom of military common sense. As for the Japanese invasion of the Pacific Coast, neither he, Hobson, nor numerous other writers on this theme had the slightest conception of the logistic difficulties of such an enterprise. Even at the height of Japan's power, in 1942, the Japanese planners apparently did not seriously contemplate such a venture.[38] The Japan of 1905–1924 was patently in no position to launch a transpacific invasion.

Because of the constant propaganda, however, many Americans became convinced that the yellow peril was upon them. In both 1907 and 1912–1913, the periods of greatest friction in California, there were full-blown war scares, manufactured by jingoes on both sides of the Pacific. Hobson, Hearst, and Lea had opposite numbers in Japan. Some historians have taken these war scares too seriously; Outten Clinnard thinks that the United States and Japan were at the "verge of war" during both scares.[39] There is no evidence for such a view. Both Theodore Roosevelt and Wilson, however, were seriously disturbed about the possibility of war. Despite many warnings of Japanese intentions to attack the United States before the completion of the Panama Canal, Roosevelt could "hardly believe that Japan is intending to strike us," but he took "every step to be ready."[40] In the later crisis, neither Taft nor Wilson, despite urgings by some advisers, took any warlike steps.[41] Since no evidence has been presented indicating warlike actions by the Japanese government, it is difficult to see the validity of this retrospective brinksmanship.

With the onset of the First World War, in which Japan was an associate rather than an enemy of the United States, the yellow peril continued to thrive. Its chief exponents were the Hearst press and the German propaganda machine within the United States. A postwar congressional investigation attempted to show that Hearst was in the pay of Germans, but never succeeded in proving the charge.

Wilhelm II, it will be remembered, was the originator of the *gelbe gefahr;* from 1907 on, anti-Japanese propaganda seems to have been a part of his policy. German sources, official and semiofficial, kept insisting to the unconvinced Roosevelt that a Japanese attack was imminent. Heinrich Werner, a visiting German officer, told reporters that "Japan has a well trained, highly efficient, standing army of 40,000 men" in California and Mexico.[42] With the coming of war, this propaganda was intensified.

In May, 1915, the German agent George Sylvester Viereck wrote to his chief of a yellow peril pamphlet of which 300,000 copies had been distributed.[43] Dozens of such pamphlets were produced and distributed in the United States between 1915 and the American declaration of war. A typical production, *Preparedness for the Pacific Coast,* was published in Seattle in 1916 under the auspices of the German Newspapers Association. It agreed that Americans should arm and prepare for war, but not against Germany, from whom the United States had nothing to fear, but against "tartaric" Japan, who "wants a foothold on the Pacific Coast."[44]

Some of the German agents wished to do more than publish pamphlets; Edward Lyell Fox, an American newspaperman and a minor cog in the German propaganda machine, hatched a plot worthy of Sax Rohmer's diabolic Dr. Fu Manchu. Fox proposed to Franz von Papen, then a captain in the German army and an inept espionage agent, that Germany provide *agents provocateurs* to foment anti-Japanese riots in California, which, Fox hoped, might embroil Japan and the United States in war. Fox pointed out that plenty of assistance would be furnished such a scheme once it was under way.

An examination of the files of the Hearst newspapers [Fox wrote] will show their bitterness toward Japan. No chance has been passed by them to warn the people against the Japs and foment trouble in California.... Any anti-Japanese move would have the support of Mr. Hearst.... There should be a play produced in New York, Chicago, San Francisco and Los Angeles that will send its audiences out of the theatres heated to the fever point against the Japanese.... The public mind thus prepared, play the trump card with trouble on the Pacific Coast.... Rioting in San Francisco, etc. against a few Japanese [would be easy to arrange with hired thugs]. The Asiatic Exclusion League, the anti-Japanese organization of the Pacific Coast, enters the plan. Its president has served a term in jail; he will do anything made worth his while.... It would be an easy matter to use some young and "innocent" prostitutes to the detriment of the Japs.[45]

This particular outrage never was perpetrated; perhaps the bumbling von Papen found it less soldierly than blowing up munitions plants. Anti-Japanese race riots on the Pacific Coast would not have been hard to incite, and, indeed, might have had serious repercussions.

As it was, the Germans and the Hearst press followed parallel courses. In October, 1915, the newspaper chain played a new variation of the yellow peril gambit. In a double-page spread in successive Sunday supplements was reproduced what purported to be a semiofficial Japanese publication; it was, in fact, a cheap pamphlet put out by Japanese jingoes predicting a fantasy invasion of California, and it read remarkably like the productions of Hobson and Homer Lea, with one notable exception: Mexico was the ally of Japan. The Japanese army and navy were victorious and the peace terms imposed on the United States included the cession of the Philippine and Hawaiian islands, unlimited immigration into the United States for Japanese, who were to have full civil rights, and the right of Japanese fishermen to catch lobsters (!) within the territorial waters of the United States.[46]

The Hearst propaganda continued in this vein up to the American declaration of war, which the Hearst press opposed vehemently. Telegrams printed by the Senate committee investigating German propaganda show that William Randolph Hearst himself concocted some of the yellow peril propaganda. On March 3, 1917, Hearst sent the following telegram to one of his editors:[47]

McCay could make strong eight column cartoon occupying in depth two thirds editorial page, showing smaller figures Uncle Sam and Germany shaking their fists at each other on left side page and on right side big head and shoulders of Japan with knife in hand leaning over into picture and evidently watching chance to strike Uncle Sam in back. Title of picture to be quote Watchful waiting unquote. Subtitle quote Look out Uncle Sam your neighbor Japan is eagerly awaiting an opportunity to strike you in the back unquote.

HEARST

Motion pictures, as well as the printed word, were used by Hearst to preach the yellow peril gospel. In 1916 the International Film Service Corporation, part of the Hearst empire, produced a motion picture called *Patria*. As described to the Senate Investigating Committee by Captain George B. Lester, of Army Intelligence,

"Patria" had a story with three barrels. Its principal excuse was preparedness. But by the time the first episodes were released [it was a ten-part serial] the country was already committed to that. Therefore only the other two elements, anti-Mexican and anti-Japanese propaganda, remained active. These showed the attempt by Japan to conquer America with the aid of Mexico. A Japanese noble, at the head of the secret service of the Emperor in America, was the chief villain. Japanese troops invaded California, committing appropriate atrocities [the chief of which was the attempted rape of the heroine, played by Irene Castle].

"Patria" was first shown in New York January 9, 1917, and about that time in other cities. The American and other Hearst papers carried the story in serial form week by week. And the story was run—as is the custom with all serials—in a large number of newspapers, one in each city. "Patria" was shown in the smaller towns and cities, the first four or five months of the war . . .[48]

President Wilson saw the film in Washington, and was incensed by it. His pressures caused the film to be severely edited, although under wartime regulations it could have been completely suppressed. According to Captain Lester, the editing produced peculiar results: all the blame was "dumped on Mexico. . . . The Mexicans were made the villains, and they changed the whole piece over to Mexico, so that the Japanese had Mexican names; but in the film they were still wearing Japanese uniforms."[49]

Besides the press and the Germans, there was one additional main source of yellow peril propaganda—officers in the armed forces of the United States. From his experience as Assistant Secretary of the Navy

(1913 to 1920), Franklin Delano Roosevelt was "quite certain ... that a very considerable part of the suspicion between [Japan and the United States] rose from the perfectly natural attitude of Army and Navy officers whose duty it has been in the past to prepare the country against the most probable enemy.' "[50] So far as the United States Navy was concerned, that enemy was Japan.[51] Josephus Daniels, Wilson's Secretary of the Navy, complains in his memoirs that Hobson and Rear Admiral Bradley A. Fiske, Chief of Naval Operations, both "obsessed with the yellow peril," often came to his office to harangue him about it.[52] Army officers were not so outspoken as their seagoing colleagues, but a few were strong proponents of the yellow peril. Lieutenant General Adna R. Chaffee, a former chief of staff and an old China hand, wrote a glowing introduction to *The Valor of Ignorance,* as did Major General J. P. Story. Since it was assumed by most serious military thinkers that any future Japanese-American war would be fought almost exclusively at sea, it was only natural that naval officers expressed the greater interest.

In the years immediately after the war, the real rather than the imagined acts of the Japanese government were of growing concern to many Americans. The continued subjugation of Korea; the Twenty-one Demands upon China; the Shantung question; the friction between Japanese and American troops in Siberia; the insistent Japanese demands for racial equality, raised at Versailles and later at Geneva; the persistent and erroneous belief, before 1922, that the Anglo-Japanese alliance was somehow aimed at the United States: these were some of the issues that caused friction between the two countries. When these were added to the hostile feeling toward Japan already created by the war scares and the yellow peril propaganda, it was not difficult to convince many non-Californians that Japan was, as V. S. McClatchy put it, "the Germany of Asia."[53]

How much effect did the yellow peril propaganda have?[54] Certainly, no quantitative answer can ever be given to such a question. It is undeniable, however, that somewhere in the Platonic entity called the American psyche a sort of anti-Japanese reflex had been conditioned. A great deal of evidence of various sorts can be marshaled to support this contention; for the present discussion two pieces of literary data will have to suffice.[55] In the years before the war, in St. Paul, Minnesota, far from the Pacific, Amory Blaine, F. Scott Fitzgerald's alter ego, "would dream one of his favorite waking dreams ... the one about the Japanese invasion, when he was rewarded by being made the youngest general in the world."[56] In the American South the yellow peril subtly fused with fear of a Negro rebellion. "We used to talk a great deal," one young Southerner wrote, "about the race war which was coming, when blacks and yellows would unite and meet the scorn of whites with violence. It was one of our favorite topics of conversation."[57]

By the end of the First World War a great reservoir of anti-Japanese sentiment had been created throughout the country. But sentiment does not automatically translate itself into legislation; before the California exclusionists could achieve their first great national victory it was necessary for them to create an effective and "respectable" middle-class organization.

CHAPTER VI

THE PRESSURE GROUPS TAKE OVER

"California was given by God to a white people, and with
God's strength we want to keep it as He gave it to us."
—William P. Canbu, Grand President, Native Sons of
the Golden West, April, 1920

FROM 1913 to 1919 exclusionist activity within California ebbed; no
significant anti-Japanese organization existed during those years. There
was an attempt, led by Paul Scharrenberg of the California State Federation of Labor, to bring about passage of a stricter alien land law by
the 1915 legislature, but this was squelched by Hiram Johnson.[1] The
governor presumably heeded the injunctions of former President Theodore Roosevelt, who argued that because of the European war any anti-
Japanese activity would be inexpedient.[2] Throughout the war years,
and beyond, responsible leaders in California either exercised restraint
or had it thrust upon them.

During the same period an entirely new force entered the picture.
For the first time, starting in 1914, an organized and vocal opposition
to the anti-Japanese movement came into being. The organized opponents of the "California position" were mostly Easterners and
generally represented one or another of three groups: Protestant missionaries working along denominational lines and through the Federal
Council of the Churches of Christ in America; businessmen working
through various commercial associations and the Japan Society of
America; and educators and other middle-class groups working, often,
through the American Peace Society.[3] These groups, well organized and
well financed, began a diversified counterattack on the allegations of
the exclusionists in the spring of 1914.

The central figure in this movement was Sidney Lewis Gulick, a Congregational missionary who had lived for many years in Japan; he
quickly became the *bête noire* of the exclusionists. Gulick seemed to be
a mass movement all by himself: he was executive secretary and organ-
izer of the National Committee for Constructive Immigration Legislation, secretary of the Committee on American-Japanese Relations, and
representative of the Commission on Relations with Japan of the Federal Council of Churches of Christ in America; between 1914 and 1924
he wrote at least twenty-four books and pamphlets, besides dozens of
magazine articles, and gave hundreds of lectures and sermons on the
Japanese question.[4] His basic position was set forth in his first major

work on the subject, *The American Japanese Problem,* published in 1914.

A goodly part of Gulick's writings consists of polemics against the California position, which was, he argued, "needless," "hysterical," "unscientific," and "un-Christian." Yet, like those of almost all the American friends of Japan, his own arguments were not entirely free from race prejudice. He was sure that Japanese were superior to immigrants from southern Europe and to Negroes. "The Japanese race," he asserted, "already contains considerable white blood." He was opposed to the "free intermarriage of the races" and to "unlimited immigration."[5]

Unlike most of the antiexclusionist writers, however, Gulick made positive proposals on the whole subject of immigration. These proposals soon became the platform of the National Committee for Constructive Immigration Legislation, and later, with modifications which completely thwarted Gulick's intentions, were written into the statute books as the Immigration Acts of 1921 and 1924. The heart of the missionary's scheme was this: "Immigration [to the United States] from any land should be allowed on a percentage rate of those from the same land who are already naturalized including their American-born children."[6]

His avowed purpose was to put Asians on exactly the same basis as all other immigrants, but he also pointed out that his scheme would "allow all probable immigration from Germany, Great Britain, and Scandinavia, while it would put a check on Russian, Austrian, and Italian immigration."[7]

Such a proposal was not original with Gulick. The United States Immigration Commission had included a similar plan in its 1911 report; that body, however, favored the literacy test, as did the Immigration Restriction League.[8] Gulick and the committees that he ran and organized were the first to stress such a plan and give it widespread publicity. Gulick marshaled much support for his plan, largely through the Committee for Constructive Immigration Legislation. This committee has been called a "liberal" group; "internationalist" would be the better word. Its membership included such diverse figures as William Howard Taft, Charles A. Beard, John Bates Clark, Frederic C. Howe, James M. Beck, Oswald Garrison Villard, George W. Wickersham, Cardinal Gibbons, and Louis F. Post.[9] Gulick's other activities, quite naturally, concentrated on mobilizing widespread sentiment in favor of Japan through the Protestant churches. A three-point argument was used. First, prejudice against the Japanese was un-Christian. Second, if

Asians were treated badly in California and the rest of the United States, the vast Protestant missionary endeavors in China and Japan would be hampered. Third, an amelioration of racial conflicts would make war less probable. Gulick's campaign began in early 1914; only after that date was there widespread protest from California pulpits against anti-Japanese agitation and legislation.

The California exclusionists were alert to the dangers that Gulick's campaign entailed. After reading Gulick's first book, Chester Rowell wrote to Montaville Flowers, who had been giving anti-Japanese Chautauqua lectures in the East, that "we will have to do some systematic organization in California" to combat such propaganda. But, Rowell complained, "the only organization of the sort that we ever had was conducted by crooks and criminals and was worse than useless."[10] Sarajevo and its aftermath occupied the attention of Rowell and most Californians, and serious talk of a new anti-Japanese organization was deferred until after the war. Flowers, however, exercised no such restraint; in 1917 he published a book-length diatribe against the Japanese in California and the forces headed by Sidney Gulick.[11]

Flowers' *Japanese Conquest of American Public Opinion* begins an entirely new phase of the anti-Japanese movement. Californians had always been sensitive to Eastern criticism, but never before had any of them made it a primary issue. According to Flowers, Gulick and his cohorts were in the grip of the "Great American Illusion"—the idea of the melting pot; he also claimed that a deliberate campaign of vilification was being waged against California, whose righteous position the bankers, missionaries, and Easterners were undermining by subtle propaganda. Although Flowers' book had no appreciable national influence, it was indicative of things to come.

Not even the Californians paid much attention to Flowers. James D. Phelan, by then a United States senator approaching the end of his term, was an exception. Throughout 1918 and 1919 Phelan sent his friends free copies of the book. Phelan, whose anti-Oriental activities dated back to the 1880's, formally launched the postwar anti-Japanese campaign before a special session of the state legislature on the evening of March 31, 1919. He insisted that the Japanese were a menace economically, socially, and militarily; he called for a more stringent alien land act, abrogation of the Gentlemen's Agreement, passage of a Japanese exclusion law, a larger navy, and strengthened coastal defenses on the Pacific slope.[12] While no one who has examined his career in detail can doubt Phelan's sincerity, it is also clear that this speech was the opening of his personal campaign for reëlection to the Senate. In 1914, when the Democratic tide was running strong and his opponents were divided, Phelan ran as a Wilson Democrat and almost completely ignored the Oriental issue. In 1919 and 1920, with the Democratic tide ebbing, Phelan made his slogan "Keep California White" and all but ignored both his invalid chief and the national ticket.

Most students of California anti-Orientalism have made far too much of Phelan's obvious opportunism and have slid over what most Californians felt or came to feel were their legitimate grievances. The Californians had been assured by Roosevelt and his successors that the Gentlemen's Agreement would halt Japanese immigration. They had seen the number of adult Japanese within California rise from 32,785 in 1910 to 47,566 in 1920, while the constant increase of native-born Japanese who had full rights of citizenship seemed even more menacing. In 1913, Governor Johnson and the legislature assured the people of the state that Japanese land acquisition had been checked—yet Japanese landholdings had increased more than fourfold in the next six years. These seemingly glaring evidences of Japanese perfidy and encroachment ensured the success of the postwar anti-Oriental campaign.

The campaign itself, although based upon years of anti-Oriental hostility, had to start almost from scratch. Before Phelan's speech at the end of March, no anti-Japanese bills had been introduced in the current session of the legislature and in the press there was no trace of a full-scale propaganda war against the California Japanese. The morning after Phelan's speech, State Senator J. M. Inman, a Republican from Sacramento County, asked permission to introduce an alien land act designed to plug the now obvious loopholes in the 1913 law and a joint resolution asking the American delegates to the Versailles conference to oppose the free immigration proposals which the Japanese delegation was supposed to be sponsoring. The legislature was in the second half of a divided session and its rules required the permission of three-fourths of the entire membership before any new business could be introduced. A minority of the legislature, strengthened in its resolve by a cablegram from Secretary of State Robert Lansing requesting no anti-Japanese action, blocked the introduction of Inman's bill and defeated his resolution. They could not, of course, prevent discussion of his proposals in the press. The only significant anti-Japanese measure passed in the 1919 legislature was a concurrent resolution ordering the state to conduct an investigation of the landholdings of "aliens ineligible to citizenship."[13]

Obviously, the still unorganized exclusionists had not originally planned any anti-Japanese legislation during the 1919 session. It seems to me highly probable that Phelan was the instigator of Inman's bill; the timing is too neat to be accidental. Why Phelan and Inman waited until late in the session to act is still not clear, but perhaps a growing alarm about what Japan might ask for and get at the peace conference served as a spur. Inman, whose Republicanism was orthodox, certainly cannot be considered as a conscious abettor of the reëlection plans of Phelan, a Democrat.

Phelan himself found it possible to believe almost anything about the Japanese. He gave a hearty second to the views of Homer Lea and Montaville Flowers. When an obviously unbalanced woman wrote to him in 1920 about a German submarine's making regular trips between Germany and San Pedro, California, and landing armament and poison gas for the use of Japanese troops in the invasion of California, Phelan believed her and insisted that his friends in naval intelligence investigate the matter thoroughly.[14] Phelan had no sympathy with Gulick and other "philanthropists who are always talking about the brotherhood of man and the fatherhood of God." He, too, could quote scripture to support his position: "The Lord made of one blood all the races of the earth [but He also] appointed the places of their habitation. This continent belongs to us. That continent belongs to them."[15] When a group of social scientists at Stanford published findings indicating that offspring of interracial marriages had intelligence quotients approximately equal to those of other children, Phelan penned a protest to Ray Lyman Wilbur, the president of the university. He insisted that it was common knowledge, even in Japan, that Eurasians were inferior to "pure bloods" of either race, and cited, rather incongruously, both Herbert Spencer and Louis Agassiz as scientists whose findings on the matter he preferred.[16] To Phelan "a Jap was a Jap," and it was his considered opinion that "the native Japanese are as undesirable as the imported."[17] All Japanese, the senator was convinced, wanted to take possession of the Pacific Coast; but "if they want it," he declared, "they will have to fight for it."[18] He did not think the Japanese inferior in all things: "their very cleverness," he declared, was "one of the dangers besetting California," and they were "capable of taking the place of the White man."[19] Unfortunately, the Japanese could not "be treated as the negro." Therefore they had to be excluded.[20]

Such were the views of the initial instigator of the postwar agitation. But Phelan was not alone, nor was his support confined to fellow Democrats. Although frustrated in the legislature, the exclusionists, with Phelan in the van, stirred up feeling throughout the state. The movement obviously lacked focus and direction; but in early September,

1919, in the offices of State Controller John S. Chambers, a Republican, the first reorganization meeting of the exclusionists was held. In a mimeographed letter, Chambers described the results:[21]

> Last Friday night a meeting was held ... to consider the Japanese situation. Briefly, the feeling expressed was this: that the Japanese now in California or in other parts of the Union, probably had acquired certain rights of which they could not be dispossessed, nor was any desire expressed to dispossess them. It was felt that ... we could take care of the Japanese now among us, and the progeny. But the future as to the immigration of the little brown men presents a very hard problem indeed—one full of menace not only to California but eventually to the United States. It was agreed that the anti-Japanese sentiment in California should be crystallized through organization, and by this means bring to pass such protective legislation as under the constitution of the State or of the United States could be rightly asked. Also, that a campaign of education should be started in the Middle West and East that the people of those regions might be taught to understand the Japanese and eventually to cooperate with us to influence Congress and the administration at Washington to enact such legislation, even if the amendment of the Constitution be necessary, as will protect the white race against the economic menace of the unassimilable Japanese. No desire to inflict injustice upon the Japanese here was expressed. No one denied them their industry, but all agreed that their loyalty was first to Japan and second, if at all, to America; that they were here in large part in pursuance of a plan to populate the Pacific Slope of America and that they were a peril, economically, politically and socially.

I do not know exactly who, besides Chambers, attended the meeting. It seems that most of those present were politicians, but the committee that ensued cut across party lines. Although candidates of various persuasions tried to convince the electorate that they, rather than their opponents, should be entrusted with "saving California from the Japs," neither the Democrats nor the Republicans succeeded in monopolizing the issue. Like so many antidemocratic movements in recent United States history, the postwar anti-Japanese campaign was truly bipartisan.

The immediate result of the Sacramento meeting was not quite what its instigators envisaged. They organized the California Oriental Exclusion League, with Senator Inman as president. The new organization failed to achieve either permanence or great influence. Almost simultaneously, similar organizations arose in other parts of the state: in the south, the Los Angeles Anti-Asiatic Association; in the Sacramento Valley, the Fourteen Counties Association; in the Imperial Valley, the Alien Regulation League; and, in the San Joaquin Valley, the Americanization League.[22] In the seeming diversity, however, there was unity. The five-point program laid down by the new Exclusion League was accepted by all the groups. It called for:

1. Cancellation of the "Gentlemen's Agreement"
2. Exclusion of "Picture Brides"
3. Rigorous exclusion of Japanese as immigrants
4. Confirmation of the policy that Asiatics shall be forever barred from American citizenship
5. Amendment of the Federal Constitution providing that no child born in the United States shall be given the rights of an American citizen unless both parents are of a race eligible to citizenship[23]

An even more important unity existed in the fact that the leaders and members of all these bodies were drawn chiefly from four organized groups within the state: the Native Sons of the Golden West and its distaff counterpart, the Native Daughters; the newly organized American Legion; the California State Federation of Labor; and various farm bodies, chiefly the California State Grange. These four pressure groups, with the assistance of professional politicians who were usually members of at least one of the four, formed the organized heart of the postwar anti-Japanese movement. Each merits separate consideration.

The Native Sons of the Golden West (N.S.G.W.) is not now important in California politics, but from just after the turn of the century until the onset of the great depression it was perhaps the most influential pressure group in the state. The views expressed by its leaders in their monthly publication, the *Grizzly Bear,* were consistently reactionary and nativist, and quite often hysterical. The very first issue of the magazine, in May, 1907, contained an article warning of "The Asiatic Peril"; in almost every subsequent issue there was at least one article which attacked the Japanese. The members of the Native Sons and Daughters, not united by common economic ties, made no bones about the basis of their antagonism to Orientals: it was blatantly racist.

"Would you like your daughter to marry a Japanese?" the *Grizzly Bear* asked. "If not, demand that your representative in the Legislature vote for segregation of whites and Asiatics in the public schools."[24] At one time the editor was convinced that "separate public schools for all aliens" were needed.[25] The women's auxiliary joined in these sentiments; one leading Native Daughter was sure that California was being "Japanized" just as the South was being "Negroized" and went on to warn her sisters that "it is not unusual these days to find, especially the 'better class' of Japanese, casting furtive glances at our young women. They would like to marry them."[26]

Another Native Daughter, Cora M. Woodbridge, who also served in the state legislature and as an officer of the California Federation of Women's Clubs, vented her spleen on the picture brides. She assured her gentle readers that the Issei mother was not entitled to any con-

sideration on account of her sex, since she was a "beast of burden up
to the time of the birth of her child and, within a day or two at most,
resumes her task and continues it from twelve to sixteen hours a day."[27]

The general political tone of the *Grizzly Bear* may be seen at perhaps
its worst in the issue of December, 1919. On one page it asked, "where
is the red-blooded American who will condemn the Centralia lynchers?,"
advocated the expulsion of Victor Berger from the country, proposed
the barring of aliens from all labor, fraternal, and civic organizations,
and bragged that the N.S.G.W. was the "only organization that limited
membership exclusively to NATIVE-BORN AMERICANS."[28]

Apart from the Japanese, the foreigner, and the radical, the Native
Sons were particularly outraged by Americans who favored decent
treatment for the Japanese immigrants and their children. After 1919,
when anti-Orientalism was given full sway in the magazine, there were
regular fulminations against the "white-Japs, who masquerade as Americans, but, in fact, are servants of the mikado."[29] Particular objects of
scorn were certain Protestant church groups and educators. The
N.S.G.W. insisted that the "Methodist Church . . . is thoroughly pro-Jap
and has been more active in the interests of the yellow pests in California than any other agency."[30] The columns of the *Grizzly Bear* were
opened to Montaville Flowers, ineligible for membership because of his
birth in Virginia; he denounced Sidney Gulick, the Japan Society, the
Federal Council of Churches of Christ in America, and the American
Peace Society. He proposed a purge of pro-Japanese professors in California universities, particularly at Stanford and the University of
Southern California.[31]

The antidemocratic activities of the American Legion are common
knowledge, and need not be calendared here. From its very first convention, at Minneapolis in November, 1919, the veterans' group adopted
a consistent and unwavering anti-Japanese policy.[32] In separate resolutions it proposed:[33]

Abrogation of the so-called "gentlemen's agreement" with Japan, and the exclusion of Japanese from the United States on the same basis as other Oriental races.

Amendment to Section one of the Fourteenth Amendment to the effect that no
child born in the United States of foreign parentage shall be eligible to citizenship
unless both parents were so eligible.

Similar resolutions were enacted at every national convention of the
Legion until Japanese exclusion became a reality. Within California
the new organization was quick to adapt itself to the state's venerable
vigilante tradition, thus adding to the anti-Japanese movement a lawless
element that had been, happily, absent from the movement since the

hooliganism of its San Francisco infancy. Shortly after the Legion joined the anti-Japanese crusade there were several instances of mass expulsions of Japanese from individual rural areas within the state, the most prominent of which occurred at Turlock, in central California, during the summer of 1921.[34]

The state's labor unions continued their long tradition of anti-Oriental activity in the postwar period, but it is clear that their old militancy was lacking; they played a distinctly subordinate role. The fear of cheap competition from Oriental labor continued to be the stated reason for the labor unions' opposition to the Japanese, but it is hard to reconcile this argument with the real economic position of the Japanese in the state. The Issei were mainly small farmers and businessmen. By the 1920's no significant number of California's Japanese was competing with organized labor, and occasional comments to this effect were heard from labor's ranks.[35] But for Paul Scharrenberg, the American Federation of Labor's chief spokesman on the Japanese question and an exclusionist of long standing, the menace of Japanese immigration was an article of faith.[36] Patently, organized labor's anti-Orientalism was an inherited position and was no longer dictated by economic interest. In fact, only if the exclusionists had been successful in dispossessing the Issei of their landholdings, as extremists among them wanted to do, would there have been any large-scale cheap-labor competition.

The final element in the coalition was the farmers. So long as Japanese in large numbers provided the "stoop labor" needed to harvest much of California's crops, organized agricultural groups refrained from adding their voices to the anti-Japanese chorus. By the postwar period, the overwhelming majority of the Issei engaged in agriculture were either tilling their own land or working for their compatriots. They had become competitors rather than employees. As noted earlier, by the end of the war Japanese farmers were reaping ten per cent of California's crops in terms of market prices. Both major California farm organizations, the Farm Bureau Federation and the State Grange, wholeheartedly supported the exclusionist position. The president of the Los Angeles County Farm Bureau testified that his organization opposed "Japanese being permitted to lease, rent or own agricultural land ... or own any lands whatsoever."[37]

Thus for the first time all the anti-Japanese forces in the state were united behind a common program, which was soon endorsed by every major political figure in the state. By November, 1919, the N.S.G.W. exclusionists had decided that the "only thing that will save California

is . . . a state law that will make it impossible for Japanese to get possession of the soil."[38] By the following March, such a law had been
drafted. As the result of petitions for which the Native Sons and
Daughters and the Legionnaires seem to have gathered most of the
necessary signatures, the proposed law was presented as an initiative
measure on the 1920 ballot instead of being held for the 1921 legislature.[39]

The new law, like Inman's earlier proposal, was designed to plug the
now obvious loopholes in the 1913 measure. It prohibited any further
transfer of land to Japanese nationals; barred any lease of land to
them; barred acquisition, by lease or purchase, of land by any corporation in which Japanese held a majority of the stock; and prohibited
Issei parents who were noncitizens from serving as guardians for their
minor citizen children, since that device had been used with great success by Issei to circumvent the 1913 law.[40] The guardianship provision,
which was crucial, could not be enforced. The courts soon ruled that to
deprive the Nisei children, who were citizens of the United States, of
their right to have their own parents as guardians of their property
was to infringe upon their right to hold property. Under the Fourteenth
Amendment no state had such power; hence that part of the initiative
measure was void.[41]

The 1920 measure was an attempt to lock the door after the horse
had been stolen. Had it been enacted in 1913, when native-born Japanese were less numerous, it would have seriously inhibited Japanese
acquisition of agricultural land. By 1920 its enactment was an empty
gesture, an ineffective irritant; it caused much litigation, but it in no
wise significantly affected land tenure in the state. The Issei were well
organized and they availed themselves of legal counsel. With a few
notable exceptions, the California courts acted impartially.[42]

The futility of the act was not apparent to the majority of the exclusionists, although the unconstitutionality of the guardianship provisions
was clear to the legally sophisticated.[43] From March to November an
intensive campaign for passage was waged. The state government declared itself unambiguously for the measure. The investigation of Japanese land tenure, ordered by the 1919 legislature, was issued in June,
1920, as a document of more than two hundred pages. *California and
the Oriental* went beyond an investigation of landholdings; it was a
full-scale statement of the whole California position. It sought not only
to influence voters for the 1920 initiative, but also to advance the whole
exclusionist cause. In a preface addressed to Secretary of State Bainbridge Colby, Governor William D. Stephens pointed out that the

pending initiative measure would "exhaust the state's power in dealing with this great race problem," which could not be solved "short of an exclusion act passed by Congress."[44]

California and the Oriental, purportedly the work solely of the State Board of Control, was actually compiled with the clandestine coöperation of the Bureau of the Census.[45] The careful reader will have noted several previous quotations from it as matters of fact; its statistics are, in themselves, accurate. In addition, in a seeming spirit of fair play, its compilers included twenty-five pages of material prepared by the Japanese Association of America. Despite this show of fairness, the state's official report is biased, inaccurate, and prejudicial. The prejudice lies not in the figures themselves, but in the use that is made of them; the whole report is a masterpiece of manipulation clearly demonstrating the old adage about figures and liars.

According to Governor Stephens, the greatest danger to white California came from the high birth rate of these alien people: "the fecundity of the Japanese race far exceeds that of any other people."[46] The report tried to prove that the Japanese birth rate was nearly three times that of the white. It showed that 15,211 Japanese women had given birth to 4,378 children in one year, while 313,281 married white women had given birth to 30,893 children in a similar period.[47] The figures prove absolutely nothing, for they are in no wise comparable. Because of the special conditions of Japanese immigration, almost all Japanese wives were, during the period cited, in the first years of marriage and of prime childbearing age. To compare such a group to a different group of women ranging from fifteen to forty-five years of age and married for widely varying periods of time was patently absurd, except for purposes of propaganda. As a point of fact, perhaps in part as a result of the lack of any religious inhibitions about birth control, the long-range Issei birth rate was somewhat below that for contemporary immigrant groups from Europe, and only slightly above the rather low native-white birth rate in the twenties and thirties. The report made similar distortions of other data; its basic assumption was that the Japanese and their children were, and would remain forever, alien and subversive elements embedded in the American body politic.

Throughout the summer of 1920 the propaganda war continued; since Phelan was making his race for the Senate at the same time, the California electorate was deluged with anti-Japanese propaganda. Although conservative Republican papers like the San Francisco *Chronicle* and the Los Angeles *Times* deprecated Phelan's jingoistic bluster, their candidate, Samuel Shortridge, was almost equally vociferous.[48] The

American Legion made and circulated an anti-Japanese movie, *Shadows of the West:* it depicted the Issei farmers as spies and sex fiends. Its inevitable climax was the melodramatic rescue of two innocent white girls from the clutches of the wily agents of the mikado; naturally, the boys from the local Legion post served as the rescuers.[49]

The overwhelming majority of California's newspapers was in favor of the land act proposed on the initiative, but none quite so vehemently as the Hearst chain. On the eve of the election, to cite only two examples, these slanted headlines appeared on the front page of the San Francisco *Examiner:*[50]

JAP ATTACKS GIRL, BEATEN BY MOTHER

JAPAN'S TREASURY POURS GOLD INTO STATE TO
BATTLE LAND LEGISLATION

The second headline, without any real basis in fact, referred to the existence within California of an organized opposition to the exclusionists. Both the Japanese Association of America and a new organization, the American Committee of Justice, were actively campaigning against the initiative measure.[51] The existence of the latter group, composed of ministers, businessmen, and educators, may certainly be attributed to Gulick's missionary endeavors. With one important exception, the membership of the American Committee of Justice included the presidents of all the large colleges in the state. The holdout was General David P. Barrows, president of the University of California. His predecessor, Benjamin Ide Wheeler, perhaps inhibited by the legislature, had been conspicuously absent from most earlier protests against anti-Japanese activity, but it should be added that he also refrained from abetting the exclusionists. Barrows, who seemed more at home in the barracks than the groves of academe, stated that it was "imperative . . . to hold in the hands of American families the ownership and tillage of the land," and added "I should wish to see [Japanese] *ownership and holdings of the soil liquidated,* but [without] financial injustice."[52]

The initiative, of course, passed, carrying every county in the state, but the results must have been disappointing to the exclusionists, who had conducted an expensive campaign. An overwhelming majority had been forecast—ten to one was a common boast—but only a three-to-one majority (668,483 to 222,086) was obtained. Phelan was defeated for the Senate, but did run well ahead of the rest of the Democratic ticket. Yet this should not be viewed solely as an endorsement for his extreme brand of Japanese baiting, since Shortridge, an old-guard Republican, cannot have had much appeal for the Progressive Republican voters, who were still a force to be reckoned with. Many of these must have remembered Phelan as an old-line progressive who had helped finance the San Francisco graft prosecution in the early years of the century.

As we have seen, the 1920 law was doomed to failure. For the rest of the decade the legislature attempted minor harassments of the Issei, but these need not concern us here. Even before election day, the eyes of the exclusionists were turning toward Washington. They knew it was there that the crucial battle would be fought. Phelan's partisan candidacy and certain other minor frictions which had developed during the campaign made it clear that a unified movement was needed in the place of the decentralized one then in existence. It also seemed clear that a leader was needed who would stand above the partisan battles that would continue to rage in California.

The exclusionist reorganization took place on September 2, 1920, in Native Sons Hall in San Francisco; the new group was christened the Japanese Exclusion League of California, and was organized as a pressure group rather than on a geographical basis. State Senator Inman was named president, and vice-presidencies were awarded to officials of the Native Sons, the American Legion, the California State Federation of Labor, the California Federation of Women's Clubs, the California State Grange, the Farm Bureau, and the Loyal Order of Moose.[53] Inman, however, soon proved to be a figurehead; the real power in the organization devolved into the hands of Valentine Stuart McClatchy, its volunteer special representative, who devoted full time to what he felt was a holy cause.

McClatchy was a leader behind whom the whole movement could rally. Because he was a retired newspaper publisher with an independent income, no motives of personal aggrandizement could be charged to him. McClatchy seemed to be on good personal terms with every leading member of the diverse exclusionist group. One of the two sons of James McClatchy, founder of the liberal and powerful Sacramento *Bee,* he had been publisher of that newspaper until just before 1920. A personal dispute with his brother Charles occasioned his retirement, although he still maintained an interest in the *Bee.* (Their differences of opinion did not include the Japanese question, for the *Bee* continued to be a vehicle for V. S. McClatchy's anti-Japanese propaganda.) As a former director of the Associated Press, McClatchy was personally acquainted with many of the molders of national opinion. But perhaps his chief friendship was with the irascible and rather frigid Hiram Johnson, after 1920 California's senior United States senator and an increasingly influential figure.[54] These two native sons, V. S. McClatchy and Hiram Johnson, formed what might be called the general staff of the exclusionist forces. They directed the final exclusionist victory.

CHAPTER VII

EXCLUSION

"California has only commenced to fight."
—Sacramento *Bee,* Nov. 4, 1920

WITH THE passage of the 1920 Alien Land Law, the exclusionists realized that California had done all it could to halt the "Japanese invasion," and they agreed with Governor Stephens that the law had to be further supplemented. By 1920 the propaganda campaign envisioned by State Controller Chambers was well under way. Articles setting forth the California position appeared with increasing regularity in national magazines, often linking the aggressive actions of the Japanese government in Asia with the fight for exclusion.[1] V. S. McClatchy's argument that Japan was the "Germany of Asia" was repeated again and again. Japan's ever-increasing potency in world affairs had earlier placed the Issei in a special position; in the postwar period it served as an additional argument for discriminatory legislation against them.

The new postwar attitude can best be seen in two anti-Japanese novels serialized nationally in 1920 and published as books in 1921: Peter B. Kyne's *Pride of Palomar* and Wallace Irwin's *Seed of the Sun.* The first, whose arguments are derived verbatim from Montaville Flowers, has for its hero a Californian of Spanish-Irish descent (Kyne refers to him as an Anglo-Saxon!) who had learned about the tricky Japanese as a member of the American Expeditionary Force sent to Siberia to fight the Bolsheviks; Irwin's hero is a stay-at-home California Irishman (with "Anglo-Saxon eyes"). In both these novels—which are sentimental magazine romances with a political message inserted—the native-son hero not only must win the girl and thwart Japanese landgrabbers, he also must indoctrinate the Eastern-born heroine with the opinions proper to California. Kyne's villain, the "potato baron" Okada, resorts to all sorts of hoodlum skulduggery to gain a few thousand more acres of California soil; Irwin's villain, the Baron Tazumi, is a more subtle type who masterminds Japanese land acquisition as part of the mikado's plan for world domination. Both novels are replete not only with denunciations of Japan and Japanese, but also of their American defenders, the missionaries and the Japan Society.[2] Like most of the exclusionist propaganda, they are directed toward a single end—congressional enactment of Japanese exclusion.

Expecting that history would repeat itself, exclusionists had long envisaged a Japanese exclusion act after the model of the 1882 statute barring Chinese. Such was not to be: the exclusion of Japanese became part of the general restriction of immigration. The postwar immigration acts were almost a complete reversal of previous American policy; perhaps a synopsis of immigration legislation is in order here.

For some time after the American Revolution legal control of immigration remained in the hands of the states. The Articles of Confederation, while instituting a national citizenship, failed to institute national control of immigration.[3] The Constitution, except for the clause referring to the slave trade, made no direct reference to immigration and its control; but it was later ruled, in a series of decisions beginning in 1849, that the commerce clause, which provides that Congress has the power "to regulate commerce with foreign nations," gives to Congress, and to Congress alone, the right to regulate immigration.[4]

This, however, was not immediately understood, and up to 1824 no contest of the right of the states to control immigration was made.[5] At that time the federal government began to take legal steps to set aside state laws which levied taxes on or required bonds of immigrants. In the Passenger Cases of 1849, laws of New York and Massachusetts which had taxed immigrants on arrival were declared unconstitutional by the Supreme Court. This decision placed the regulation of immigration under the exclusive purview of Congress, except for matters concerning health and public safety, which were adjudged within the competence of the several states.[6]

Congress, however, passed no real immigration legislation until after the Civil War. The infamous and short-lived Alien Act of 1789 provided for the deportation of aliens at the discretion of the President, while the Act of March 2, 1819, merely provided for the enumeration of immigrants at ports of entry.[7] No other immigration legislation existed.

The first restrictive immigration act was passed in 1875 and barred the entry of "women for the purposes of prostitution" and criminals "whose sentence has been remitted on condition of emigration."[8] Seven years later the first Chinese Exclusion Act was passed; in the same year a head tax of fifty cents was levied on all incoming alien passengers to "defray the expense of regulating immigration . . . and for the care [and relief] of immigrants." At the same time, the Secretary of the Treasury was charged with the enforcement of all immigration laws.[9]

In 1885 and 1887 laws were enacted prohibiting contract labor; in 1891 the excluded category was widened to include "all idiots, insane persons, paupers or persons likely to become a public charge, persons suffering from a loathsome or dangerous contagious disease, persons who have been convicted of a felony or other infamous crime or misdemeanor involving moral turpitude, [and] polygamists." The same act also forbade the solicitation of immigration, except by a state or by relatives and friends of the migrant.[10] In 1895 Congress created the office of Commissioner General of Immigration and eight years later transferred that office from the Treasury Department to the newly formed Department of Commerce and Labor.[11]

The Act of March 3, 1903, marked a further departure in immigration limitation; for the first time Congress demanded an inspection of the political opinions of entrants. In words that have since become all too familiar, the law added to the excluded list "anarchists, or persons who believe in or advocate the overthrow by force and violence of the Government of the United States . . . or the assassination of public officials." The same act increased the head tax to two dollars and set up a rather elaborate bureaucratic apparatus for the inspection and regulation of immigrants.[12]

A series of minor acts in the next fourteen years made no substantial changes in basic immigration policy. Then in 1917 two major changes were made: a literacy test was established (any recognized language or dialect including Hebrew and Yiddish was permitted), and, by means of a barred zone, expressed in latitude and longitude, all Asian immigrants except Japanese were excluded.[13]

Thus, by the end of the First World War, the once free and unrestricted immigration policy of the United States had been limited in seven major ways: Asians (except for Japanese), criminals, persons who failed to meet certain moral standards, persons with various diseases, paupers, certain radicals, and illiterates had been denied admission. Many felt that the bars should be raised still further. By late 1920, amid scare stories predicting a flood of undesirable immigrants from eastern and central Europe in the immediate future, it was clear that Congress was about to pass the most stringent immigration law in history.

At the beginning of the Lame Duck session of the 66th Congress, in December, 1920, Representative Albert Johnson (Republican, Washington), chairman of the Committee on Immigration and Naturalization, introduced a bill suspending all immigration for one year.[14] The House of Representatives approved the bill by a vote of 296 to 42 a week later and sent the measure to the Senate.[15] There, the chairman of the Committee on Immigration, Senator William P. Dillingham (Republican, Vermont), substituted an entirely different measure: a quota system based on national origins and designed to check the new immigration from southern, central and eastern Europe.

The original Dillingham bill provided that the "number of aliens of any nationality who may be admitted in any . . . year shall be limited to five percent of the number of foreign-born persons of such nationality resident in the United States as determined by the [1910] census." The bill continued all the inhibitory provisions of previous acts and recognized the Gentlemen's Agreement by providing that the act should not apply to "aliens coming from countries immigration from which is now regulated in treaties and agreements."[16] The substitute bill was agreed to in both houses by overwhelming majorities; in the process the number of immigrants to be admitted was reduced to three per cent.[17] President Wilson disposed of the bill by pocket veto. An identical measure was introduced in the House on April 18, 1921.[18] In less than a month the new Congress approved it.[19] Admittedly a temporary measure, it was to expire on June 30, 1922; Congress later extended it two additional years.[20]

Surprisingly enough, none of the California delegation even attempted to have Japanese exclusion written into the bill. Yet, as we shall see, Hiram Johnson, now the senior senator from California, was organizing congressional support for exclusion while the bill was being debated. Although I can find no positive evidence, it seems probable that the two Johnsons, Albert and Hiram, had a gentlemen's agreement of their own. The Californians must have agreed to defer their attempt for exclusion until a later date. I imagine they received some sort of assurances of future support from Albert Johnson and other congressional leaders. The Californians were willing to go a long way to secure the coöperation of the congressman from the state of Washington: Albert Johnson, because of his position as chairman of the Committee on Immigration and Naturalization, could deal a deathblow to their hopes. Although he came from a Pacific Coast state which had a Japanese problem of its own, Johnson was continually flirting with the idea of allowing the Japanese a token quota. His original bill in 1920 made no reference to the Japanese at all; when the topic was injected into the debate in the House, Johnson quickly changed the subject.[21]

During the winter of 1920 Hiram Johnson and McClatchy seem to have had hopes that exclusion might be brought about by treaty.[22] Discussions were then taking place in Washington between United States Ambassador Roland Morris and Japanese Ambassador Kijuro Shidehara toward that end, and Johnson was made privy to them. If the California exclusionists seriously thought that these discussions would satisfy their demands, they were quickly disabused. Just after the new year, Johnson gave McClatchy the gist of the discussions:[23]

The Japanese insist the discrimination rests fundamentally upon the denial... of citizenship.... Morris says that he is inclining personally to what he designates as Roosevelt's original position—that citizenship must be given to those who are here and total exclusion then enforced.... I feel the only way to deal with Japan is to stand upon what we have the jurisdiction and the right to do.

Morris' proposal was, of course, repugnant to Johnson, and the Californian quickly spelled out his reasons.

The naturalization of Japanese [he wrote to the ambassador] would be most abhorrent to our people, and, of course, be vigorously resisted. From the broader standpoint, too, the national weal, no class of citizens within our borders should be made citizens who do not in reality become American citizens. It is an incontrovertible fact that the Japanese continue ever Japanese, that their allegiance is always to Tokio, and even in the event of naturalization, they would continue alien, and their loyalty would ever be, not to the United States, but to Japan.[24]

Later in the year Johnson and McClatchy attempted to convert the State Department to their point of view, but with little success. McClatchy, after Johnson had arranged for him to see Secretary of State Charles Evans Hughes, complained that Hughes had given him only ten minutes, and a rather cool and formal ten minutes at that; McClatchy, who could expound on the Japanese question for hours, was politely but firmly shown the door and asked to submit his views in writing. At about this time the exclusionist leaders seem to have despaired of diplomatic relief.[25]

In the spring of 1921 Hiram Johnson began organizing congressional sentiment for the exclusion fight to come. First, the entire California delegation met and was addressed by V. S. McClatchy. There was no need to convince the delegation of the Japanese menace; what was important was to get the delegation to agree on unified action.[26] This done, Johnson proceeded to organize what he called the "Executive Committee of Western States"—actually it was a steering committee for anti-Japanese measures. It included one senator and one representative from each of eleven Western states and was to work in coöperation with the California delegation. The committee cut across party lines and included some illustrious names.[27] Although it is not clear whether this committee continued meeting through 1924, its existence is indicative of the methodical course the exclusionist movement pursued after Johnson and McClatchy took charge. In April, 1921, the Western congressmen were given a lengthy exposition of the exclusionist case by McClatchy.

Johnson and McClatchy were willing to bide their time. Sometime in 1921 they seem to have decided to defer all attempts at exclusion until Congress should next take up the immigration question. Meanwhile, the exclusion movement was having organizational difficulties, the problem being money. The bylaws of the new Exclusion League called for contributions from member organizations; as early as November, 1920, John S. Chambers was complaining that the money was not coming in.[28] In the spring of 1921 professional fund raisers were employed, but to no avail. By the spring of 1922 the League stopped functioning altogether as a membership organization; its executive committee continued to meet. Phelan and McClatchy agreed jointly to subsidize the whole anti-Japanese movement themselves. McClatchy continued to devote his time to anti-Japanese activities. The pressure groups continued to render support in the form of resolutions, but it is clear that McClatchy was now managing the movement. He thus described the new policy:

> It has been decided [that] the Japanese Exclusion League will not figure publicly. It has also been decided that it would be unwise to make this an anti-Japanese campaign, but rather to conduct it... simply as a movement which no good American citizen can fail to endorse.[29]

McClatchy wanted no undue vulgarity. In 1922–23 organized anti-Japanese groups in Los Angeles started a "Swat the Jap" campaign designed to make life miserable for all Japanese residing there. Its general character may be judged from the following leaflet:[30]

JAPS

You came to care for lawns,
 we stood for it
You came to work in truck gardens,
 we stood for it
You sent your children to our public schools,
 we stood for it
You moved a few families in our midst,
 we stood for it
You proposed to build a church in our neighborhood
 BUT
We DIDN'T and WE WON'T STAND FOR IT
You impose more on us each day
 until you have gone your limit
WE DON'T WANT YOU WITH US
SO GET BUSY, JAPS, AND
GET OUT OF HOLLYWOOD

This was just the sort of thing, McClatchy felt, that might undo the exclusionist cause, and he did everything in his power to put an end to it.[31] McClatchy was personally on speaking terms with many Issei and Nisei leaders, and was always willing to discuss matters with them. He insisted that he, himself, wished to do nothing to disturb those

Japanese already resident here, yet he never repudiated the plank in the exclusionist platform which called for a constitutional amendment to deprive the Nisei of their citizenship.

In November, 1922, a decision of the United States Supreme Court simplified matters for the exclusionists by validating their long-standing contention that Japanese were "aliens ineligible to citizenship." This assumption was challenged by Takao Ozawa, who had been denied citizenship by a district court in Hawaii in 1914. Ozawa had lived most of his life in the United States and Hawaii, was a graduate of Berkeley High School, and had attended the University of California for several years. He was a Christian, and the English language was used in his home. The court conceded that he was "well qualified by character and education for citizenship."[32]

Even so, the court unanimously rejected Ozawa's petition, holding that the statutes—whose basic language dated from 1790—limited naturalization to "free white persons and aliens of African nativity." The contention of Ozawa's counsel, George W. Wickersham, a former Attorney General of the United States, was that the absence of any specific congressional prohibition against Japanese meant that they were eligible. The court ruled, however, that since Japanese were not specifically included in the language of the act they could not be admitted to citizenship.[33] This decision meant that Congress could now safely use the time-honored "aliens ineligible to citizenship" formula, which had been hitherto restricted to state and municipal statutes.

The exclusionists continued to bide their time. In January, 1923, McClatchy notified his executive committee that:

Senator Hiram W. Johnson advises me that in his judgment no immigration bill will be reported out this session, but if one *is* reported out it will contain the ineligible alien provision ... [It] would be an impossibility to get before the Senate, now, a constitutional amendment referring to Japanese [which] could not possibly be passed at this session.[34]

Hiram Johnson's predictions were proved correct. No general immigration bill was considered until the 68th Congress, which met in December, 1923.[35] The bill as originally reported by Albert Johnson in the House, called for a quota of only 2 per cent—and this based on the predominantly "Nordic" census of 1890; the bill also contained a prohibition against the admission of any "alien ineligible to citizenship." The anti-Japanese feature of the bill aroused only token opposition in the House.[36] Even Adolph Sabath of Chicago, an immigrant congressman and the leader of the fight against a discriminatory quota system, announced himself in favor of excluding the Japanese.[37] It soon became apparent that if Japanese exclusion were to be defeated, that outcome would depend on action in the Senate, traditionally more sensitive to the international implications of its acts.

Realizing this, the exclusionists directed their heaviest batteries upon the Senate. In March, 1924, a three-man exclusionist delegation came to Washington to testify and to lobby; its leader, V. S. McClatchy, was seconded by former Senator Phelan and the Attorney General of California, Ulysses S. Webb. McClatchy, in a long presentation before the Senate Committee on Immigration, made the ultimate apologia for the California position. He denounced the Japanese for "violations" of the Gentlemen's Agreement, specifying the picture brides and their successors and the allegedly astronomical birth rate. He cited as dangers to California's Anglo-Saxon civilization the increased landholdings of the Issei and their clannishness, and made the usual assertion that all Japanese were loyal only to Japan. He cited their foreign-language schools and the fact that many Japanese sent their children to Japan to be educated as proofs of his contention. But the essence of McClatchy's position, as the essence of the California position had been all along, was racism.

The Japanese [McClatchy argued] are less assimilable and more dangerous as residents in this country than any other of the peoples ineligible under our laws. . . . With great pride of race, they have no idea of assimilating in the sense of amalgamation. They do not come here with any desire or any intent to lose their racial or national identity. They come here specifically and professedly for the purpose of colonizing and establishing here permanently the proud Yamato race. They never cease being Japanese. . . . In pursuit of their intent to colonize this country with that race they seek to secure land and to found large families. . . . They have greater energy, greater determination, and greater ambition than the other yellow and brown races ineligible to citizenship, and with the same low standards of living, hours of labor, use of women and child labor, they naturally make more dangerous competitors in an economic way. . . . California regards herself as a frontier State. She has been making for 20 years the fight of the nation against incoming of alien races whose peaceful penetration must in time with absolute certainty drive the white race to the wall, and prior to that time inevitably provoke international trouble across the Pacific.[38]

McClatchy boasted that the House Committee on Immigration had already been converted to the California position, and he predicted that the then unfriendly Senate committee would be brought round in time. His detailed presentation seemed to have been in vain. In the upper house an entirely different bill was brought in, and this bill proposed leaving the Gentlemen's Agreement alone. As Senator LeBaron Colt (Republican, Rhode Island), chairman of the Immigration Committee, put it, "we have left the Japanese question to be settled by diplomacy."[39]

The manager of the bill, Senator David Reed (Republican, Pennsylvania), expressed willingness to put the Japanese under a quota, as several senators had suggested. (Under the percentage scheme finally adopted, a Japanese quota would have been a hundred immigrants per year.) Speaking for the committee, Reed said that he would prefer to postpone what he had to say on Japanese exclusion "until the matter is argued by someone who wants to offend the Japanese." He meant Hiram Johnson, who was absent, campaigning for the Republican presidential nomination in the Middle West. Reed added: "We feel that the preservation of the gentlemen's agreement more effectively keeps down Japanese immigration than any exclusion law we could possibly adopt."[40]

With Hiram Johnson still absent, the junior senator from California, Samuel Shortridge, put forth the exclusion case four days later and offered an amendment barring aliens ineligible to citizenship. Shortridge had little influence in the Senate; he complained that senators were leaving the chamber during his violently anti-Japanese speech.[41] In the ensuing debate several senators expressed themselves in favor of a quota for Japan and it began to appear that exclusion might have rough sledding.

The views of the administration were also brought to bear by Secretary of State Hughes. In words similar to Reed's, he came out strongly for a quota for Japan, plus continuance of the Gentlemen's Agreement. This, Hughes said, would provide

a double control of immigration from Japan. It contemplates the continuation of the gentlemen's agreement whereby we have the cooperation of the Japanese Government in excluding laborers. It also provides for a check on immigration from Japan by means of the quota restriction. On account of our long frontier lines I am of the opinion that such a double control would be more effective to prevent the entry of undesirable aliens than an exclusion provision.[42]

During the course of the debate, in both houses, the complaint had been made that the Gentlemen's Agreement was a secret document which no one had ever seen. The same complaint had been made by Hughes's colleague in the cabinet, Secretary of Labor James J. Davis.[43] Actually, the terms of the agreement were generally known: Senator Colt had accurately described them earlier in the session.[44] Nevertheless, Hughes felt uneasy about this charge, and on March 27, 1924, he suggested verbally to Japanese Ambassador Masanao Hanihara that "the Ambassador could write a letter to the Secretary [in which] the [Gentlemen's] Agreement could be summarized in a brief and definite fashion and could be presented authoritatively."[45]

After consulting with his government, Hanihara wrote the desired letter on April 10, 1924. Hughes transmitted it to the Senate the next day. Three days later, in the shrewd hands of Henry Cabot Lodge, the Hanihara letter became the instrument with which Japanese exclusion was forced through the Senate.⁴⁶ The first part of the letter was a long and accurate exposition of the substance of the Gentlemen's Agreement and its workings. The ambassador expressed the willingness of his government to modify the agreement if the United States so desired. Then Hanihara addressed himself to the bill pending.

... a certain clause, obviously aimed at the Japanese as a nation, is introduced in the proposed immigration bill, in apparent disregard of the most sincere and friendly endeavors on the part of the Japanese Government to meet the needs and wishes of the American Government and people, is mortifying enough to the Government and people of Japan. They are, however, exercising the utmost forbearance at this moment, and in so doing they confidently rely upon the high sense of justice and fair-play of the American Government and people, which, when properly approached, will readily understand why no such discriminatory provision as above referred to should be allowed to become a part of the law of the land.

It is needless to add that it is not the intention of the Japanese Government to question the sovereign right of any country to regulate immigration to its own territories. Nor is it their desire to send their nationals to the countries where they are not wanted. On the contrary, the Japanese Government showed from the very beginning of this problem their perfect willingness to cooperate with the United States Government to effectively prevent by all honorable means the entrance into the United States of such Japanese nationals as are not desired by the United States, and have given ample evidence thereof, the facts of which are well known to your Government. To Japan the question is not one of expediency, but of principle. To her the mere fact that a few hundreds or thousands of her nationals will or will not be admitted into domains of other countries is immaterial, so long as no question of national susceptibilities is involved. The important question is whether Japan as a nation is or is not entitled to the proper respect and consideration of other nations.

... The manifest object of the [exclusion clause] is to single out Japanese as a nation, stigmatizing them as unworthy and undesirable in the eyes of the American people. And yet the actual result of that particular provision, if the proposed bill becomes law as intended, would be to exclude only 146 Japanese per year. On the other hand the Gentlemen's Agreement is, in fact, accomplishing all that can be accomplished by the proposed Japanese exclusion clause except for those 146. It is indeed difficult to believe that it can be the intention of the people of your great country, who always stand for principles of justice and fair play in the intercourse of nations, to resort—in order to secure the annual exclusion of 146 Japanese—to a measure which would not only seriously offend the pride of a friendly nation, that has always been earnest and diligent in its efforts to preserve the friendship of your people, but would also seem to involve the question of good faith and therefore of the honor of their Government, or at least of its executive branch.

Relying on the confidence you have been good enough to show me at all times, I have stated or rather repeated all this to you very candidly and in a most friendly spirit, for I realize, as I believe you do, the grave consequences which the enactment of the measure retaining that particular provision would inevitably bring upon the otherwise happy and mutually advantageous relations between our two countries.[47]

Three days after the delivery of this note, Lodge asserted, and almost the whole Senate professed to believe, that the phrase "grave consequences" was in fact a "veiled threat" against the United States, and that, since no one could threaten the United States with impunity, Japanese exclusion must become law. Even considering the fact that in 1924 international diplomacy had not yet degenerated to its current level of daily abuse and counterabuse, the Lodge construction was a bit farfetched. Although the fact that Hughes had asked Hanihara to write the letter was not then known, it was quite clear to any intelligent observer that Hughes and the Japanese ambassador were coöperating. Even James D. Phelan, perhaps the most jingoistic of the exclusionists, could see nothing exceptional in Hanihara's note. In a statement for the California organization, he merely characterized the letter as a part of Japan's bid for racial equality and called on his former colleagues to ignore the letter and enact the House bill.[48] As matters stood on April 14, 1924, three days after the publication of Hanihara's letter, it still seemed possible that the Senate would reject exclusion. Phelan privately claimed to have "more than fifty votes" lined up for exclusion, but with strong administration pressure—1924 was an election year—this majority might well have evaporated.[49] It should be noted that this was far from the two-thirds majority necessary to override a veto.

When the question of Japanese exclusion came up for further discussion on the floor of the Senate, Henry Cabot Lodge, hitherto silent on the Japanese question, moved that the Senate go into executive session, where it remained for fifty minutes.[50] After the doors were reopened, Lodge, with alleged reluctance, restated "what I had said behind closed doors." Plucking the phrase "grave consequences" out of context, Lodge, who spoke with particular authority in matters diplomatic, insisted that

the letter addressed to our State Department by the ambassador from Japan seems to me a letter improper to be addressed by the representative of one great country to another friendly country. It contains, I regret much to say, a veiled threat.... The United States can not legislate by the exercise by any other country of veiled threats.[51]

Lodge, with his instinct for the jugular, turned the discussion into a stampede. Senator Reed, of Pennsylvania, hitherto a leader in the fight for a Japanese quota, said he now felt "compelled ... to vote in favor of exclusion."[52] So did almost all his colleagues. The provision containing an endorsement of the Gentlemen's Agreement was defeated by a vote of 76 to 2.[53] Although there were a whole series of later maneuvers, this vote effectively sealed the fate of the Gentlemen's Agreement and made Japanese exclusion the law of the land for twenty-eight years.

Lodge's action—and the action of the Senate in following him—can only be described as wanton. As an act of studied international insolence it makes the rejection of the Versailles Treaty seem a veritable judgment of Solomon. As we know, Lodge had helped Roosevelt arrange the preconditions for the Gentlemen's Agreement. Roosevelt himself, in a state paper Lodge helped to prepare, had used the superlative of Hanihara's phrase—"gravest consequences"—in referring to the possible consequences of discrimination against the Japanese.[54] Why then did Lodge wreck an understanding he had helped establish? It is impossible to say; it is also impossible to take his statements at face value. He was far too sophisticated not to realize that Hanihara and Hughes were acting in concert, although this fact may have escaped some of his more rustic colleagues. Lodge may well have wanted to embarrass the Coolidge administration—there was no love lost between Lodge and Coolidge and his Secretary of State—or he may have wanted merely to demonstrate that his talent for wrecking international agreements was still unimpaired. At any rate, his "veiled threat" speech was the last major act of a long career. He died on November 9, 1924.

An even more fundamental question than the actions of an individual remains. Why did the exclusionists risk the grave consequences of total exclusion, when even the granting of a token quota would have satisfied Japan's pride? It is not enough to point out, as some writers have, that the exclusionists were stubborn men who had long struggled toward a fixed goal, although in this connection it should be remarked that Americans seem to have an almost fatal weakness for not-too-meaningful slogans: "Free Silver," "Unconditional Surrender," and the like. Perhaps the crux of the problem was that the American people—along with much of Congress—had developed a deep-seated distrust of the State Department and diplomacy. Although the original basis for this distrust probably lay somewhere in the dark recesses of the American psyche—the very lineaments and phrases of diplomacy are, after all, European—the exclusionists had good reason to feel that diplomacy had been used to thwart their cause in the past. The State Department's continued insistence that the Gentlemen's Agreement had been a success, when it actually produced results undreamed of by Roosevelt and Root, served only to make a bad situation worse.

The private position of the State Department was entirely different. In one of its background papers prepared for the American delegation at the Washington Conference of 1921–22, the State Department admitted that "it was never anticipated at the time the agreement was concluded that large numbers of women would be brought to this country." It was also argued that "the features of the 'Gentlemen's Agreement' that have caused most of the ill-favor in which it is held . . . have been the secrecy with which it has been surrounded," and that "These conditions are psychologic and are not likely to be affected by statistics."[55] Despite these realizations of its defects, the State Department continued to insist publicly that the agreement was exactly what Roosevelt and Root had ordered, and did nothing to lift the veil of secrecy until the Hanihara letter.

Most critics of Hughes' course in the Hanihara letter incident have concentrated their fire on his failure to realize the possible effects of the "grave consequences" phrase. Actually, the phrase could have passed unnoticed, and since the Senate might have acted at any moment—Hughes had been waiting for Hanihara's letter for two weeks—it is easy to see how the possible grave consequences were not anticipated. It seems to me that more fundamental criticisms are to be directed at the Secretary. It is one thing for an executive officer to oppose a bill pending in Congress—in fact, it is often his duty to do so—and quite another to do so in league with a foreign ambassador. The results Hughes wanted could have been just as readily obtained had he written the letter putting forth the terms of the agreement, with perhaps a covering letter by Hanihara endorsing Hughes's statements. In the final analysis, however, the most serious blunder seems to have been the stubbornness of both governments in clinging to an obsolete agreement. Despite Hughes's and Hanihara's insistence on the superior efficiency of a "double control," any quota arrangement for Japan would have made the Gentlemen's Agreement meaningless and superfluous. Had the State Department been willing to scrap the Gentlemen's Agreement and make the fight solely on a token quota for Japan, without the unnecessary subtleties of the Hanihara letter, it is just possible—but not probable—that the exclusionists might have been denied total victory. Instead, Hughes and Hanihara became the unwitting accomplices of the exclusionists.[56]

The Californians, of course, were ecstatic. "I [am] repaid for my efforts," Phelan gloated; "the Japs are routed."[57] But the exclusionists' other great demand—a constitutional amendment depriving Nisei and other native-born Asians of their citizenship—was never seriously considered by Congress. After 1924, what energies the exclusionists could muster were devoted to rebutting the counterattacks of the American friends of Japan, still led by Sidney Gulick, who persistently, but futilely, tried to get a quota for Japan.[58]

After the passage of the Immigration Act of 1924, the Japanese Exclusion League, which had been dormant for two years, was dissolved, and in its place the California Joint Immigration Committee was substituted. It was supported by the Native Sons, the American Legion, the A.F. of L. and the Grange. V. S. McClatchy continued his nativist labors for that group until his death in 1936, but the crusading fervor of most of the exclusionists gained no more victories in peacetime. Only after Pearl Harbor did the exclusionists again influence public policy: Manzanar, Gila River, Tule Lake, White Mountain and the other relocation camps are the last monuments to their patriotic zeal.

An account of the exclusion movement is thus a sort of American success story, and, like so many American success stories, it leaves a rather bitter taste in the mouth. The taste must be made even more bitter by the realization that the accomplishment of exclusion was not merely the work of a little band of willful men. Had Japanese exclusion been put to a national referendum in the 1920's, there is little doubt that it would have received the sanction of the vast majority of the electorate. Like the racist restriction of immigration which it accompanied, it was popular. Liberal historians too often make the American past a sort of perpetual morality play in which the wicked conservatives continually thwart the democratic aspirations of the people. Certainly there are many episodes in our history which justify this sort of scenario. But there have been times when the role of the conservative has been to try to foil the undemocratic aspirations of the people. Demos has a dark side too; the anti-Japanese movement was one of its aspects.

CHAPTER VIII

CONCLUSION

As we have seen, California's anti-Oriental tradition has roots reaching back to her gold-rush past. The Issei's first American legacy was the hate and the fear of Orientals which had been generated in the anti-Chinese crusade. First inspired by economic competition and restricted largely to organized labor, the anti-Japanese movement soon received at least passive support from the overwhelming majority of California's population.

Prejudice, the sociologists tell us, is learned behavior. Twentieth-century Californians learned the lesson well. Although racial prejudice, directed at various ethnic groups, flourished throughout the United States during the period under discussion, nowhere north of the Mason-Dixon line did any single group encounter the sustained nativist assault that was directed against California's Japanese. There seem to be four chief reasons for this. First, the Japanese were of a distinct racial group; no amount of acculturation could mask their foreignness. Second, unlike the Chinese, they rapidly began to challenge whites in many businesses and professions—as a group, Japanese in the United States became very quickly imbued with what, in Europeans, would be called the Protestant ethic. Third, the growing unpopularity of their homeland—an unpopularity that was, to a certain degree, deserved—further served to make immigrants from Japan special objects of suspicion. These three conditions would have made any large group of Japanese a particularly despised minority anywhere in the United States. Finally, the fact that most of the Japanese were in California probably made things worse, for California probably had a lower boiling point than did the country at large.

California, by virtue of its anti-Chinese tradition and frontier psychology, was already conditioned to anti-Orientalism before the Japanese arrived. Other special California characteristics abetted the success of the agitation. In the prewar years, the extraordinary power of organized labor in northern California gave the anti-Japanese movement a much stronger base than it would have enjoyed elsewhere; in the postwar years, open-shop southern California proved almost equally hospitable to an agitation pitched to middle-class white Protestants. In the two periods anti-Japanese sentiment flourished among completely disparate populations: the first- and second-generation immigrants who were the backbone of California's labor movement, and the

Midwestern *émigrés* who came to dominate the southern California scene. For most of these Californians, opposition to the Japanese was based upon fears which were largely nonrational.

It is instructive to note that these nonrational fears were nowhere more persistent than in the minds of those middle-class leaders whom we have come to call progressive. If it seems paradoxical that a reform group dedicated to what one of its number called "the promise of American life" should lead so blatant an antidemocratic movement, it ought to be pointed out that one of the most glaring and too often unremarked deficiencies of the progressive was his utter disregard for civil liberties in general. Nowhere in the long debate over Japanese exclusion have I found even a suggestion that alien immigrants might have civil rights. Not until discrimination against immigrants after the First World War had reached its climax did some progressives begin to realize that even the rights of noncitizens must be protected if the liberties of all were to remain unimpaired.

The discriminations against the Japanese recounted here, as well as those of a later date, are clearly blots on the democratic escutcheon which we prize so highly. But the consequences of the anti-Japanese movement were more than moral. The existence of this prejudice helped to poison relations between the United States and Japan. As George F. Kennan has pointed out, in his provocative series of lectures on *American Diplomacy, 1900–1950,* the "long and unhappy story" of United States–Japanese relationships in this century was constantly worsened by the fact that "we would repeatedly irritate and offend the sensitive Japanese by our immigration policies and the treatment of people of Japanese lineage . . . in this country."

APPENDIXES

APPENDIX A

(Figures consolidated from *Annual Reports*,
Commissioner General of Immigration)

Year ending June 30	Immigrants	Emigrants[b]
1901[a]	5,249	.....
1902	14,455	.....
1903	20,041	.....
1904	14,382	.....
1905	11,021	.....
1906	14,243	.....
1907	30,842	.....
1908	16,418	5,323
1909	3,275	3,903
1910	2,798	4,377
1911	4,575	3,351
1912	6,172	1,501
1913	8,302	733
1914	8,941	794
1915	8,609	825
1916	8,711	780
1917	8,925	722
1918	10,164	1,558
1919	10,056	2,127
1920	9,279	4,238
1921	7,531	4,352
1922	6,361	4,353
1923	5,652	2,844
1924	8,481	2,120
Totals	244,483	43,901

[a] Perhaps 30,000 Japanese came to the United States before 1901. The census of 1900 recorded 24,326 Japanese residents.
[b] No accurate figures available before 1908.

APPENDIX B

[Executive Mansion]
[Sacramento]
June 21, 1913

MY DEAR COLONEL ROOSEVELT:

This week I finished with the extraordinary number of bills that had been passed by the Legislature and presented to me for approval or disapproval. This is my first breathing spell and I wished above all things to utilize it in giving you some sort of a narrative of the events which led finally to the enactment of the alien land bill.

Early in January, during the first part of the legislative session (you know we have what is termed a bifurcated session,—first a meeting of thirty days, and then an adjournment for at least thirty days, and then a continuation of the session until the work is completed) there was some little agitation among legislators in reference to the Japanese. The question for many years has been a smouldering problem in California, now and then bursting into acute activity. The encroachment of the Japanese upon certain of our farming communities has been very marked of late years, and wherever they gained a foothold there they continued until the American farmers moved out and the Japanese farmers' supremacy was unquestioned. You are very familiar with the attempts of past legislatures to deal with the subject and the causes which led, in each instance, to postponement. I think you will remember two years ago I had some correspondence with the national administration in which a distinct threat was made by the State Department speaking in behalf of the President to which I responded with some degree of firmness, and presented then the California view of our right to legislate exactly as I had presented it this year. Two years ago a bill undoubtedly would have passed, but for the fact that it reached the Assembly after passage in the Senate just at the close of the session and was bottled up with many other bills under the rules governing the particular time. At the commencement of our session, in January, the Panama-Pacific Exposition officials came to Sacramento, and stated that it had been conveyed to them, and they conveyed it therefore to us, that Japan would regard as an unfriendly and offensive act any legislation of an alien land bill, any discussion of the subject or even the introduction of such a measure into our legislature. The Exposition people were extremely frightened and they begged that nothing be done, that discussion be stilled and that the subject be not mentioned, because they asserted that if there were the slightest agitation, Japan would refuse to exhibit at the 1915 Exposition at San Francisco and that the most attractive part of the Exposition,—the part relied upon to bring European exhibitors would be eliminated and the Exposition would be transmuted from a great international institution into a mere local affair. So very earnest and insistent were the Exposition Officials that I brought them in contact in my office with various delegations in the Legislature, and they presented their case in detail. At the time of the presentation of their case, the Exposition people assumed to answer for the Press

[112]

and the Labor people, who had been foremost in anti-Japanese legislation. There was no very great disposition among the legislators then to proceed and the Exposition officials might have succeeded in their purpose had it not been for the farmers of a few communities in the state. These farmers insisted that an alien land bill was absolutely essential for their protection, and necessary for the future welfare of California. They presented the stories of their communities with such detail and the demonstration was so complete that they completely won many of the legislators who had not before been particularly interested in the subject. The result was that bills were introduced despite the Exposition people, and those bills rested during the February intermission, and took their regular course in the Legislature. During the second session, I arranged for a public hearing in the Assembly Chamber, when publicly the Exposition people could present their case to the legislators. At that hearing the farmers appeared, and the debate between the very plain rugged, untutored and uncultured men from the fields and our astute and educated, plug-hatted brigade who represented the Exposition was most interesting and memorable. When it had ceased the Exposition people retired crestfallen; the audience roared its approval of the farmers and the Committee in charge of the bill immediately and unanimously reported that it "do pass." Then I began to receive telegrams from various people in Washington, always intimating the desires of the federal government and suggesting delay; the direful results that would come to us from action by the Legislature and how carefully we were being safeguarded by the present administration. Finally, to one of those telegrams, from Congressman Kent, which he supplemented with a second stating that he was speaking authoritatively, I responded, saying that the national government had not hesitated in the past to express its wishes to the government of the State of California, and if the federal authorities had anything to say concerning legislation pending, I was unable to comprehend why it could not do so, in the ordinary fashion to the duly constituted authorities of the state. This dispatch to Kent brought me the first wire from Bryan. I then with the utmost courtesy and in detail, explained the pending bills, their exact status, and their possibilities. It was then thought that a general alien land bill would be passed, and I so stated to Mr. Bryan. The Bradford bill of the Assembly about this time passed the Assembly and it contained the clause "ineligible to citizenship." Certain Senators prepared a general alien land bill and presented it to the members of the Senate for their acquiescence before pressing its passage, and then we found that the sentiment of the legislature was overwhelmingly against a general alien land bill. Not only was this so but the state began to be agitated from one end to the other and we were deluged with telegrams and communications which were of sufficient moment to convince' the legislators that a general alien land bill would be disastrous to investments in the state and to our development. During this period, I kept Washington advised and finally wired them that a general alien land bill would not be passed and we were unable to see how the use of the words "ineligible to citizenship" constituted a discrimination against Japan. During the exchange of telegrams the Washington government was constantly in communication with democratic senators here who were advising the administration just how to act so that they might be in the clear, and the entire burden be assumed by the State administration. Undoubtedly, because of this underground method of communication, the President and Mr. Bryan were saying to me in dispatches continuously [that] after the bill passed both houses of the legislature, and was in my hands, they desired it delayed until reasons could be presented to me concerning the vetoing of the bill, ever declining to present any real arguments concerning the measure. Just as often as I would receive a wire from Mr. Bryan, or the President, upon the subject, I would advise them that it was necessary if they had anything to communicate concerning the measure that they communicate it at once so that it could be transmitted by me to the Legislature. Finally, came the peculiar telegram of the President in which he referred to our national obligations, the hope that we would not pass the legislation etc., and then my response was made concerning what we conceived to be our right and our duty and defending the particular measure then pending before the legislature. At last came the wire asking if we would receive Mr. Bryan and we prepared our reply from both houses of the legislature that while we insisted upon the right of the state to legislate as it chose, we were perfectly willing to have Mr. Bryan come to confer or consult. We acted with the utmost circumspection in dealing with the government at Washington, and I think that our correspondence was always respectful although I trust that it was at no time ambiguous. We delayed action in the Senate on the bill pending Mr. Bryan's arrival. We all thought, of course, that he was coming here with something of great importance to import, and the gravity of the situation was during this period of waiting, more keenly felt than at any other time. When Mr. Bryan arrived, immediately we arranged for his consultation with the legislature, and that consultation, at his suggestion, was made *executive*. The very suggestion aroused to the highest pitch the interest of the legislators, and the first meeting with Mr. Bryan was held with the idea prevalent that he would make such disclosures as would render imperative postponement of our measure. We sat with Mr. Bryan for some hours that day. He invited discussion and various members—not always the most influential, nor the ablest—presented their views. Before consultation he met with many of the democratic senators, nearly all of whom are candidates for federal office, and unquestionably with them arranged upon his plan of action. After sitting all day, Mr. Bryan presented absolutely nothing that could not have been transmitted within the limits of a night letter, without using all of the allotted words, and at the conclusion of the first consultation, there was a feeling among the legislators not only of disappointment, but that they had been decoyed more or less into a postponement without any real reasons, and that their time in consultation and conference had simply been frittered away. That night, at my home, I told Mr. Bryan that when he concluded on the following day, because he wished again to meet with the legislators, the Webb bill which had been prepared at my instance by the Attorney General would be introduced in the Senate and pressed forward for passage. I handed to him then a copy of the bill, and this was twenty four hours before it was presented, asking him to wire it to the President, and ascertain definitely if there was any objection to it. He did wire the bill to Washington, but he never presented to me any response. On that first day's consultation, we had continued until about seven o'clock, talking of nothing particularly and having nothing presented to us of importance and in the last moments of the conference, I talked to the legislators for not to exceed three minutes in the endeavor to clear the atmosphere, and to bring them back to the one point at issue and I was delighted at the expiration of the brief talk to have our legislators with almost unanimity—excepting, of course, the democratic senators who were candidates for federal jobs,—applaud most heartily.

The following day more of the same nonsense occurred,—Mr. Bryan talking always easily and quietly and tactfully, but presenting nothing, and that evening I had the President pro-tem of the Senate, who was presiding, turn to Mr. Bryan finally and ask if he had anything further that he desired to submit to the conference and he said he had nothing further, and then I announced to Mr. Bryan in accordance with what I had told him, on the previous day, that the Webb bill would go forward, and immediately it was introduced in the Senate. Then commenced a struggle that will ever be memorable to me, and that to me forms the historic aspect of this incident. We had provided Mr. Bryan with the Lieut. Governor's office, directly across the hall from the Senate Chamber. There he sat for the period of a week, representing the President of the United States, and the government of the United States, engaged during that period in sending for democratic senators and assemblymen, interviewing many others as well, and engaged in a parliamentary battle with the administration of the State. Immediately above my office he was marshalling the forces of the federal government, determined to enact only such legislation in a State as the federal government should desire, while I with a like determination, gathered the forces of the state government to pass legislation desired by the state.

This struggle for days continued, and it was a spectacle that I daresay has never before been witnessed in the United States. I would not describe Mr. Bryan's activity during that time as lobbying, but it consisted in dealing directly and personally with every standpatter with whom he could deal in our legislature and all of the democratic legislators, and in preparing with these the mode of procedure upon an alien land bill in the legislature of the state and directing that procedure. The first attempt was to postpone action and it was currently reported that the resolution introduced by Senator Curtain in that regard, was actually, in part, prepared by Mr. Bryan. Mr. Bryan admitted to me that he read the resolution and made some suggestions concerning it. The democrats whipped into line by the national administration were in a most peculiar position. Their party, and theirs alone, had adopted an anti-alien land law plank in its last platform. They were pledged to an anti-alien land law. We were not. They had made their campaign in a great degree upon this plank and upon an anti-Japanese cry, and yet on the motion to postpone which, of course, meant no bill, all of the democrats but two in the Senate, voted to postpone, while on the other hand, I marshalled all of the Progressives but two against postponement.

After the defeat of the motion to postpone, various amendments were attempted, with a desire to kill the bill; the democrats struggling in every fashion to prevent its passage, but it was passed by the Senate a little after midnight Friday, and immediately transmitted to the Assembly Saturday morning. I knew the necessity for immediate action, so I had the Assembly suspend the Constitution, read the bill twice and then in the afternoon put it upon its final passage. Here again, the same bitter fight was made by the democrats; the same effort to postpone, the same attempts to amend,—all of which were voted down. On Saturday afternoon, during the debate, Mr. Bryan requested a last conference and when asked for what purpose, he stated that he wished to bid the members of the Legislature Good-bye. In the very midst of the debate upon the bill, this last conference was held and instead merely of bidding the members Good-bye, he repeated the arguments that he had previously made. After his departure, the debate was resumed. At midnight Saturday night, the bill passed the Assembly, and then it came to me for signature.

The different parts of our state have different kinds of people. The problems that agitate the northern part and the central part, do not disturb, sometimes, the southern part of the State. The Japanese problem was peculiarly a problem of the northern and central part of the state. Our brethren in the south were little interested; but they stood by me most loyally during this very trying period. Some of them, however, Mr. Bryan argued with privately, sometimes persuasively and sometimes speciously. It was perfectly obvious to me that when we had started upon our course, there was nothing to do but to go through with it and pass our bill. Of course, all of our timid legislators would have liked to recede, and at times I had extraordinary difficulty in making them understand that having started we must finish, and I really believe that many of them went through with the matter more in personal loyalty than because they had any stomach for the particular kind of legislation. The big thing to me of this incident was the breaking down of the barrier that has heretofore existed between the nation[al] government and legislation in the states; the direct repudiation of the doctrine of State's rights, by a democratic administration and the remarkable and astounding scene of the United States Government, through its Secretary of State, for the period of a week struggling in every conceivable fashion as against a state administration, upon a particular measure pending in that state legislature. Of course, I have not been able to express myself publicly upon this phase of the situation, and during the time that Mr. Bryan was here, inasmuch as he was my guest, it was impossible for me to express myself as I desired in this particular. I did say to him during one of the trying times, however, that his position was an anomalous one, and that possibly no other man than himself could have occupied that anomalous situation for a period of sixteen seconds without a public explosion from the state administration.

Now, you may not know the other side of this Japanese question, a side that I did not consider during the time of our fateful days with the legislature. Last year, however, in this state, the Japanese question was made an issue and the Democratic Party abused you roundly for your stand during the time that you were President. Mr. Wilson in his usual elegant diction presented to the voters of the State of California, his views upon the subject and during the campaign, cards literally by the hundreds of thousands were distributed throughout the State of California, bearing on the one side what purported to be a statement of your position and on the other the letter of Mr. Wilson on the subject. I enclose herein a copy of the matter appearing on that card. To say that at least ten thousand votes were lost in this state upon this issue, I think is conservative. I did not know until I returned to California after the election the hammering we had undergone by democrats and reactionaries on this point and so you can pardon, perhaps a little malicious pleasure, that I took out of the attitude of our democratic brethren, and the democrats of the national administration.

During Mr. Bryan's visit a friend of mine related in my presence to Mr. Bryan ,an incident that occurred just after the election, and this is an absolutely true story. Raphael Weill of San Francisco, gave a banquet to Democrats in celebration of the Democratic victory in November, last. The most blatant of the democrats, Senator Sanford, was present at one of the tables at that banquet. Sanford has always been a bloviating blustering demagogue, his chief stock in trade,—the Japanese question. At the banquet Sanford announced to those near him, that on the first day of the session, he was going to introduce an alien land bill, and that he would have that fellow Johnson side stepping and climbing over the capitol dome during all the rest of the session with that bill. The democrat sitting next to him said, "Be careful, Senator, remember there will be then a democratic national administration, and you may have that administration side stepping." Sanford's boasting reply was, "Don't trouble about that. Mr. Bryan and Mr. Wilson know all about this question and we will have Johnson jumping during this whole session." Mr. Bryan didn't laugh as heartily at this narrative as my friend had thought he would. I might remark, parenthetically, Sanford is still side stepping. He was one of the democrats [who] is a candidate for a job.

I think we have laid the ghost. I know that never again in California can the Japanese question be a political question, except as we shall want it to be. I do not think there is any danger of war, and I believe we have vindicated our right to legislate as we see fit upon a matter clearly and wholly within our jurisdiction and I believe too, that we have shown the democratic doctrine of "State's rights" to be sham and pretense, insisted upon when it is their state that is affected but denied when they represent the federal government and our State is affected.

I haven't attempted to describe to you any particular phase of the Japanese problem with us. I think you understand that quite as well as I do. Suffice it to say, the question is one that had to be met sooner or later and it came about in such fashion at this session of the legislature that I deemed it our duty to meet it, and to meet it with firmness. If you will read carefully the words of Mr. Wilson as set forth in an enclosed copy of the campaign card, circulated, last year, and then compare those words with Mr. Bryan's utterances during our conference you must reach I think, as I reached, one of two conclusions—either Mr. Wilson played the demagogue in California last year in his utterances or he has in the interim thoroughly changed his views. The latter conclusion, in Mr. Wilson's case, would not be startling in view of our experience with him on other public questions; but the whole manner of the conduct of the campaign by the democrats in California last year, with the method of utterance of Mr. Wilson at that time upon a subject concerning which he doubtless knew little or nothing, might justly lead us to the conclusion first suggested.

I am sending you by this mail a copy of the stenographic report of the conference with Mr. Bryan at [that?] legislature. I do not know that you will care to read even all of this letter, but I thought there might come a time in the future when possibly you would desire to refer to recent occurrences here.

Pardon this discussive letter. It is dictated hastily as I am about to leave on a brief vacation.

Permit me to congratulate you not only on the result of your recent libel case, but upon your usual courage in forcing it to trial. I hope that you have forever set at rest the false and malicious story to which this libel gave public utterance.

Mrs. Johnson joins me in love to you and Mrs. Roosevelt.

Sincerely,

NOTES

NOTES

[1] The Japanese terms "Issei" ("first generation," for immigrants from Japan) and "Nisei" ("second generation," for their children born in the United States or Hawaii) will be used frequently for precision. The terms "Japanese-Americans" and "Americans of Japanese ancestry" are not appropriate for the period under discussion because the vast majority of the adult population (except for a handful of Issei "illegally" naturalized) were "aliens ineligible to citizenship" and remained, in law, Japanese nationals. Therefore I will often use the term "Japanese" to cover both immigrants and their citizen offspring, although it is to be understood that many of both generations had more of the spirit of America in them than some whose forefathers were the first to settle the land. For linguistic and historic convenience, the terms "Caucasian" and "white" are used as if they were altogether meaningful, which of course they are not. The semantic problems involved in doing otherwise in a work of this nature are dreadful to contemplate.

[2] For statistics of Japanese immigration see Appendix A.

[3] Z. Nuttall, "Earliest Historical Relations Between Mexico and Japan," *University of California Publications in American Archaeology and Ethnology*, 4 (1906), 1–47.

[4] William Lytle Schurz, *The Manila Galleon* (New York, 1959), p. 15.

[5] Sacramento *Union*, Dec. 14, 1876; San Francisco *Alta California*, March 5, 6, 17–20, 22, and 23, and April 5, 1871; the *Alta* for Feb. 21 and March 2, 1852, gives a running account of one group of castaway Japanese.

[6] For the stories of two wandering Japanese of this period see Joseph Heco, *The Narrative of a Japanese; What He Has Seen and the People He Has Met in the Course of the Last Forty Years* (Tokyo, 1895) and Hizakazu Kneko, *Manjiro, the Man Who Discovered America* (Boston, 1956).

[7] San Francisco *Alta California*, Sept. 19, 1855; C. Yanaga, "The First Japanese Embassy to the United States," *Pacific Historical Review*, 9 (March, 1940), 113–138.

[8] *Reports of the Immigration Commission* (Washington, 1911), Vol. 23, p. 5.

[9] San Francisco *Chronicle*, June 17, 1869.

[10] Paolo Sioli, *Historical Souvenir of El Dorado County, California* (Oakland, 1888), p. 112. *Alta California*, June 16 and Oct. 24, 1869. Sacramento *Union*, June 5, 7, 18, 19, and 21, and Oct. 24, 1869; March 2, April 5, June 11, Sept. 1 and 3, and Dec. 31, 1870; April 7, 1871.

[11] San Francisco *Chronicle*, June 17, 1869. One suspects that the expectation of a thriving tea and silk industry weighed heavily with the editor. The West's lack of manufactures was a chronic complaint in California newspapers. For an even later favorable comment see the Sacramento *Union*, Jan. 19, 1888.

[12] That is, absorbed literally. California then could take interracial marriage in its stride. On Jan. 12, 1877, the Sacramento *Union* published in its exchanges a report from the Truckee *Republican* telling of a marriage between "a large good looking white man" and "a delicate fragile looking Japanese woman." There was no derogatory comment. Twenty-eight years later, California would be in an uproar because Japanese boys sat in the same classrooms with Caucasian girls.

[13] *Japan Weekly Mail*, Dec. 20, 1884, quoted in Hilary Conroy, *The Japanese Frontier in Hawaii, 1869–1898* (Berkeley and Los Angeles, 1953), pp. 61–62. As the notes will show, this chapter relies heavily on Professor Conroy's excellent monograph.

[14] *Ibid.*, pp. 11–12, quoting from the *Hawaiian Gazette*, Jan. 19, 1870. See also

[121]

Ralph Kuykendall, *The Earliest Japanese Labor Immigration to Hawaii* (Honolulu, 1935). For a good account of the Chinese coolie trade see Persia Campbell Crawford, *Chinese Coolie Emigration to Countries Within the British Empire* (London, 1923). Strictly speaking, there was never any "coolie" emigration to the United States.

[15] Conroy, *op. cit.*, pp. 15, 21.

[16] *Report of the Commissioner of Labor on Hawaii, 1901* (Washington, 1902), p. 26.

[17] Quoted by Conroy, *op. cit.*, p. 133.

[18] Donald Rowland, "The United States and the Contract Labor Question in Hawaii, 1862–1900," *Pacific Historical Review*, 2 (Sept., 1933), 249–269.

[19] *Report of the Commissioner of Labor on Hawaii, 1901*, pp. 26, 34.

[20] Quoted by Conroy, *op. cit.*, p. 58.

[21] *Ibid.*, p. 154.

[22] See the map in Yosaburo Yoshida, "Sources and Causes of Japanese Immigration," *Annals of the American Academy of Political and Social Science* (hereinafter cited as *Annals*), 34 (Sept., 1909), 161.

[23] *Ibid.*

[24] Conroy, *op. cit.*, pp. 82–83. Irwin had doctors inspect the laborers as part of the selection process and naturally chose as good physical specimens as he could, since the work on the plantations was grueling. As Conroy notes, this means that the later physical comparisons of Nisei children with those in Japan (Nisei were larger) do not prove as much as once was thought, the original migrants having been selected for their superior physical qualities (see pp. 80–89).

[25] Yoshida, *op. cit.*, pp. 160–162.

[26] Conroy, *op. cit.*, p. 28.

[27] *Ibid.*, Appendix E, p. 154. Romanzo Adams, *The Japanese in Hawaii* (New York, 1924), Table C, p. 12, gives the numbers as 712. For an excellent fictional treatment of the Japanese in Hawaii from about 1900 on see James A. Michener, *Hawaii* (New York, 1959), particularly the section entitled "From the Inland Sea."

[28] Contract labor was abolished by sec. 10 of the Act of April 30, 1900, 31 Statutes at Large 141, chap. 339 (2 Supp., Revised Statutes 1141); *Report of the Commissioner of Labor on Hawaii, 1901*, p. 19; *Reports of the Immigration Commission*, Vol. 23, p. 6.

[29] San Francisco *Call*, June 25, 1892.

[30] See, for example, the affidavit of Cleveland L. Dam, former deputy labor commissioner of the State of California, Feb. 16, 1900, in *Reports of the Industrial Commission* (Washington, 1901), Vol. 15, pp. 767–768. For a federal official's reminiscences, see Hart H. North, "Chinese and Japanese Immigration to the Pacific Coast," *California Historical Society Quarterly*, 28 (Dec., 1949), 343–350. For an adverse appraisal of North's treatment of Chinese immigrants see letter, Theodore Roosevelt to Victor H. Metcalf, June 16, 1905, in E. E. Morison (ed.), *The Letters of Theodore Roosevelt* (Cambridge, Mass., 1951), IV, 1235–1236; hereinafter cited as Roosevelt Letters.

[31] Quoted in *Reports of the Immigration Commission*, Vol. 23, p. 14.

[32] Varden Fuller, "The Supply of Agricultural Labor as a Factor in the Evolution of Farm Organization in California," in *Hearings before a Subcommittee of the Committee on Education and Labor, United States Senate, Seventy-Sixth Congress, Third Session pursuant to S. Res. 266 (74th Congress)*, (Washington, 1940), Part 54, p. 19778. Another authority comments that California's specialized farming "was made possible by a long continued supply of cheap migrant labor. . . . In the years preceding the First World War [the Japanese] constituted the primary

supply.... By the 1920's [many] had migrated to cities or had set themselves up as farmers." Clarke A. Chambers, *California Farm Organizations* (Berkeley and Los Angeles, 1952), pp. 1–2.

[33] See the testimony of John Powell Irish, a large-scale California agriculturist and long-time advocate and defender of Orientals, in U. S. Congress, House of Representatives, Committee on Immigration and Naturalization, *Hearings on Japanese Immigration* (Washington, 1921), pp. 43–49.

[34] Fuller, "The Supply of Agricultural Labor ... ," *op. cit.*, pp. 19827–19833.

[35] *Ibid.*, pp. 19834–19835. The employer's complaint is in the *California Fruit Grower*, 28 (Aug. 15, 1903), 2. The Immigration Commission shrewdly comments, on this stated preference, that it must be remembered that "these opinions are expressed ... after the [Chinese] had largely disappeared from the industry.... There is at least a question whether the Chinese have not risen in the appreciation of the growers with their scarcity and at the expense of the reputations of the races at present employed." *Reports of the Immigration Commission*, Vol. 24, p. 108.

[36] Shichiro Matsui, "Economic Aspects of the Japanese Situation in California" (Unpublished M.A. thesis, University of California, Berkeley, 1922), p. 93; *Reports of the Immigration Commission*, Vol. 23, pp. 33–45.

[37] Data for 1900, 1904, 1909 are in *Reports of the Immigration Commission*, Vol. 23, p. 79; for 1919 in California State Board of Control, *California and the Oriental* (Sacramento, 1922), p. 48.

[38] *California and the Oriental*, p. 49.

[39] The date of arrival is variously given as 1888, 1889, and 1890; but see letter, Shima to Hiram Johnson, Feb. 11, 1911 (Johnson MSS, Bancroft Library, Berkeley).

[40] The sketch of Shima is drawn from: Kaizo Naka, "Social and Economic Conditions among Japanese Farmers in California" (Unpublished M.A. thesis, University of California, 1913), pp. 55–60. K. K. Kawakami, *The Real Japanese Question* (New York, 1921), pp. 44–47. San Francisco *Chronicle* March 8, 1909; Jan. 6, April 7, and Dec. 15, 1910; Jan. 21, Sept. 1 and 16, 1911; June 25, 1912; Jan. 19 and 26, 1917; Nov. 20, 1919; March 27, 28, 29, and 30, and April 18, 1926; July 19, 1927; April 26, 1952. San Francisco *Examiner* Feb. 23, 1917. Dorothy Swaine Thomas, *The Salvage* (Berkeley and Los Angeles, 1942), pp. 181 ff. The home incident is from the *Chronicle* of March 13, 1909.

[41] Statistics from *Reports of the Immigration Commission*, Vol. 23, pp. 183–184. Viewers of television may recall that the "western" serial show "Have Gun, Will Travel" has repeatedly used a stereotyped Chinese servant as a late-nineteenth-century status symbol; see also the Californian novels of Gertrude Atherton.

[42] *Reports of the Immigration Commission*, Vol. 23, pp. 97–99.

[43] Gunnar Myrdal, *An American Dilemma* (New York, 1944), I, 310.

[44] A student of the Japanese in the State of Washington finds that "cultural differences have tended to isolate the Japanese and make of them a discrete unit ... [They have developed] a complementary economic organization." John A. Rademaker, "The Japanese in the Social Organization of the Puget Sound Region," *American Journal of Sociology*, 40 (Nov., 1934), 338–343.

[45] *Reports of the Immigration Commission*, Vol. 23, pp. 99–103; Matsui, *op. cit.*, pp. 53–57.

[46] *Fourteenth Census of the United States, 1920* (Washington, 1920), Vol. 3, pp. 109–110. The term "southern California" traditionally refers to the area south of the Tehachapi Mountains which are north of Los Angeles.

[47] *Reports of the Immigration Commission*, Vol. 23, pp. 3–4, 7–8.

[48] *Thirteenth Census of the United States, 1910* (Washington, 1910), II, 159.

Fourteenth Census of the United States, 1920 (Washington, 1920), II, *passim.* Among all immigrants to the United States from 1865 to 1924 the ratio was about 6.5 males to 3 females according to Harry Jerome, *Migrations and Business Cycles* (New York, 1926), p. 38. For the best treatment of the problems immigration laws caused Oriental families see R. D. McKenzie, *Oriental Exclusion* (Chicago, 1928), pp. 79–97.

⁴⁹ For an excellent chart see Dorothy S. Thomas and Richard Nishimoto, *The Spoilage* (Berkeley and Los Angeles, 1946), p. 31. The same work states that the "average modal age of Issei was 56, of Nisei 21" (p. 68). It is obvious that the Issei figure refers to males only, but not clear whether those figures have relevance outside the particular camp under discussion (Gila River). See also, *ibid.*, p. 4.

⁵⁰ One of the best treatments of the problems of the Nisei is in Carey McWilliams, *Prejudice* (Boston, 1944), pp. 96–105. For generalizations about American immigration see Marcus L. Hansen, "The History of American Immigration as a Field for Research," *American Historical Review*, 32 (April, 1927), 500–518.

⁵¹ Aiji Tashio in *New Outlook*, Sept., 1934, quoted in McWilliams, *op. cit.*, p. 99. Tashio's parents were undoubtedly much better educated than the average Issei, since they read to him in English; but all Nisei would, by their attendance in public schools, have comparable experience.

⁵² Matsui, *op. cit.*, p. 98.

⁵³ Without being able to cite any data, I would also suggest that "new immigrants" in California—Italians, Armenians and Greeks in particular—were economically better off than their contemporary compatriots in the East.

CHAPTER II: LABOR TAKES THE LEAD

¹ For the best treatment see Elmer C. Sandmeyer, *The Anti-Chinese Movement in California* (Urbana, Ill., 1939), which is much superior to the earlier Mary Roberts Coolidge, *Chinese Immigration* (New York, 1909).

² John Bigler, *Governor's Special Message on the Subject of Chinese Coolie Immigration* (Sacramento, 1852), p. 4.

³ Lucille Eaves, *A History of California Labor Legislation* (Berkeley, 1910), p. 6.

⁴ C. P. Dorland, "The Chinese Massacre at Los Angeles in 1871," Historical Society of Southern California, *Proceedings*, 3 (1894), 22–30. For Chinese testimony see *People* v. *Hall*, 4 Cal. 399. The "obituary" appeared in the Los Angeles *Times*, Feb. 15, 1882.

⁵ For the Workingmen's program and the convention of 1879 see Winfield J. Davis, *History of Political Conventions in California, 1849–92* (Sacramento, 1893), pp. 384–386, 390–392. For the 1880 platforms see Kirk H. Porter and Donald B. Johnson, *National Party Platforms, 1840–1956* (Urbana, Ill., 1956), pp. 57–58.

⁶ *Smith* v. *Turner; Norris* v. *The City of Boston*, 48 U. S. 283 (1849); for details see chap. vii.

⁷ *Cal.Stat.* (1855), p. 194; *People* v. *Downer*, 7 Cal. 169; for comments upon this and other anti-Chinese legislation see Carl Brent Swisher, *Stephen J. Field* (Washington, 1930), pp. 207–208.

⁸ For Hayes's and Arthur's vetoes see James D. Richardson, *Messages and Papers of the Presidents* (Washington, 1911), VIII, 4466, 4699. For the Chinese Exclusion Act see 22 U. S. Stat. 58.

⁹ Richard Hofstadter speaks of a "status revolution" at about this time, while other historians, using more traditional language, talk of the rise of the "new" middle class. A part of the problem here, which is more than semantic, is that the earlier division—which is much clearer in the rather rudimentary society of nine-

teenth-century California than in the older area of the United States—was a relatively straightforward reflection of economic status. The rise of a middle class—in
the United States, at least—was as much dependent on attitudes as on assets. The
middle-class attitude—particularly that phase of it that came to be called "progressive"—was, it seems to me, more of a denial of class position than the converse. The
attitude of the typical progressive to both extremes of the class structure was one
of "a plague on both your houses," as a reading of any of Theodore Roosevelt's
annual messages will demonstrate. The progressive almost automatically assumed
that *he* spoke with the voice of enlightened mankind and that *he* was actuated by no
"sordid" interests, economic or otherwise, as opposed, say, to "the malefactors of
great wealth" on the one hand and the "agitators" and "anarchists" on the other.
Cf. Richard Hofstadter, *The Age of Reform* (New York, 1955), pp. 131–172, and
George E. Mowry, *The California Progressives* (Berkeley and Los Angeles, 1951),
chap. iv.

¹⁰ *Coast Seaman's Journal*, July 25, 1888. The Sailor's Union of the Pacific barred
Asians from membership, as did almost all West Coast unions. See Paul S. Taylor,
The Sailor's Union of the Pacific (New York, 1923), p. 156. The only unions in the
Far West to accept Japanese as members seem to have been the Western Federation
of Miners and the United Mine Workers in Wyoming. *Report of the Immigration
Commission*, Vol. 23, p. 170.

¹¹ Letter, MacArthur to Ira Cross, March 13, 1935 (MacArthur MSS, Bancroft
Library). Strikebreaking by Japanese in the United States was rare, and occurred
mainly outside California. The other known instances are in coal mining in Utah
and Colorado, smelting in Utah, and meat packing in Nebraska, and in the shops
of one western railroad. All these incidents occurred in the period 1903–1907 and
involved relatively few persons. See *Reports of the Immigration Commission*, Vol.
23, pp. 53, 57.

¹² San Francisco *Morning Call*, May 4, 1892.

¹³ *Ibid.*, May 6, 1892.

¹⁴ *Ibid.*, May 18, 1892.

¹⁵ *Ibid.*, June 25, 1892.

¹⁶ *Ibid.*, May 29, 1892; Sacramento *Daily Record-Union*, July 7, 1892. The anti-
Semitism was an innovation for Kearney; he had probably been reading Populist
tracts during his retirement. For the anti-Semitic tinge of much of Populism see Hofstadter, *op. cit.*, pp. 60–93.

¹⁷ San Francisco *Chronicle*, March 10, 21, 22, 27, and 31, and May 16, 23, and 26,
1900; San Francisco *Bulletin*, March 27, 1900; San Francisco *Examiner*, March 12,
1900; San Francisco *Call*, March 29 and May 29, 1900, May 24, 1901; see also
Appendix to the Journals of the Senate and Assembly of the State of California,
34th sess., 1901, I, 7–18. The "plague scare" was to prove intermittently troublesome for the rest of Phelan's political career. The bathhouse report is in the *Call* of
Sept. 23, 1898.

¹⁸ The first anti-Japanese meeting in the United States was held in Seattle on
April 19, 1900, according to R. D. McKenzie, *Oriental Exclusion* (Chicago, 1928),
p. 30. Seattle had the largest concentration of Japanese in the country outside of
California. For the agitation in adjoining British Columbia see Charles H. Young,
et al., *The Japanese Canadians* (Toronto, 1938), pp. 119–146.

¹⁹ The estimate of Phelan is based on a perusal of the Phelan MSS in the Bancroft
Library. (Robert Hennings, "James D. Phelan and the Wilson Progressives of California," unpublished Ph.D. dissertation, University of California, Berkeley, 1961,
throws much additional light on both the man and the period.) Phelan's remarks
are quoted from the San Francisco *Examiner* and the San Francisco *Chronicle*, both
for May 8, 1900.

[20] *Ibid.*

[21] Porter and Johnson, *op. cit.*, pp. 115, 118, 123.

[22] As cited in Samuel Gompers, *Meat vs. Rice* (Washington, 1901), p. 25.

[23] *Appendix to the Journals of the Senate and Assembly of the State of California,* 34th sess., 1901, II, 6–7.

[24] San Francisco *Bulletin,* Nov. 21, 22, and 23, 1901; San Francisco *Chronicle,* Oct. 8 and Nov. 22, 1901. For the text of the memorial see U. S. Congress, Senate, *Some Reasons for Chinese Exclusion,* 57th Cong., 1st sess., Doc. 137 (Washington, 1902), pp. 25–30.

[25] Fresno *Republican,* April 28, 1900; Rowell MSS, Bancroft Library. Rowell's carbon copies are cited here, rather than the newspaper editorial.

[26] Eleanor Tupper and George E. McReynolds, *Japan in American Public Opinion* (New York, 1937), p. 1.

[27] The campaign continued with varying intensity for more than a year. The headlines quoted are in the San Francisco *Chronicle,* Feb. 23 to March 13, 1905, *passim.* Since it was winter, there would have been more Japanese in San Francisco than at the height of the agricultural growing season. On the first day of the campaign, twenty of forty-eight "situations wanted" insertions were by Japanese, mostly "schoolboys."

[28] Richard Austin Thompson, "The Yellow Peril, 1890–1924" (Unpublished dissertation, University of Wisconsin, 1957).

[29] John P. Young, "The Support of the Anti-Oriental Movement," *Annals,* 34 (Sept., 1909), 234–235. Young deliberately underplays the role of the unions. For imputations of interest on the part of de Young see Thomas A. Bailey, *Theodore Roosevelt and the Japanese-American Crises* (Stanford, Calif., 1934), pp. 10–11. Roosevelt also ascribed an ulterior motive (the failure to get an ambassadorship). He, along with many other progressives, liked to feel that his "wicked" opponents were actuated by "selfish" motives as opposed to his disinterestedness. See letter, Roosevelt to Lloyd C. Griscom (July 15, 1905), *Roosevelt Letters,* IV, 1274–1275. In 1901 de Young had served on the executive committee of the Chinese Exclusion Convention; see San Francisco *Call,* Nov. 26, 1901.

[30] San Francisco *Chronicle,* Feb. 21 and March 1 and 21, 1905.

[31] Kaizo Naka, "Social and Economic Conditions among Japanese Farmers in California" (Unpublished M.A. thesis, University of California, 1913), p. 85, and M. Fujita, "The Japanese Associations in America," *Sociology and Social Research,* Jan.–Feb., 1929, pp. 211–212, both agree as to its semiofficial character; but see also Yamato Ichihashi, *Japanese in the United States* (Stanford, Calif., 1932), pp. 224–226, for a vehement denial. The latter work, which is the standard authority, is a mine of information, but it is not always accurate, and it breathes the spirit of apology rather than of scholarship.

[32] *Journal of the Senate of the State of California,* 1905, pp. 1164–1165; hereinafter cited as *Journal, Senate.* Points V–VIII asserted, in similar language, that Japanese were contract laborers, that they worked in gangs, that their wages were below the minimum level of white subsistence, that they were driving out white labor, and that they would, if not checked, reduce the white laborers to misery.

[33] An old law prohibiting the "importation of Chinese and Japanese women for sale" was reënacted (195 Cal. 656, chap. 497).

[34] Actually the organization was called the Japanese and Korean Exclusion League until December, 1907. To avoid confusion it is here called the Asiatic Exclusion League throughout. The founding organizations included a handful of political clubs, the Ligue Henri IV (a Franco-American fraternal group), and the Associated Dry Goods Merchants of San Francisco. The rest were labor unions. Some writers date the League's existence from the previous Sunday, but at that meeting no actual organization was formed.

[35] Born in Ireland, Norway, Scotland, and Sweden, respectively. For McCarthy

see Walton Bean, *Boss Ruef's San Francisco* (Berkeley and Los Angeles, 1952), pp. 12–14. For Furuseth see Hyman Weintraub, *Andrew Furuseth* (Berkeley and Los Angeles, 1959), p. 2; Weintraub says that "few labor men, even on the West Coast, outdid Furuseth in anti-Oriental chauvinism" (p. 113), but he does not record Furuseth's connections with the anti-Japanese movement. A further demonstration of Furuseth's bias is given in Jerrold S. Auerbach, "Progressives at Sea: The La Follette Act of 1915," *Labor History*, 2 (Fall, 1961), 344–360. For MacArthur see MacArthur MSS, Bancroft Library. Tveitmoe has been variously described as a Finn, Norwegian, and Swede, but the third designation is most frequent. He had a criminal record and was convicted, but later discharged, of complicity in the 1910 bombing of the Los Angeles *Times*. See Raymond Leslie Buell, "The Development of the Anti-Japanese Agitation in the United States," *Political Science Quarterly*, 37 (Dec., 1922), 617. Carey McWilliams, *Prejudice* (Boston, 1944), asserts that "most of the leaders of the anti-Oriental movement, in its early phases, were Irish" (p. 20), and assumes that the Glasgow-born MacArthur fitted this description. The allegation of Irish dominance of the movement is false, although some contemporary Protestant advocates of the Japanese made this charge, for obvious reasons.

[36] Asiatic Exclusion League, *Proceedings* (San Francisco, 1907–12), May, 1910, pp. 13–14.

[37] *Ibid.*, March, 1910, pp. 10–11, and April, 1908, p. 23.

[38] See the testimony of William T. Bonsor at the 1920 hearings of the House Committee on Immigration and Naturalization, *Hearings on Japanese Immigration* (Washington, 1921), p. 590. For the congruence of the two organizations, compare letterheads in Hiram Johnson MSS, Part I, Box 37, Bancroft Library.

[39] Asiatic Exclusion League, *Proceedings*, April, 1908, p. 4; May, 1908, p. 6; May, 1910, p. 15; May, 1911, p. 115; May, 1912, p. 222. Tveitmoe's statement is in the Asiatic Exclusion League of North America, *Proceedings* (San Francisco, 1908), p. 55. This latter league was a short-lived coalition of anti-Japanese groups from California, Washington, Nevada, Colorado, and British Columbia. It held a "First International Convention" in Seattle, Feb. 3–5, 1908, and after a squabble over distribution of offices (which went to Tvietmoe and his associates) seems to have collapsed under internal pressures.

[40] H.R. 3160 and 8975; see *Congressional Record*, 59th Cong., 1st sess., pp. 115, 568. Curiously, the first Japanese exclusion bills were introduced by a Democratic representative from Indiana, James M. Robinson. They were similarly bottled up and their sponsor never referred to them on the floor. See *Cong. Rec.*, 57th Cong., 1st sess., p. 7615, and 58th Cong., 1st sess., p. 516.

[41] *Cong. Rec.*, 59th Cong., 1st sess., pp. 3747–3753.

[42] Ira Kipnis, *The American Socialist Movement, 1897–1912* (New York, 1952), p. 279.

[43] Cameron H. King, Jr., "Asiatic Exclusion," *International Socialist Review*, 8 (May, 1908) 669. For a minority view see Louis B. Boudin, "Immigration at Stuttgart," *Internat. Socialist Rev.* (Jan., 1908), 489–497. Debs always avoided racism, but did not combat it in his comrades. It is interesting to note that "Big Bill" Heywood, whose Western Federation of Miners was one of the rare unions which admitted Issei, testified that they were fighting unionists. See Kipnis, *op. cit.*, p. 284.

[44] *Ibid.*, pp. 276–286.

[45] Quoted in Phillip Foner, *Jack London* (New York, 1947), p. 59.

[46] Kipnis, *op. cit.*, p. 227.

CHAPTER III: SEGREGATION AND DIPLOMACY

[1] A recent account of the 1901 strike is in Hyman Weintraub, *Andrew Furuseth* (Berkeley and Los Angeles, 1959), pp. 60–71. For the Union Labor party and municipal politics this chapter generally follows Walton Bean, *Boss Ruef's San*

Francisco (Berkeley and Los Angeles, 1952). The best account of the whole school board affair and its consequences is Thomas A. Bailey, *Theodore Roosevelt and the Japanese-American Crises* (Stanford, Calif., 1934), which focuses on the international aspects. Eleanor Tupper and George E. McReynolds, *Japan in American Public Opinion* (New York, 1937), has been helpful throughout in assessing the national climate of opinion.

[2] Many pro-Japanese writers have tried to show San Francisco as the epitome of evil, and many contemporary San Franciscans, out of some sort of perverse civic pride, "remember" similarly. R. L. Buell, "The Development of the Anti-Japanese Agitation in the United States," *Political Science Quarterly*, 37 (Dec., 1922), p. 611, refers to a "period of political corruption which would make the blackest deeds of Boss Tweed look as harmless as politics in a woman's club." For a saner view see Bean, *op. cit.* Lincoln Steffens, *The Shame of the Cities* (New York, 1904), is a collection of reports on various American cities.

[3] San Francisco *Call*, Sept. 7, 1901. Actually, Chinese had been segregated since 1858. Lucille Eaves, *A History of California Labor Legislation* (Berkeley, 1910), p. 37. At least four subsequent acts confirmed this segregation. See *Cal. Stat.* (1885), p. 100, chap. 117; *Cal. Stat.* (1891), p. 160, chap. 129, sec. 18; *Cal. Stat.* (1893), chap. 193, sec. 33; *Cal. Stat.* (1903), p. 86, chap. 77. They may be found in the various editions of the *California Political Code*, sec. 1662. For an early (c. 1860) account of these schools see Ernest Frignet, *La Californie* (2d ed.; Paris, 1867), pp. 284–285.

[4] George Kennan, "The Japanese in San Francisco Public Schools," *Outlook*, June 1, 1907, p. 207. The uncle of George Frost Kennan, the diplomat-historian, George Kennan was also an expert on Russia; he was a correspondent (pro-Japanese) during the Russo-Japanese War. His is perhaps the best contemporary treatment.

[5] U. S. Congress, Senate, *Japanese in the City of San Francisco, Cal.*, 59th Cong., 2d sess., Doc. 147 (Washington, 1907). This is the report of Roosevelt's Secretary of Commerce and Labor, Victor H. Metcalf; hereinafter cited as *Metcalf Report*. The Board's resolution is on p. 3.

[6] See note 3. Local authorities were allowed discretion because most communities had few, if any, Oriental children. At one time Negroes were segregated in San Francisco, but this practice ceased before the turn of the century. Segregation was unsuccessfully contested by a San Francisco Negro parent in 1874. The California Supreme Court proclaimed the "separate but equal" doctrine, foreshadowing the national case of *Plessy* v. *Ferguson* (1896), in 48 Cal. 36 (Feb. 24, 1874). Professor Brainerd Dyer called this case to my attention.

[7] Bailey, *op. cit.*, p. 17.

[8] *Metcalf Report*, pp. 35–41; Herbert B. Johnson, *Discrimination Against Japanese in California* (Berkeley, 1907), pp. 74–75.

[9] *Metcalf Report*, p. 8.

[10] *Ibid.*, pp. 7–12, 33–38.

[11] *Ibid.*, pp. 12–17.

[12] Secretary of State Root knew of the order by Oct. 23, 1906. See Philip C. Jessup, *Elihu Root* (New York, 1938), II, 9; for a detailed analysis of press reactions see Bailey, *op. cit.*, pp. 29 ff.

[13] Letter, Roosevelt to Kentaro Keneko, Oct. 26, 1906, in *Roosevelt Letters*, V, 473.

[14] Roosevelt to George Kennan, May 6, 1905. In a letter to Henry Cabot Lodge, June 5, 1905, he calls the "feeling on the Pacific slope . . . as foolish as if conceived by the mind of a Hottentot." *Ibid.*, IV, 1168–1169, 1205.

[15] An earlier analyst reached a different conclusion. Bailey, *op. cit.*, p. 124, states that Roosevelt's "correspondence for 1905 . . . reveals an utter inability to understand why the bigoted Californians should create a disturbance over the presence of a few Japanese coolies." Presumably, he did not see the letter to Kennan and

thus found a shift in Roosevelt's attitude from 1905 to 1906 when there really was none.

[16] Roosevelt to Lloyd C. Griscom, July 15, 1905. See also the letter to Cecil Arthur Spring-Rice, July 24, 1905, for his early determination to thwart the agitation. *Roosevelt Letters*, IV, 1274–1275, 1286.

[17] James D. Richardson (ed.), *Messages and Papers of the Presidents*, X, 7388–7389.

[18] Roosevelt's interest in power as opposed to principle in foreign affairs is nowhere better demonstrated than in the following handwritten postscript to his Secretary of State: "We can not possibly interfere for the Koreans against Japan. They couldn't strike one blow in their own defence." Letter to John Hay, Jan. 28, 1905, in *Roosevelt Letters,* IV, 1112.

[19] Letters to: Theodore Roosevelt, Jr., Feb. 10, 1904; Cecil Arthur Spring-Rice, March 19 and June 13, 1904; George von Lengerke Meyer, Dec. 26, 1904. *Ibid.*, pp. 724, 760, 829–833, 1079–1081.

[20] Letters to: Cecil Arthur Spring-Rice, June 13, 1904 (describing a lunch with Kaneko and Japanese Minister Kogoro Takahira on June 6), and John Hay, July 26, 1904. *Roosevelt Letters, Ibid.*, pp. 829–833, 865.

[21] Letter to Chief No Shirt, May 18, 1905. *Ibid.*, pp. 1185–1188.

[22] Letter to Kentaro Kaneko, Oct. 26, 1906. The parenthetical characterization of Kaneko is from a letter to Elihu Root, July 26, 1907. For stylistic reasons parts of two adjoining sentences have been combined within the parentheses. *Ibid.*, V, 473, 729.

[23] Letters to: Elihu Root, Oct. 29, 1906, and Victor Howard Metcalf, Nov. 27, 1906. *Ibid.*, pp. 484, 510–511. For a list of the President's chief callers see *ibid.*, VI, Appendix 4. It was characteristic of Roosevelt to think of using troops. A year earlier, on hearing of disturbances among the Japanese plantation workers in Hawaii, he directed Taft, then Secretary of War, to find out if the governor needed "a regiment or two of troops." Letter to William Howard Taft, Feb. 9, 1905, *Ibid.*, IV, 1118.

[24] The Metcalf interview is in San Francisco *Examiner*, May 18, 1905. One of the reasons it was not "remembered" is that the morgues of all the major San Francisco newspapers were destroyed in the earthquake and fire. Metcalf's promotion, which was effective on Dec. 12, 1906, is often attributed to Roosevelt's satisfaction with the report, but the change had been long slated and was publicly announced in October as forthcoming. See *Roosevelt Letters*, V, 461n.

[25] Richardson, *Messages and Papers of the Presidents*, X, 7433–7436.

[26] Booker T. Washington dined with the President on Oct. 16, 1901. News of this created a furor in the South, and much severe criticism of Roosevelt developed. He publicly insisted on his right to show hospitality to anyone, but never again did he choose to invite a Negro to share a White House meal. See *Roosevelt Letters*, III, 181n.

[27] Chester H. Rowell, who knew Roosevelt, wrote after the former President's death: "I knew from Roosevelt personally that his [proposal to naturalize Japanese] was intended for Japanese consumption and . . . to hold over [California] the big stick of such a law." Letter to Raymond Leslie Buell, Oct. 26, 1920 (Rowell MSS, Bancroft Library). Rowell was a man of unquestioned probity. It can, of course, be argued that Roosevelt, who had a convenient memory, might well say this sort of thing to a California supporter who had definite anti-Japanese sentiments.

[28] Letter, Elihu Root to Luke E. Wright, United States Ambassador to Japan, Feb. 6, 1907, quoted in Jessup, *op. cit.*, II, 19.

[29] For press reactions in 1906 and 1907 see Bailey, *op. cit.*, pp. 96 ff., and Tupper and McReynolds, *op. cit.*, pp. 28 ff. For Bryan see *Roosevelt Letters*, V, 533n.

[30] *Metcalf Report*, pp. 17–18. Most of the Nisei pupils were in the normal grade

for their age in a day when it was still possible to fail a grade in the public schools of California. Two bright seven-year-olds were in the third grade, forerunners of thousands of Nisei who have charmed generations of California school teachers. None of the anti-Japanese literature quotes teachers who actually had experience with Japanese pupils.

[31] San Francisco *Argonaut*, Jan. 5, 1907, as cited in Bailey, *op. cit.*, p. 115. Metcalf retired from the cabinet in 1908 and lived in Oakland until his death in 1936. He never again participated in public life. A scrapbook, obviously one of several, of newspaper clippings that was prepared for him to aid in the preparation of his report is in the Bancroft Library. There is no biography of Metcalf, and he was omitted from the appropriate Supplement of the *Dictionary of American Biography*.

[32] Jessup, *op. cit.*, p. 11. Simultaneous suits were filed in the California Supreme Court and the local federal district court; neither came to trial. The California defense was that (1) the rights and privileges included in the treaty did not entitle Japanese to attend schools, and (2) if such rights were granted in the 1894 treaty they were unconstitutional because "(a) it is in excess of the authority given to the President and Senate as a treaty making power; (b) it is repugnant to the fundamental principles of government; and (c) it trespasses upon the reserve powers of the several states." William G. Burke, *The Japanese School Segregation Case; Respondent's Brief* ([San Francisco ?, 1907 ?]), p. 4.

[33] Letter, Root to Luke E. Wright, Jan. 16, 1907, in Jessup, *op. cit.*, pp. 7–8.

[34] Letter, Roosevelt to Victor Howard Metcalf, Nov. 27, 1906, *Roosevelt Letters*, V, 510–511. See also the letters of Root to Luke E. Wright, Jan. 16 and Feb. 1, 1907, in Jessup, *op. cit.*, pp. 7–8, 18–19.

[35] *Ibid.*, pp. 15–16. Hawaiian business interests continued to need fresh supplies of labor, and since Japan was still the most convenient source available the government did not want to cut off the Japan-Hawaii migration.

[36] *Journal, Senate*, 1907, pp. 51–52.

[37] *Ibid.*, p. 334; for Assembly action see *Journal of the Assembly of the State of California*, 1907, p. 361; hereinafter cited as *Journal, Assembly*. The measures included resolutions condemning Roosevelt's naturalization proposal, asking for exclusion, and affirming the right of California to regulate its own schools; there were bills strengthening the segregation provisions of the school law, limiting alien land tenure, and calling for a referendum on the subject of Asiatic immigration. These were Senate Resolutions 1 and 7, Senate Joint Resolution 11, Senate Bills 460 and 930, Assembly Concurrent Resolutions 2 and 9, and Assembly Bill 404. See *Journal, Senate*, 1907, pp. 181, 268, 444, 1144, 1244, 1477, 1522, 1582, 1593, 1621, 1651–1652, and *Journal, Assembly*, 1907, pp. 97, 164–165, 174, 1204, 1367, 1560, 1692, 1762.

[38] *Journal, Senate*, 1907, p. 334; *Journal, Assembly*, 1907, p. 361.

[39] Letter to James Norris Gillett, March 9, 1907; see also the letters to Gillett, March 11, 1907, and to Root, March 10, 1907. *Roosevelt Letters*, V, 608–614. For Gillett's messages to the legislature see *Journal, Assembly*, 1907, pp. 1787, 1855–1856.

[40] 34 *Stat.* 898, sec. 1.

[41] Letter, Root to Lodge, Feb. 11, 1907, in Jessup, *op. cit.*, p. 16.

[42] Executive Order 589, March 14, 1907. This remained in force until revoked by President Truman in Executive Order 10,009, Oct. 18, 1948.

[43] The notes themselves were not published until 1939. See Department of State, *Foreign Relations of the United States, 1924* (Washington, 1939), pp. 339–369.

[44] Letter, Japanese Foreign Office to the American Embassy, Feb. 18, 1908, *ibid.*, p. 365.

[45] For details see Bailey, *op. cit.*, pp. 193 ff.

[46] The *Chronicle*'s shift of position is clear by Feb. 20, 1907, although there are signs of moderation before that date. The Hearst position is more difficult to pinpoint. The San Francisco *Examiner* had always been anti-Oriental, like almost all

of the California secular press, but the attitude seems to begin to become a fixation only after Roosevelt's intervention in the school board affair. Attacking the President was a favorite Hearst gambit; those who remember only Hearst's sordid senescence will find it difficult to believe that during this period he was regarded—and in many quarters feared—as a possible future president.

CHAPTER IV: THE PROGRESSIVES DRAW THE COLOR LINE

[1] See San Francisco *Call*, Sept. 8, 1908.

[2] Fresno *Republican*, Oct. 29, 1908.

[3] Long Beach *Press*, Oct. 30, 1908. See also San Luis Obispo *Breeze*, Oct. 31, 1908, and Watsonville *Register*, Nov. 1, 1908.

[4] Assembly Bills 14, 32, and 78; Senate Bill 71; see *Journal, Assembly*, 1909, pp. 17, 74, 78, and *Journal, Senate*, 1909, p. 61.

[5] Letter, Roosevelt to James Norris Gillett, Jan. 16, 1909. See also letters to: Gillett, Jan. 26, and Feb. 4, 6 and 10, 1909; Philip Ackley Stanton (speaker of the California Assembly), Feb. 6 and 8, 1909; Theodore Roosevelt, Jr., Feb. 6, 1909, and Philander Chase Knox, Feb. 8, 1909. *Roosevelt Letters*, VI, 1477–1478, 1483–1486, 1502, 1505, 1506, 1509–1514.

[6] Letter to William Howard Taft, Feb. 13, 1909, *ibid.*, p. 1519.

[7] The resolution is printed in Franklin Hichborn, *Story of the Session of the California Legislature of 1909* (San Francisco, 1909), pp. 215–216. Hichborn, a reformer and prohibitionist, had decided anti-Japanese views and does not always tell the whole story, as his correspondence shows. His papers are in the Bureau of Governmental Research, University of California, Los Angeles. Much of Hichborn's work was subsidized by two reform-minded San Francisco millionaires, Rudolph Spreckels and James D. Phelan. For Gillett's message see *Journal, Assembly*, 1907, pp. 265–268, 430–432. The bill, much to everyone's surprise, proved a boomerang; Labor Commissioner John D. MacKenzie, a conservative Republican from San Jose, apparently took his cue from large ranchers and reported that Japanese or other Oriental laborers were necessary to the agriculture of the state. The report was denounced by much of the state press (*e.g.*, Fresno *Republican*, May 30, 1910) and officially condemned by the legislature; see *Journal, Senate*, 1910, p. 39. The full report was suppressed; if a copy is still extant no researcher has yet unearthed it from the state archives.

[8] As cited in Hichborn, *op. cit.*, p. 207.

[9] *Journal, Senate*, 1909, pp. 1155–1156. The New England press was more antipathetic to the California position than any other segment of the country's press.

[10] Asiatic Exclusion League, *Proceedings*, Feb. 1909, p. 7; letter, J. B. Sanford to James D. Phelan, Jan. 29, 1909 (Phelan MSS, Bancroft Library).

[11] *Journal, Senate*, 1909, p. 317; see also *Journal, Assembly*, 1909, pp. 279–280.

[12] San Francisco *Chronicle*, Jan. 9, 1909. For similar views see the San Francisco *Call*, Dec. 18, 1909.

[13] Letter, Phillips to C. C. Moore, April 25, 1913 (Panama-Pacific International Exposition MSS, Bancroft Library); letter, Rowell to Ernest Harvin, June 25, 1919 (Rowell MSS, Bancroft Library).

[14] George E. Mowry, *The California Progressives* (Berkeley and Los Angeles, 1951), p. 154.

[15] This paragraph is, I believe, a synthesis not only of Chester H. Rowell's views, but also of that rather elusive abstraction, the progressive mind. Each set of quotation marks denotes a separate statement; all are from the Rowell MSS in the Bancroft Library. In order: Editorials, Fresno *Republican*, Sept. 26, 1900; May 18, 1916; Jan. 4, 1910, Letter, Rowell to Charles P. Huey, Sept. 1, 1915. Editorial, Fresno *Republican*, May 6, 1913. Letter, Rowell to David Starr Jordan, April 26, 1913. Typescript of a speech [Aug. ?] 1921. This was the sort of position that most middle-class Californians took on the subject, but it was often stated in cruder

terms. For his relative moderation, Rowell was sometimes attacked as a "pro-Jap."

[16] Asiatic Exclusion League, *Proceedings*, Sept., 1910, pp. 53–55. One reason that Johnson had little to do with the League was that it was under the control of P. H. McCarthy, who led the antireform wing of the unrepentant Union Labor party. Johnson won his first fame as the prosecutor of Schmitz and Ruef, and on any account would have had little to do with their heirs.

[17] As cited by Franklin Hichborn, *Story of the Session of the California Legislature of 1913* (San Francisco, 1913), pp. 223–224.

[18] *Cf.* Carey McWilliams, *Prejudice* (Boston, 1944), p. 25.

[19] Letter, Hiram Johnson to Theodore Roosevelt, March 24, 1911 (Johnson MSS, Bancroft Library).

[20] Assembly Bills 30, 34, 132, 196, 322, 395, 486, 1072, 1132, 1134, 1372, 1432; Senate Bills 2, 24, 35, 167, 620, 1020, 1074, 1075, 1076; Assembly Joint Resolutions 2, 7, 12; Senate Joint Resolution 12; Senate Constitutional Amendment 29. None of these passed both houses. See *Journal, Assembly*, 1911, and *Journal, Senate*, 1911, *passim*.

[21] See letter, Uchida to Japanese Foreign Office, Dec. 9, 1910, quoted in Teruko Okada Kachi, "The Treaty of 1911 and the Immigration and Alien Land Law Issue between the United States and Japan, 1911–1913" (Unpublished dissertation, University of Chicago, 1957). Kachi's work, based on microfilms of the Japanese archives, has added an otherwise inaccessible dimension to this chapter.

[22] Johnson to Knox, Jan. 6, 1911 (Johnson MSS). Altogether, twenty-two letters and telegrams passed between Johnson and the administration between Jan. 6 and March 11, 1911.

[23] See Milton R. Konvitz, *The Alien and the Asiatic in American Law* (Ithaca, N.Y., 1946). The whole naturalization process was in great confusion until it was reformed late in Theodore Roosevelt's second administration. See United States Department of Justice, *Annual Report of the Attorney General of the United States, 1903* (Washington, 1903), pp. 393–399. One report indicates that at least 420 Japanese had been "illegally" naturalized by 1910; see United States Bureau of the Census, *Chinese and Japanese in the United States, 1910*, Census Bulletin 127 (Washington, 1914), p. 10. See also chap. vii of the present work.

[24] California State Library, "Alien Ownership of Land; Select List of References to Material in the California State Library," *News Notes of California Libraries*, Vol. 9 (1914), gives references to contemporary laws and discussions of them. Many of the earlier antialien land bills were aimed at foreign corporations rather than individuals.

[25] Robert Karl Reischauer, "Alien Land Tenure in Japan," *Transactions of the Asiatic Society of Japan*, 2d ser., 13 (July, 1936), 112. Furthermore, a foreigner in Japan could incorporate under Japanese law and become a Japanese "legal person." The only major discrimination against foreign corporations in Japan was that they could not receive government subsidies. *Ibid.*, pp. 87 ff. I ignore the special problem of perpetual leases. The laws as described above were in effect throughout the whole period under discussion.

[26] The pertinent part of the Treaty of Feb. 21, 1911, between the United States and Japan provided that "the citizens or subjects of each of the High Contracting Parties shall have the liberty to enter, travel and reside in the territories of the other to carry on trade, wholesale and retail, to own or lease and occupy houses, manufactories, warehouses and shops, to employ agents of their choice, *to lease land for residential and commercial purposes* [italics added], and generally to do anything incident to or necessary for trade on the same terms as native citizens or subjects." United States Department of State, *Papers Relating to the Foreign Relations of the United States, 1911* (Washington, 1919), p. 315. A separate note signed the same day confirmed the Gentlemen's Agreement and continued it. *Ibid.*, p. 319. The provisions of the treaty thus made it possible for California to legislate against the agri-

cultural holdings of Japanese nationals. There had been similar provisions in the treaty of 1894. For a complete analysis of the treaty and the negotiations see Kachi, *op. cit.*

[27] The Panama-Pacific International Exposition came to symbolize the rather grandiose dreams of many Western businessmen, particularly San Franciscans. Spurred on by the age-old dream of a passage to India and the riches of the Orient, many of the commercial leaders of the Pacific Coast felt that with the opening of the Panama Canal their seaports would become centers of international trade; some even dreamed that the financial center of the western world, then in the process of crossing the Atlantic, might continue its westward migration all the way to the Golden Gate. Anything that tended to impair good relations between the United States and Japan and China would be opposed by these businessmen and their organizations. Similarly, Japanese businessmen deplored anti-American demonstrations in Japan provoked by California discriminations and affronts.

[28] Kachi, *op. cit.*, pp. 86–87, citing Taft and Knox MSS.

[29] *Journal, Assembly*, 1911, p. 700.

[30] The legislature appropriated $5 million. A further $5 million was raised by a special San Francisco bond issue.

[31] Johnson to Knox, Jan. 31, 1911 (Johnson MSS).

[32] Knox to Johnson, Feb. 8, 1911 (Johnson MSS).

[33] Johnson to Gilson Gardner, Feb. 24, 1911 (Johnson MSS). For the published telegraphic correspondence between Sacramento and Washington, see *Journal, Senate*, 1911, pp. 1147–1148.

[34] The committee report, *ibid.*, p. 2032; the text of the substitute bill, pp. 2172–2173; the vote, p. 2264. Despite their unfavorable report, 13 members of the Judiciary Committee voted for the bill and only 2 were recorded as opposed. Five committee members were absent; 4 of them had been present a few minutes before the bill was voted upon.

[35] Huntington Wilson to Johnson, March 23, 1911 (Johnson MSS). In his *Memoirs of an Ex-Diplomat* (Boston, 1945), Huntington Wilson does not refer to the 1911 controversy, but does offer, perhaps unconsciously, a revealing insight into the unstated assumptions of the professional diplomats of the prewar years.

[36] Letter, Johnson to Theodore Roosevelt, March 24, 1911 (Johnson MSS).

[37] Telegram, Johnson to Huntington Wilson, March 24, 1911 (Johnson MSS).

[38] Telegrams, Johnson to Huntington Wilson, March 25, 1911; Knox to Johnson, March 25, 1911 (Johnson MSS).

[39] *Journal, Assembly*, 1911, pp. 2348–2349, 2565 ff; *cf.* Hichborn, *Story of the Session of the California Legislature of 1911* (San Francisco, 1911), pp. 342–344.

[40] Sanford to Phelan, April 6, 1911 (Phelan MSS).

[41] See letter, Phelan to Woodrow Wilson League, Oct. 7, 1911 (Phelan MSS).

[42] Arthur S. Link, *Wilson: The Road to the White House* (Princeton, N.J., 1947), p. 381. In subsequent pages Professor Link discusses how Wilson's characterization of the new immigrants was used against him in the East, but does not discuss the California phase of the immigration controversy, which has been almost completely ignored by historians.

[43] Woodrow Wilson, *A History of the American People* (New York, 1902), V, 213–214. Just preceding this passage, Wilson wrote of the coming of "multitudes of men of the lowest class from the south of Italy and men of the meaner sort out of Hungary and Poland, men out of the ranks where there was neither skill nor energy nor any initiative of quick intelligence; and they came in numbers which increased from year to year, as if the countries of the south of Europe were disburdening themselves of the more sordid and hapless elements of their population." (pp. 212–213). For a detailed treatment of American historical writings about European immigrants, see Edward N. Saveth, *American Historians and European Immigrants* (New York, 1948).

[44] Phelan to McCombs, Jan. 27, 1912 (Phelan MSS).

[45] Letters, Phelan to McCombs, Feb. 2 and Mar. 6, 1912, and McCombs to Phelan, Mar. 20, 1912 (Phelan MSS).

[46] Phelan to Wilson, Apr. 20, 1912 (Phelan MSS). There are several drafts of this letter, dated over a period of a month; the texts are substantially the same. That quoted from here seems to have been the one actually sent.

[47] Letter, Phelan to McCombs, Apr. 26, 1912, contains Phelan's draft statement; Wilson to Phelan, May 3, 1912, is the same over Wilson's name (Phelan MSS). Wilson's statement was published in the San Francisco *Daily News*, May 4, 1912. For much of the material in this note I am indebted to Professor Robert Hennings.

[48] Phelan to McCombs, May 8, 1912 (Phelan MSS). In the California Democratic primary, May 14, 1912, Clark defeated Wilson by 43,163 to 17,214. Wilson's subsequent nomination made Caminetti and Phelan the state's leading Democrats. In 1913 Wilson appointed Caminetti United States Commissioner of Immigration, partly to offset hostility among new immigrants, who would presumably be mollified by his Italian lineage, and partly, as Phelan wrote when he suggsted the appointment, because "a Californian in that office ... would help us on the Oriental question." Phelan to Charles W. Fay, Dec. 12, 1912 (Phelan MSS).

[49] The card and the platform are quoted in Hichborn, *Story of the Session of the California Legislature of 1913*, pp. 212–213. One of the actual cards is in the Johnson MSS, Part One, Box 37.

[50] The figures:

Roosevelt (Prog., Rep.)	283,610
Wilson (Dem.)	283,436
Debs (Soc.)	79,201
Chafin (Prob.)	23,366
Taft (Rep.) [write-in]	3,914

[51] In previous California presidential elections the Democratic party's percentage of the vote had been:

1908	33
1904	27
1900	41
1896	41
1892	45

[52] Letter, Phelan to McCombs, Nov. 11, 1912 (Phelan MSS).

[53] Letter, Johnson to Roosevelt, June 21, 1913 (Johnson MSS).

[54] George Shima to C. C. Moore, Jan. 22, 1912 (Panama-Pacific International Exposition, MSS). Shima was writing as president of the Japanese Association of America and said that he based his statement on conversations with the Japanese consul.

[55] Telegram, A. C. Baker to Robert S. Hudspeth, Dec. 31, 1912 (Panama-Pacific International Exposition MSS). For Hudspeth see Link, *op. cit.*, p. 151 and *passim*.

[56] For Chinda's despatches see Kachi, *op. cit.*, p. 222.

[57] Notice to directors, Jan. 6, 1913 (Panama-Pacific International Exposition MSS). There are numerous memoranda and other documents in the Exposition files which give unusually full details of the lobbying processes.

[58] Memorandum, "Sacramento Legislative Trip," Jan. 6–7, 1913 (Panama-Pacific International Exposition MSS).

[59] C. C. Moore to Ira Bennett, May 20, 1913 (Panama-Pacific International Exposition MSS).

[60] Memorandum, "Sacramento Legislative Trip," Jan. 6–7, 1913. In addition to the delegation, which was publicized, the Exposition directors put much undercover pressure on legislators, a surprising amount of which is frankly recorded in memoranda in the MSS. See also Hichborn, *Story of the Session of the California Legislature of 1913*, pp. 219–221.

[61] The major alien land bills were Senate Bills 5, 27, and 416 and Assembly Bills 10, 113, 183, and 194. See *Journal, Senate*, 1913, and *Journal, Assembly*, 1913, *passim.*

[62] Chinda's despatches, as cited by Kachi, *op. cit.*, pp. 103–106, 120, 224–225.

[63] Ray Stannard Baker, *Woodrow Wilson: Life and Letters* (New York, 1931), IV, 78. It is not clear whether Baker is citing a letter from Wilson to Bryan or Bryan's subsequent letter to Lister, March 23, 1913.

[64] Kachi, *op. cit.*, p. 236.

[65] Letter, Johnson to Rowell, March 17, 1913 (Rowell MSS).

[66] On March 23 Johnson notified Rowell: "Have informed [Assemblyman E. S.] Birdsall [sponsor of a general antialien land bill] that he may act if he desires" (telegram, Johnson MSS).

[67] Letter, Rowell to C. C. Moore, March 12, 1913 (Rowell MSS); letters, Rowell to Johnson, March 16, 1913, and Johnson to Rowell, March 23, 1913 (Johnson MSS). Rowell, a Johnson appointee to the Exposition Commission, performed most of the liaison between the governor and the Exposition. At least one of the directors feared that the whole procedure might backfire, but the rest seemed willing to trust the governor's judgment.

[68] Letter, Johnson to Theodore Roosevelt, June 21, 1913 (Johnson MSS). See also Hichborn, *op. cit.*, pp. 226-235. Democratic interpretations differed. Phelan felt that "the progressives in control have been forced to agree to pass the law by the Democratic minority." Phelan to Senator Thomas P. Gore (Dem., Okla.), April 5, 1913 (Phelan MSS), Caminetti, more realistically, believed that "political capital no doubt is at the bottom of it all" in regard to the switch of the Progressive majority. Letter, Caminetti to Bryan, April 22, 1913, as cited in Kachi, *op. cit.*, p. 241. Even Chester Rowell, one of Johnson's advisers, was at first left "in the dark" by the switch from a general antialien bill to the more discriminatory measure. Another Johnson supporter, Franklin Hichborn, who publicly praised the measure, also felt that a general antialien land bill would have been preferable. Letters: Rowell to C. C. Moore, April 14, 1913, and Hichborn to Rowell, Sept. 25, 1913 (Rowell MSS).

[69] For Newman see letter, A. P. Bettersworth to Phelan, Dec. 25, 1913 (Phelan MSS). Bettersworth, one of Phelan's clients, was then editor of the Elk Grove *Citizen*. Elk Grove, just south of Sacramento, was in the heart of one of the heaviest concentrations of Issei farmers in the state.

[70] Hichborn, *op. cit.*, pp. 230-231. Newman's oration was well publicized; his former clerical status was not.

[71] *Ibid.; Grizzly Bear*, Nov. 1920, p. 25; letter, Phelan to Gore, April 5, 1913 (Phelan MSS). Scharrenberg represented the reform wing of the San Francisco labor movement. He, too, was European, having been born in Hamburg, Germany. See Paul S. Taylor, *The Sailor's Union of the Pacific*, p. 172. Despite threats to the contrary, Japan eventually exhibited at the 1915 Exposition. Since most European exhibits were cancelled because of the war, the Japanese exhibits were even more important than they would have been otherwise. There was much sentiment in Japan against exhibiting, but her business leaders, putting interest ahead of pride, prevailed in their view.

[72] Kent to Johnson, April 7, 1913 (Johnson MSS). On the formula proposed by Wilson here, Arthur S. Link comments: "it was a transparent ruse, but, as future events were to prove, it would have been enough to satisfy the Japanese government." He then cites a Japanese *aide-mémoire* of July 13, 1913. This was after the final passage of the bill. While the bill was under consideration the Japanese consul informed the Exposition directors that "he had been instructed to say, by his government, that the provision permitting aliens to acquire land after taking out their first papers was regarded by his government as discriminatory." Letter, Rowell to Johnson, March 16, 1913 (Johnson MSS). Link's argument is in *Wilson: The New Freedom* (Princeton, N.J., 1956), p. 291. Kent actually supported Johnson's final

position, and had long been a proponent of anti-Japanese measures. See letters, Kent to Johnson, April 26, 1913, in the Sacramento *Bee* of the same date, and Kent to Bryan, April 7, 1913, in Roy Watson Curry, *Woodrow Wilson and Far Eastern Policy, 1913–1921* (New York, 1957), p. 49; see also Asiatic Exclusion League, *Proceedings*, Aug., 1912, p. 243.

[73] Telegram, Johnson to Kent, April 8, 1913 (Johnson MSS).

[74] Letter, Rowell to Johnson, April 9, 1913 (Rowell MSS).

[75] Telegram, Bryan to Johnson, April 10, 1913 (Johnson MSS). The request for the bill was superfluous since Senator Caminetti was keeping Bryan supplied with copies of bills and a running account of the course of the legislation. See Kachi, *op. cit.*, pp. 221, 241.

[76] Telegram, Johnson to Bryan, April 11, 1913 (Johnson MSS).

[77] Telegram, Johnson to Bryan, April 16, 1913 (Johnson MSS).

[78] Letter, Johnson to Rowell, April 18, 1913 (Rowell MSS).

[79] Link, *op. cit.*, p. 293.

[80] Kachi, *op. cit.*, p. 238. The "picture bride" question, which later became a major complaint of the California exclusionists, had been raised as early as 1910, when the Exclusion League complained of the "importation of Jap women for sinister purposes, by so-called picture marriages under the guise of a marriage by proxy in Japan, remarried here as a mere matter of form, and after a month or a year of so-called married life deserted, or cast into a crib [house of prostitution] is another way of getting women into the country for immoral purposes." Asiatic Exclusion League, *Proceedings*, May, 1910, p. 14.

[81] Bryan's sole contributions seem to have been two rather impractical suggestions: for the Japanese government to withhold voluntarily passports from all landholders (Root had specifically included landholders as admissible under the Gentlemen's Agreement) and a farfetched proposal to distribute California's Japanese equally among the other states. See Kachi, *op. cit.*, p. 238. Bryan returned to this latter idea in 1915, when he wrote to the President: "I see but one way of relieving the Japanese situation on the Coast and that is by the dispersion of the Japanese in this country so as to relieve the economic pressure which has aroused protest [because] the question is not a race question but purely an economic question." Wilson dismissed the idea. Bryan probably was sincere, but it is difficult to see how this population dispersion could have been effected. See letters, Bryan to Wilson, March 8, 1915, and Wilson to Bryan, March 8, 1915, in United States Department of State, *Papers Relating to the Foreign Relations of the United States: The Lansing Papers, 1914–1920* (Washington, 1940), II, 400–402.

[82] Printed in *Journal, Senate*, 1913, p. 1717.

[83] Telegram, Johnson to Woodrow Wilson, April 22, 1913 (Johnson MSS).

[84] Telegrams: Wilson to Johnson, April 23, 1913; Johnson to Wilson, April 23, 1913; Bryan to Johnson, April 23, 1913. Johnson MSS.

[85] The full text of the so-called Webb-Heney Act may be most conveniently found in United States Department of State, *Papers Relating to the Foreign Relations of the United States, 1912–1913* (Washington, 1920), p. 627. It was 206 Cal. Stats. chap. 113. Article 1 sets forth the rights of all aliens eligible to citizenship. The rest of the bill inhibits the rights of Japanese and incidentally other Asians by referring to "all aliens other than those mentioned in Section 1."

[86] Letter, Johnson to Theodore Roosevelt, June 21, 1913 (Johnson MSS).

[87] *Ibid.*

[88] The complete transcript of the executive sessions is in Johnson MSS, Box 41, Part 1. The quotation is on p. 79.

[89] Telegram, Wilson to Bryan, April 29, 1913, as quoted in Baker, *op. cit.*, p. 80.

[90] Phelan, the leading Wilson Democrat in the state, continued to press for the land bill, and he and the President corresponded about it on friendly terms. Wilson wrote: "I think I understand the gravity of the situation in California and I have

never been inclined to criticize. I have only hoped that the doing of the thing might be so modulated and managed as to offend the susceptibilities of a friendly nation as little as possible." Wilson to Phelan, April 9, 1913, as quoted in Baker, *op. cit.*, p. 78.

[91] *Journal, Senate*, 1913, p. 2324; *Journal, Assembly*, 1913, p. 2495.

[92] The timing here is typical of the formal correctness of Johnson's relations with the federal government. He allowed one more day than the normal four days which it then required for mail between Sacramento and Washington before he signed the bill; the letter to Bryan is dated May 14. Johnson also appreciated the formal courtesy which marked Bryan's dealings with him. Wilson was sarcastic; one of his wires to Johnson begins: "Thank you for your patriotic telegram." Wilson to Johnson, April 23, 1913 (Johnson MSS).

[93] Johnson to Bryan, May 14, 1913 (Johnson MSS). When Americans were being discriminated against, Johnson's idea of "justified offense" was somewhat broader. Writing to a California rabbi about Russia's refusing passports to American Jews, he argued: "I take it that one of the prerequisites to a nation's vitality is the protection of its citizens. Where the citizens of any one nation are debarred from the privileges that are freely accorded those of another, that nation, itself, is the sufferer, and the question far transcends in importance the personality of the individual debarred." Johnson to Rabbi Martin A. Meyer, Dec. 15, 1911 (Johnson MSS).

[94] Johnson to Roosevelt, June 21, 1913 (Johnson MSS). This long letter, which has been cited several times, is a narrative of the whole course of the land act, and is given in full in Appendix B. A recent study has characterized Theodore Roosevelt as Hiram Johnson's "political father confessor." See A. Lincoln, "Theodore Roosevelt, Hiram Johnson, and the Vice Presidential Nomination of 1912," *Pacific Historical Review*, 28 (Aug., 1959), 283–298.

[95] Rowell to Johnson, April 11, 1913 (Rowell MSS).

[96] For clarification of some of the legal devices used to circumvent the various alien land laws, I am indebted to the late Guy C. Calden, of Berkeley, who explained the matter to me in August and September, 1959. Calden and his partner were the leading attorneys for Japanese in northern California. They were employed both by individuals and by the Japanese Association of America.

[97] For the exchanges see United States Department of State, *Papers Relating to the Foreign Relations of the United States, 1912–1913*, pp. 629–653.

[98] See Eleanor Tupper and George E. McReynolds, *Japan in American Public Opinion* (New York, 1937), pp. 62–63, and the survey of press opinion in *Oriental Review*, 3 (May-June, 1913), 485.

[99] Letter, Anti-Jap Laundry League to Johnson, Jan. 25, 1915 (Johnson MSS). The Laundry League, not a part of McCarthy's machine, had consistently favored anti-Japanese measures. It was, however, never a significant influence, owing to its restricted membership, which was confined solely to laundry workers in and around San Francisco. The dying Exclusion League continued its opposition. See the San Francisco *Chronicle*, May 19, 1913.

[100] San Francisco *Chronicle*, May 7, 1913. Bell's threatened action worried both Johnson and Phelan. Johnson hired private detectives to determine Bell's course of action. See letters, W. A. Mandell to Al McCabe (Johnson's secretary), May 31, 1913 (Johnson MSS). Phelan warned the President of his rival's activities in a letter showing his agreement with Wilson's policy. "I think I understand the attitude of the administration on the Japanese question. You admit the evil and seek by the least offensive means to cure it. Reactionary politicians are talking of a referendum, which will utterly fail, and, at the same time, it may do great injury to the party prestige in California." Phelan to Wilson, May 8, 1913 (Phelan MSS).

[101] Los Angeles *Times*, April 23, 1913. The San Francisco *Chronicle* was similarly opposed; see its editorial of May 2, 1913. The Hearst papers and most of the rest of the California press supported the act. See Los Angeles *Examiner*, April 22, 1913;

Sacramento *Bee*, Jan. 8, 1913; Sacramento *Union*, Jan. 8, 1913. The smaller news-papers of central California were almost unanimously in favor of the act; the Visalia *Times*, March 22, 1913, is perhaps typical.

[102] *California Christian Advocate*, May 8, 1913.

Chapter V: The Yellow Peril

[1] The degree to which a racist ideology permeated American thought from the 1880's to the 1930's has only recently begun to be a subject of investigation for historians, partly because so many historians themselves subscribed to racist think-ing. The best treatment is the chapter "Racism—Toward the History of an Idea" in John Higham, *Strangers in the Land* (New Brunswick, N.J., 1955), pp. 131–157. There are extremely perceptive comments in Oscar Handlin, *The American People in the Twentieth Century* (Cambridge, Mass., 1954), especially pp. 14–46; see also his *Race and Nationality in American Life* (New York, 1957). A fine monograph by Barbara Miller Solomon, *Ancestors and Immigrants* (Cambridge, Mass., 1956), delineates the ruling assumptions of the Brahmins of the Immigration Restriction League; Edward N. Saveth's *American Historians and European Immigrants* (New York, 1948), dissects the biases of historians; Richard Hofstadter's *Social Darwin-ism in American Thought* (Philadelphia, 1944), is invaluable for the climate of opinion in which intellectual nativism flourished. The works of early continental racists seem not to have had a crucial influence in the formation of American racism. Count Arthur de Gobineau's *Essai sur l'inégalité des races humaines* (1853) seems to have had no American edition between 1856 and 1915, and Houston Stewart Chamberlain, *Grundlagen des neunzehnten Jahrhunderts* (1899) remained happily inaccessible to most Americans until its translation in 1910. Two English works, however, were quite influential: Charles H. Pearson, *National Life and Character* (London, 1893) and Benjamin Kidd, *The Control of the Tropics* (New York, 1898). Both took extremely pessimistic views of the ability of the white races to control tropical areas and discussed the possibility of whites everywhere being swamped by the sheer numbers of their colored "inferiors." Theodore Roosevelt reviewed Pear-son's book in *Sewanee Review*, 2 (May, 1894), 365–367. An enlightening account of scientific attitudes toward race in America before the Civil War is William Stanton, *The Leopard's Spots* (Chicago, 1960).

[2] 163 U.S. 537. John W. Burgess, an influential academic, wrote approvingly in 1898 that: "the Republican party, in its work of imposing the sovereignty of the United States upon eight millions of Asiatics, has changed its view in regard to the political relations of races and has at last virtually accepted the ideas of the South on that subject." Cited in C. Vann Woodward, *Origins of the New South, 1877–1913* (Baton Rouge, 1951), p. 325.

[3] Of course, non-Anglo-Saxon Americans, like Finley Peter Dunne's Mr. Dooley, often didn't agree. "An Anglo-Saxon," according to the sage of Archey Road, "is a German that's forgot who was his parents." *Mr. Dooley in Peace and War* (Boston, 1898), p. 54.

[4] In the same year, a character in William Dean Howells' *A Traveler from Altruria* (New York, 1894), assumes the imminent restriction of immigration (p. 92).

[5] Although Woodrow Wilson and the League of Nations are properly cited as casualties of this postwar reaction, it is too often forgotten that Wilson exacerbated rather than eased nativist tendencies. Speaking at Pueblo, Colorado, Sept. 25, 1919, in a typical passage he blamed all opposition to the League on foreign elements. "I find, moreover, that there is an organized propaganda against the League of Nations and against the treaty proceeding from exactly the same sources that the organized propaganda proceeded from which threatened this country here and there with disloyalty, and I want to say—I can not say too often—any man who carries a hyphen about with him carries a dagger that he is ready to plunge into the vitals of this Republic whenever he gets ready. If I can catch any man with a hyphen in

this great contest I will know that I have got an enemy of the Republic. My fellow citizens, it is only certain bodies of foreign sympathies, certain bodies of sympathy with foreign nations that are organized against this great document which the American representatives have brought back from Paris." Albert Shaw (ed.), *Messages and Papers of Woodrow Wilson* (New York, 1924), pp. 1113–1114. Other attacks on hyphenates were less restrained. In a not atypical passage Walter Hines Page insisted that "we Americans have got to throw away our provincial ignorance ... hang our Irish agitators and shoot our hyphenates and bring up our children with reverence for English history and in the awe of English literature." Letter, Page to Edwin A. Alderman (president of the University of Virginia), June 22, 1916, in Burton J. Hendrick (ed.), *Life and Letters of Walter Hines Page* (New York, 1923), II, 144. Oscar Handlin has astutely commented that the hyphenate designation "never seemed to apply to the link in Anglo-American." *The American People in the Twentieth Century*, p. 121.

⁶ The equation of radicalism with foreigners seems to have become prevalent after the Haymarket riots of 1886 and been heightened by Czolgosz' assassination of McKinley in 1901. As early as 1892 Chauncey Depew could view immigrant radicalism with alarm. "The ranks of anarchy and riots number no Americans. The leaders boldly proclaim that they come here not to enjoy the blessings of liberty and to sustain our institutions but to destroy our institutions, cut our throats, and divide our property." Quoted in Merle Curti, *The Growth of American Thought* (New York, 1951), p. 494. Henry May, *The End of American Innocence* (New York, 1959), points out that responsibility for the white-slave rings was also laid at the door of new immigrants (p. 347).

⁷ Their most widely read works were Grant's *The Passing of the Great Race* (New York, 1916) and Stoddard's *The Rising Tide of Color Against White World-Supremacy* (New York, 1920) and *Revolt Against Civilization: The Menace of the Under Man* (New York, 1922). Both of these writers were later "discovered" by the Nazis; between 1933 and 1937 Stoddard had six editions in the Third Reich, while Grant had four. *Deutsches Bücherverzeichnis*, Vol. 17, p. 1012; V⁻¹. 18, p. 1168; Vol. 20, p. 934; Vol. 21, p. 1093.

⁸ Madison Grant, Introduction to Stoddard's *Rising Tide of Color*, pp. xxix–xxxii.

⁹ *Ibid.*, pp. 297–303.

¹⁰ *Ibid.*, p. 305.

¹¹ *Ibid.*, p. 309.

¹² The only full-length treatment is Richard Austin Thompson's "The Yellow Peril, 1890–1924" (Unpublished dissertation, University of Wisconsin, 1957). He speaks of a "cultural peril," an "economic peril" and a "military peril." This division probably confuses more than it clarifies. My own definition of the term yellow peril is the fear of the imminent invasion of the continental United States, by named or unnamed Oriental powers, usually Japan. Thompson discusses at much greater length most of the "scare" literature mentioned here, plus a vast body of other material.

¹³ For perhaps the earliest American notice of Wilhelm II's phobia see *Review of Reviews*, 12 (Dec., 1895), 474.

¹⁴ New York *Tribune*, May 1, 1869. For an early amplification of this theme see H. J. West, *The Chinese Invasion* (San Francisco, 1873).

¹⁵ P. A. Dooner, *The Last Days of the Republic* (San Francisco, 1880); Lorelle, "The Battle of the Wabash," *The Californian*, 2 (Oct., 1880), 364–366; Robert Woltor, *A Short and Truthful History of the Taking of California and Oregon by the Chinese in the Year A.D. 1899* (San Francisco, 1882). None has the slightest trace of any literary merit.

¹⁶ Alfred Vagts, *Landing Operations* (Harrisburg, Pa., 1946), discusses "Overseas Invasion-Fear as a State of Modern Mind" (pp. 425–438) and gives many examples of this type of literature, none of which concerns the yellow peril. He suggests that "nations in an insular position will above everything else react violently to an

invasion threat." Such fears often lay heavily upon Americans; on various occasions in the late nineteenth and the twentieth centuries the expected attacker has been Germany, England, and even poor, decrepit Spain!

[17] Quoted in John A. Garraty, *Henry Cabot Lodge* (New York, 1953), p. 199. In 1895 Lodge warned Congress that the Japanese "understand the future; they realize the prospects which are opening up before them. . . . There they are, our nearest neighbor on the Pacific; there they are with Hawaii lying halfway between us. Remember that they are a new people; they have just whipped somebody, and they are in a state of mind when they think that they can whip anybody." *Ibid.*

[18] U.S. Congress, Senate, *Annexation of Hawaii*, 55th Cong., 2d sess., Report 681 (Washington, 1898), p. 31. Italics in original. Apart from the war scares of 1906–1907 and 1912–1913, when discussion was concentrated, this sort of antagonism toward Japan is scattered throughout the *Congressional Record* and other official documents, particularly in the hearings on naval appropriation bills.

[19] His newspapers boasted of it. See their advertisement—"For More Than 50 Years the Hearst Newspapers Kept Warning America about Japan"—in *Business Week*, Sept. 1, 1945, pp. 34–35. The advertisement asserts that they had maintained a consistent anti-Japanese policy since the 1890's.

[20] Baron K. Suyematsu, "There Is No Yellow Peril," San Francisco *Examiner*, July 2, 1905.

[21] *Ibid.*, Sept. 8, 1905.

[22] *Ibid.*, Dec. 20, 1906. See also issues of Feb. 4 and 7, and Sept. 1, 1907. No attempt has been made to catalogue all the Hearst yellow peril "news stories." Even the comic strips were called into play. At the time of the round-the-world cruise of the American fleet Mutt and Jeff were shown watching the fleet enter the Golden Gate. Mutt exclaims, "Does not yon sight make you want to punch a Jap in the nose?" Issue of May 6, 1908.

[23] *Ibid.*, excerpted from issues of Jan. 1 and 10, 1907. This story, in one form or another, is still being repeated in California. I have talked to several persons who said that they knew someone who saw such drilling—variously placed in Hawaii, Mexico, and California. There is no evidence that Japanese immigrants at any time formed military organizations, actual or potential, in the Western Hemisphere. Some of the Issei, in common with some European immigrants of the period emigrated in order to avoid military service at home.

[24] Letter, Phelan to Chicago *Tribune*, n.d. (probably Dec., 1906, or Jan., 1907), in Phelan MSS.

[25] Elting E. Morison, "Richmond Pearson Hobson," *Dictionary of American Biography*, Supplement Two, pp. 308–309. Hobson later became a crusader of a different sort, fulminating against the liquor interests and the narcotics traffic. He was also active in the jingoistic Navy League, as was James D. Phelan, who helped Hobson arrange lecture tours and lent money to him.

[26] San Francisco *Examiner*, Nov. 3 and 10, 1907. He expanded upon the theme in three articles for Hearst's *Cosmopolitan* magazine the next year. Hobson first made these assertions in a Washington interview in September, 1907. Strangely, the *Examiner* denounced him editorially, stating that "there is no [war] cloud in the sky . . . the clouds [are] in the mentality of Captain Richmond Pearson Hobson." Issue of Sept. 13, 1907. Whether this was a subordinate's blunder or deliberate policy I am not prepared to say.

[27] *Ibid.*, May 7, 1908. Naturally, Hobson drew a great amount of criticism. A magazine often described as the editorial spokesman for Roosevelt commented that "Captain Hobson belongs to the small but noisy army of those who are beating the tom-tom on the Japanese question and doing all they can to stir up trouble." "Captain Hobson Corrected," *Outlook*, 88 (Feb. 29, 1908), 470. See also "The Superhuman Japanese," *Nation*, 86 (Jan. 16, 1908), 51.

[28] Herbert G. Wells, *The War in the Air* (London, 1908), p. 229.

[29] There is no biography of Lea. Frederick L. Chapin, in "Homer Lea and the Chinese Revolution" (Unpublished Senior thesis, Harvard University, 1950), has accumulated much Lea material and is the only writer to use Lea's papers, but his work is devoid of analysis and mainly acritical. The best analysis of Lea's thought is John F. Mallan, "Roosevelt, Brooks Adams and Lea: The Warrior Critique of the Business Civilization," *American Quarterly*, 8 (Fall, 1956), 216–237. Mallan is somewhat unfair to both Lea and Roosevelt. Many of the points he makes were indicated earlier in Hofstadter, *Social Darwinism in American Thought*, chap ix.

Much of the Lea legend is based on two books by the journalist Carl Glick: *Double Ten: Captain O'Bannion's Story of the Chinese Revolution* (New York, 1945) and *Swords of Silence: Chinese Secret Societies Past and Present* (New York, 1947). Glick's information about Lea rests mainly on the statements of O'Bannion, a former sergeant in the U.S. Marine Corps, who helped Lea drill a few Chinese in the United States. O'Bannion later was convicted of smuggling Chinese into the United States and was sent to prison. Memoir accounts of Lea's California activities are: Harry Carr, *Riding the Tiger* (New York, 1934), and Marco R. Newmark, "Homer Lea," *Historical Society of Southern California Quarterly*, 37 (June, 1955), 177–184. A contemporary military opinion may be found in the obituary "Concerning Homer Lea," *Infantry Journal*, 9 (Nov.–Dec., 1912), 403. See also the New York *Times* and New York *Tribune* for Nov. 2, 1912. Paul Kaufman, "Homer Lea," in the *Dictionary of American Biography* (XI, 69–70), overestimates Lea's importance in China and does not even have all the vital data correct; e.g. he states that Lea never married, which is incorrect. The Lea MSS, or parts of them, are in the possession of Lea's stepson, Mr. Joshua B. Powers, a New York publisher's representative.

Mrs. Luce's elaboration of the Lea legend first appeared as "Ever Hear of Homer Lea?" in the *Saturday Evening Post*, March 7 and 14, 1942. It was used as identical Introductions to the reissues of Lea's books in 1942. She embraced all the extravagances of the earlier writers and added a few picturesque details of her own. Compare Lea, *The Day of the Saxon*, pp. 25–26 (1942 ed.), with Carr, *op. cit.*, p. 173, on which it is based.

Valeriu Marcu in his article "American Prophet of Total War" attempts a serious appraisal of Lea as a military thinker, but entirely misses the point. *American Mercury*, 54 (April, 1942), 413–480. Lea's thinking, which was based on the assumption that only large-scale professional armies with long-term enlistments could function effectively, was obsolete after the French Revolution, as the results of the Franco-Prussian War demonstrated. Lea, like his contemporary Mahan, took his sociopolitical assumptions from the nineteenth century, which gave a pseudo-modern cast to his military thought, which would not have been alien to Frederick the Great.

[30] The two most important Lea works are *The Valor of Ignorance* (New York, 1909) and *The Day of the Saxon* (New York, 1912). Both of these were republished in early 1942. The second told of the decline of the British Empire. Lea planned, but did not complete, a third major work, *The Swarming of the Slav*, which, had it ever been published, would undoubtedly have been reissued about 1946. Lea earlier had published a very bad novel, *The Vermillion Pencil: A Romance of China* (New York, 1908), about which the less said the better. Four short articles, first uncovered by Chapin, *op. cit.*, seem to round out the Lea corpus: "Can China Fight," *World Today*, Feb., 1907; "How Socialism Failed in China," *Van Norden's Magazine*, Sept.–Oct., 1908; "The Aeroplane at War," *Harper's Weekly*, Aug. 20 and 27, 1910; and "The Legacy of Commodore Perry," *North American Review*, June, 1913.

[31] *The Valor of Ignorance*, pp. 307–308.

[32] *Ibid.*, pp. 116–134.

[33] *Ibid.*, pp. 7–8.

[34] *The Day of the Saxon*, p. 7

[35] *The Valor of Ignorance*, chart facing p. 252.

[36] Chief of Staff to Secretary of War, Dec. 21, 1907, quoted in Outten J. Clinnard, *Japan's Influence on American Naval Power* (Berkeley and Los Angeles, 1947), p. 62.

[37] See Louis Morton, "War Plan Orange: Evolution of a Pacific Strategy," *World Politics* (Jan., 1959), 221–250.

[38] The statement of Admiral Yamamoto in December, 1941, about "dictating peace in the White House" was not the vain boast that American propagandists made it out to be, but a sober warning to the other militarists that the only way to defeat the United States was by an invasion of the North American continent, which the majority of Japanese military leaders knew was beyond their capabilities. Generally, the naval officers, who had seen more of the world, were more cautious than Japanese army officers. In the United States the converse situation seems generally to have prevailed.

[39] Clinnard, *op. cit.*, p. 89.

[40] Letter, Roosevelt to Charlemagne Tower (U.S. Ambassador to Germany), Nov. 19, 1907, in *Roosevelt Letters*, V, 853. There is a good account of the 1907 war scare in Thomas A. Bailey, *Theodore Roosevelt and the Japanese-American Crises* (Stanford, Calif., 1934), pp. 228–260; see also his "The Root-Takahira Agreement of 1908," *Pacific Historical Review*, 9 (March, 1940), 19–37

[41] These were really two separate scares. Late in Taft's administration the Hearst press fabricated a report that the Japanese government had bought Magdalena Bay, in Baja California, from Mexico. Henry Cabot Lodge, for one, was quite alarmed. See Eugene Keith Chamberlin, "The Japanese Scare at Magdalena Bay," *Pacific Historical Review*, 34 (Nov., 1955), 345–66. A second scare developed early in 1913 in connection with the Japanese protests against the California Alien Land Act; see Arthur S. Link, *Wilson: The New Freedom* (Princeton, N.J., 1956), pp. 90 ff.

[42] Cleveland *Plain Dealer*, May 11, 1913. This was a wire-service story and was printed throughout the country.

[43] Letter, Viereck to Bernhard Dernberg, May 14, 1915, in United States Congress, Senate, *Brewing and Liquor Interests and German and Bolshevik Propaganda*, 66th Cong., 1st sess., Doc. 62 (Washington, 1919), Vol. 2, p. 1426; hereinafter cited as *German Propaganda Hearings*. See also Viereck's own account, *Spreading Germs of Hate* (New York, 1930), pp. 110 ff.

[44] A. Roadmaker [Otto Frederick Wegner], *Preparedness for the Pacific Coast* (Seattle, 1916).

[45] *German Propaganda Hearings*, pp. 1458–1459.

[46] San Francisco *Examiner*, Oct. 3 and 10, 1915.

[47] *German Propaganda Hearings*, pp. 1613–1614. The cartoon, in a slightly different version, appeared in most Hearst papers on March 13, 1917, and is reproduced in Samuel Hopkins Adams, "Invaded America," *Everybody's Magazine*, 37 (Dec., 1917), 9–16, 86. Adams's article, placed by the Creel committee, is an attack on various types of antiwar propaganda.

[48] *German Propaganda Hearings*, pp. 1675–1676. For *Patria* see also James P. Mock and Cedric Larson, *Words That Won the War* (New York, 1939), pp. 143–147.

[49] *German Propaganda Hearings*, pp. 1675–1676. The yellow peril theme was well exploited by Hollywood. Another 1916 film, *The Flying Torpedo*, was a science-fiction fantasy in which the Oriental invaders were unnamed. For a critique of Hollywood anti-Orientalism see Jacobus tenBroek, Edward N. Barnhart and Floyd W. Matson, *Prejudice, War, and the Constitution* (Berkeley and Los Angeles, 1954), pp. 29–32.

[50] Letter, Franklin Delano Roosevelt to George Foster Peabody, Sept. 26, 1923, as quoted in William L. Neumann, "Franklin D. Roosevelt and Japan, 1913–1933," *Pacific Historical Review*, 22 (May, 1953), 148. See also Roosevelt's "Shall We Trust Japan?" *Asia*, 23 (July, 1923), 475–478, 526, 528. Professor Neumann says its original title was "The Japs—A Habit of Mind." The future President was

highly critical of the yellow peril and was sanguine about the future of Japanese-American relations.

[51] Clinnard, *op. cit.*, p. 2.

[52] Josephus Daniels, *The Wilson Era: Years of Peace, 1913–1917* (Chapel Hill, N.C., 1944), p. 168. Daniels was cordially hated by most professional naval officers on two counts: he barred liquor from all ships and tried to introduce more democracy into the service. He was one of the few service secretaries in recent history who succeeded in maintaining an essentially civilian outlook.

[53] Valentine Stuart McClatchey, *The Germany of Asia* (Sacramento, 1919).

[54] What Lenin correctly called a "vast literature" has only been sampled here. It must be remembered that the yellow peril was much more effective outside California, where Japanese were relatively unknown, than within it. The stereotype of the bucktoothed, nearsighted "Jap," who mangled English, hissed "so sorry," knew jujitsu, and, incidentally, was a spy, was essentially a creation of the years after 1924 and need not concern us. The earliest example of a stereotype seems to be Wallace Irwin, *Letters of a Japanese Schoolboy* (New York, 1909).

[55] For digests of newspaper opinion see Tupper and McReynolds, *op. cit.*, and the *Literary Digest*. For samplings of individual opinion see Edward K. Strong, *The Second-Generation Japanese Problem* (Stanford, 1934), and Emory S. Bogardus, *Immigration and Race Attitudes* (New York, 1928).

[56] F. Scott Fitzgerald, *This Side of Paradise* (New York, 1920), p. 19.

[57] Rollin Chambliss, "What Negro Newspapers of Georgia Say about Some Social Problems" (Unpublished M.A. thesis, University of Georgia, 1934), quoted in Gunnar Myrdal, *An American Dilemma* (New York, 1944), II, 1195.

Chapter VI: The Pressure Groups Take Over

[1] Franklin Hichborn, *Story of the Session of the California Legislature of 1915* (San Francisco, 1915), pp. 231–232.

[2] On Nov. 16, 1914, Roosevelt wrote to Johnson that "our great object should be to avoid anything that may cause serious trouble with Japan, until the European world-war has come to an end." He sent the governor a similar letter two weeks later. In letters dated Nov. 30 and Dec. 8, 1914, Johnson expressed agreement with Roosevelt's view and assured him that the Progressive majority would prevent passage of any anti-Japanese legislation. All letters in Johnson MSS, Bancroft Library.

[3] For the Japan Society see Lindsay Russell (ed.), *America to Japan* (New York, 1915) and a companion volume, Naoichi Masaoka (ed.), *Japan to America* (New York, 1914). The views of religious leaders and educators can be found most conveniently in the *Independent*, a New York weekly.

[4] The Gulick-Rowell correspondence (Rowell MSS, Bancroft Library) gives an interesting development of Gulick's position as he tries, not entirely without success, to convert a moderate California exclusionist. After 1920 Rowell parted company with the exclusionists.

[5] Sidney L. Gulick, *The American Japanese Problem* (New York, 1914). Gulick's main polemic against the Californians is on pp. 184–196. His views on Southern Europeans are on p. 72; on Negroes, pp. 152–153; on intermarriage, 157–160.

[6] *Ibid.*, p. 304.

[7] *Ibid.*, p. 288. Other facets of Gulick's original proposal included stricter provisions for citizenship and voting, for both native and foreign born, registration of all aliens, and federal authority to curb newspapers which misrepresent international news (see pp. 281 ff.).

[8] "The limitation of the number of each arriving each year to a certain percentage of that race arriving during a given period of years"—*Reports of the Immigration Commission*, Vol. 1, p. 47. For the literacy test see Barbara Miller Solomon, *Ancestors and Immigrants* (Cambridge, Mass., 1956), pp. 115–117 and *passim*. Since the literacy test could be taken in any language and the Japanese immigrants

had a relatively high rate of literacy, this form of restriction found little favor among the California exclusionists. They sometimes suggested that the United States adopt the literacy test scheme used in Australia and New Zealand, under which the inspector, not the immigrant, chose the language. Thus a literate Japanese might be excluded for failing to read an obscure language—e.g. Sanskrit.

⁹ See the list in John Higham, *Strangers in the Land* (New Brunswick, N.J., 1955), pp. 302–303.

¹⁰ Rowell to Flowers, April 27, 1914 (Rowell MSS).

¹¹ Montaville Flowers, *The Japanese Conquest of American Public Opinion* (New York, 1917).

¹² A typescript of the speech is in the Phelan MSS, Bancroft Library.

¹³ *Journal, Senate,* 1919, pp. 999, 1028, 1047, 1065, 1137, 1277, 1317, 1442, 1328, 1524, 1987, 2010. *Journal, Assembly,* 1919, pp. 1408, 1825, 2095. Lansing's message, April 8, 1919, stated in part: "In view of the present situation in international affairs here in Paris, it would be particularly unfortunate to have these bills introduced at this time."

¹⁴ Letters: Phelan to Admiral Jayne (Commandant, 12th Naval District), Aug. 27, 1920, and Commander Wallace Bertholf to Phelan, Oct. 10, 1920 (Phelan MSS).

¹⁵ *Grizzly Bear,* March, 1911, p. 13.

¹⁶ Letter, Phelan to Wilbur, Dec. 6, 1922 (Phelan MSS).

¹⁷ Letter, Phelan to V. S. McClatchy, Nov. 22, 1923 (Phelan MSS).

¹⁸ Letter, Phelan to Sequoia Parlor 160, Native Sons of the Golden West, n.d. (Phelan MSS).

¹⁹ Letter, Phelan to Charles L. Donohoe, Feb. 21, 1923 (Phelan MSS).

²⁰ Letter, Phelan to *The Freeman,* July 19, 1923 (Phelan MSS).

²¹ John S. Chambers to Chester H. Rowell, Sept. 10, 1919 (Rowell MSS).

²² The groups associated with all these are too numerous to list; their activities are best covered in the *Grizzly Bear,* the Sacramento *Bee,* the Los Angeles *Examiner* and the San Francisco *Examiner.* A partial listing of the organizations which formed the Los Angeles Anti-Asiatic Association would include the Los Angeles County Employees Association, Union League Club, Los Angeles Columbus Club, United Church Brotherhood of Pasadena, Democratic County Central Committee, Republican County Central Committee, Eclectic Home Protective Association, Phi Alpha Delta Law Fraternity, Heavy Odd Contractors Association, New York State Society, Los Angeles Employees Association, California League, Boyle Heights Improvement Association, California Congress of Mothers, Parent-Teacher Association, Ebell Club, American Legion, Veterans of Foreign Wars, Native Sons of the Golden West, Native Daughters of the Golden West, Fraternal Order of Eagles, Knights of Pythias, Loyal Order of Moose, Michigan State Society, Jinnistan Grotto, Central Labor Council, United Spanish War Veterans, and Ohio State Society.

²³ Taken from the League's letterhead; see also *Grizzly Bear,* Dec., 1919.

²⁴ *Grizzly Bear,* March, 1913, p. 6.

²⁵ *Ibid.,* Aug., 1913, p. 6. Clarence M. Hunt was editor throughout the period covered here.

²⁶ *Ibid.,* July, 1923, p. 27.

²⁷ Cora M. Woodbridge, "Now's the Time to Take a Stand against the Japs," *Grizzly Bear,* Oct., 1920.

²⁸ *Grizzly Bear,* Dec., 1919, p. 8.

²⁹ *Ibid.,* Feb., 1921, p. 5.

³⁰ *Ibid.,* March, 1922, p. 22.

³¹ Montaville Flowers, "The Third Conflict," *Grizzly Bear,* Dec., 1919. Flowers also proposed that California libraries censor or label pro-Japanese material. Later, V. S. McClatchy was allowed to label the pamphlets in the California State Library. He rather pedantically set up a three-way code—pro-Japanese, pro-California, and offensive to both sides. He failed to find any in the third category.

[32] For the most recent analysis of general Legion attitudes see Roscoe Baker, *The American Legion and American Foreign Policy* (New York, 1954).

[33] As cited in Ruth Kern, "Political Policy and Activities of the American Legion" (unpublished M.A. thesis, University of California, Berkeley, 1926), p. 8.

[34] For the Turlock incident see Raymond L. Buell, "The Development of Anti-Japanese Agitation in the United States," *Political Science Quarterly*, 38 (Mar., 1923) 73, and most California newspapers July 19, 1921 and after. There are also accounts in the New York *Times*.

[35] E.g., Sacramento *Labor Tribune*, Sept. 10, 1920.

[36] See his article "The Attitude of Organized Labor towards the Japanese," *Annals*, 93 (Jan., 1921), 34–38. This issue was devoted to immigration and contains twenty-two short articles on the Japanese question alone, representing various points of view. It is a good sampling of the debate on the more polite levels.

[37] U.S. Congress, House, *Japanese Immigration Hearings*, 66th Cong., 2d sess. (Washington, 1921), Part 3, p. 940. See also Part 2, p. 480, and Part 3, pp. 942, 1008.

[38] *Grizzly Bear*, Nov., 1919, p. 10.

[39] For Legion activities see U.S. Congress, House, *Japanese Immigration Hearings*, Part 2, pp. 475–476. For Native Sons and Daughters see the *Grizzly Bear*, issues of March to July, 1920, *passim*.

[40] Interview with Guy C. Calden, Sept., 1959. (See chap. iv, n. 96.)

[41] The leading case is the Yano case, 188 Cal. 645; the court said in part: "The act of the petitioner in securing conveyances of land to his daughter, while confessedly carried out because the laws of California did not permit him to buy it for himself, was in no sense unlawful since the daughter is a citizen of the United States and entitled to acquire and own real estate."

[42] A notable exception was the Hon. R. J. Thompson of the Superior Court of Sonoma County. In the course of a routine decision involving the 1920 act he delivered the following obiter dicta: "The purpose of the Alien Land Law . . . is to protect our rapidly vanishing fertile soil against the invading horde of brown men who come here and shatter our standards of living and citizenship; who substitute their philosophy of politeness and cunning for the enforcement of the 'golden rule'; who bring to us their Oriental ideas and religion. . . . This is the same race that circumvented . . . the 'gentlemen's agreement,' and brought their women into California for propagation purposes in the guise of 'picture brides.' Over 5,000 of them were born in California last year and 4,300 the previous year, each of whom is a citizen of our country and state. They monopolize our richest fields. Their standards of living are so low we do not wish to compete with them." He went on to praise a current anti-Japanese novel. (Under the laws of California, superior court judges are elected periodically.) Case 8468, Superior Court of Sonoma County, as cited in Consulate General of Japan, San Francisco, *Documental History of Law Cases Affecting Japanese in the United States, 1916–1924* (San Francisco, 1925), II, 929–930.

[43] The final section of the initiative read: "If any section, subsection, clause or phrase of this act is for any reason held to be unconstitutional, such decision shall not affect the validity of the remaining portions of this act. The people hereby declare that they would have passed this act, and each section, subsection, sentence, clause and phrase thereof, irrespective of the fact that any one or more other sections, subsections, sentences, clauses or phrases be declared unconstitutional."

[44] California State Board of Control, *California and the Oriental* (Sacramento, 1922), p. 13. I cite the 2nd, slightly revised edition throughout. Governor Stephens was at first reluctant to climb aboard the anti-Japanese band wagon. His refusal to call a special session of the legislature to deal with the Japanese question caused

the *Grizzly Bear* to denounce him as the "master sleeper." By the summer of 1920 his position was almost identical with that of the exclusionists.

[45] This was arranged by Senator Phelan; see letter, Phelan to Marshall de Motte (chairman, State Board of Control), Dec. 10, 1919 (Phelan MSS). Exclusionists were often able to secure the assistance of agencies of the federal government in their campaign, even though such assistance was in direct opposition to the stated policy of the administrations in power. There is frequent evidence of this lack of discipline in the Phelan and Johnson papers. The most striking case was that of Anthony Caminetti, whose appointment as Commissioner of Immigration was arranged by Phelan in 1913. His appointment, Phelan argued, would quiet the criticism of Wilson by new immigrant groups, and "a Californian in that office ... would help us on the Oriental question...." Letter, Phelan to Charles Fay, Dec. 12, 1912 (Phelan MSS). Caminetti's reports as Immigration Commissioner often paraphrased the exclusionist position, and often attacked the Gentlemen's Agreement, which the State Department was trying desperately to maintain and defend. There are many letters in the Phelan MSS showing that highly placed Army and Navy officers furnished *sub rosa* assistance to the exclusionists. For example, military intelligence officers were intercepting the mail of K. K. Kawikami, a leading Japanese publicist in San Francisco. Senator Phelan was furnished with copies of his letters, including some to Gulick. See letter, Lewis Williams to Phelan, Nov. 25, 1919 (Phelan MSS). See also K. K. Kawikami, *Senator Phelan, Dr. Gulick, and I* (San Francisco, 1920) for the publicist's suspicions.

[46] California State Board of Control, *California and the Oriental*, p. 9.

[47] *Ibid.*, pp. 37–41. From similar figures Phelan warned that "in ninety years there will be more Japanese in California than whites if the present birthrate continues," a calculation which ignores the well-known fact that a vast percentage of California's population came there after being born elsewhere. All the exclusionist population projections seem to have assumed, without mentioning it, that the migration of Caucasians to California would cease. *Grizzly Bear*, Feb., 1920, p. 21. The wildest prediction I have found was that of V. S. McClatchy: "Under the Gulick plan ... Japanese immigration would be increased.... Careful tables of increase of the Japanese population in the United States under that plan ... place the total in 1923 at 318,600; in 1933 at 542,000; in 1943 at 875,000; in 1963 at 2,000,000; in 2003 at 10,000,000; and in 2063 at 100,000,000." "Indisputable Facts and Figures," *Grizzly Bear*, Dec., 1919, p. 2. For less credulous audiences, McClatchy's indisputable facts and figures were somewhat toned down.

[48] A Shortridge advertisement in the *California Legion Monthly*, Oct., 1920 (p. 17) reads: AMERICA FIRST. PROTECTION FOR CALIFORNIA. Twenty-five years ago Shortridge said: 'The Japanese must not come. We do not covet their land, and we are unalterably determined that they shall not possess ours.' "

[49] See Raymond Leslie Buell, "The Development of the Anti-Japanese Agitation in the United States," *Political Science Quarterly*, 38 (March, 1923), 71.

[50] San Francisco *Examiner*, Nov. 1 and 2, 1920. Of roughly one hundred daily and weekly California newspapers examined, only the five following seem to have opposed the 1920 act: San Jose *News*, Richmond *Independent*, Fresno *Republican*, Los Angeles *Express*, and Los Angeles *Times*.

[51] For their side of the story see John P. Irish, *The Anti-Japanese Pogrom* (Oakland, Calif. [1920], and George Shima, *An Appeal to Justice* (Stockton, Calif., [1920]).

[52] Quoted in Tasuku Harada, *The Japanese Problem in California* (San Francisco [1920 or later]). This pamphlet consists of replies to a questionnaire sent out by Harada to a number of prominent Americans. Albert Bushnell Hart was "totally opposed to permanent Japanese immigration [because] it would create a body of residents who are bound to retain a large part of their national characteristics" (p. 62).

⁵³ The leadership of the league was as follows: J. M. Inman, president; Albert E. Boynton, treasurer; Frank C. Tracey, secretary and manager; John S. Chambers, chairman, executive committee; William I Traeger (N.S.G.W.), vice president; Daniel C. Murphy (A. F. of L.), vice president; Fred T. Bebergall (American Legion), vice president; Walter McGovern (Moose), vice president; Mrs. Aaron Schloss (California Federation Women's Clubs), vice president. The executive committee included: James D. Phelan, Mrs. Bradford Woodbridge, H. C. Lichtenberger, Buron A. Fitts, James F. Hoey, William J. Mitchell, Joseph A. Garry, and Waldo F. Postel. The finance committee included Matt I. Sullivan, Louis H. Mooser, and Clarence M. Hunt. See letter, Joseph A. Garry to Phelan, March 28, 1921 (Phelan MSS).

⁵⁴ Most of this information is gleaned from the McClatchy-Johnson and McClatchy-Phelan correspondence in the Bancroft Library. See also Gladys Hennig Waldron, "Antiforeign Movements in California, 1919–1929" (Unpublished dissertation, University of California, Berkeley, 1956).

CHAPTER VII: EXCLUSION

¹ Montaville Flowers, "The Third Conflict," *Grizzly Bear*, December, 1919.

² Peter B. Kyne, *The Pride of Palomar* (New York, 1921); Wallace Irwin, *Seed of the Sun* (New York, 1921). An earlier novel on the same theme, Griffing Bancroft, *The Interlopers* (San Francisco, 1917), had very little circulation. For an analysis of other racist views held by Kyne see Carl Bode, "Cappy Ricks and the Monk in the Garden," *Publications of the Modern Language Association*, 64, March, 1949, 59–69. Cornelius Vanderbilt, Jr., *The Verdict of Public Opinion on the Japanese-American Question* (New York, 1920), is a tub-thumping pamphlet for Kyne's novel by one then trying to gain a foothold in West Coast newspaper publishing.

³ Art. IV.

⁴ Art. I, sec. 8; *Chae Chan Ping* v. *U.S.*, 130 U.S. 581 (1889); *Edye* v. *Robertson, Collector*, 112 U.S. 580 (1884); *Chy Lung* v. *Freeman*, 92 U.S. 275 (1875).

⁵ U.S. Congress, Senate, *The Immigration and Naturalization Systems of the United States* (Washington, 1953), p. 93.

⁶ *Smith* v. *Turner; Norris* v. *The City of Boston*, 48 U.S. 283 (1849).

⁷ 1 Stat. 570; 3 Stat. 489; the former was allowed to expire in June, 1800.

⁸ 18 Stat. 370.

⁹ 22 Stat. 58, 214.

¹⁰ 23 Stat. 232; 24 Stat. 414; 26 Stat. 1084.

¹¹ 28 Stat. 780; 32 Stat. 825.

¹² 32 Stat. 1213.

¹³ 39 Stat. 874.

¹⁴ *Cong. Record*, 66th Cong., 3d sess., p. 10.

¹⁵ *Ibid.*, p. 286.

¹⁶ *Ibid.*, p. 3443.

¹⁷ *Ibid.*, pp. 3937, 3973.

¹⁸ *Cong. Record*, 66th Cong., 3d sess., p. 417.

¹⁹ 42 Stat. 5.

²⁰ 42 Stat. 540.

²¹ *Cong. Record*, 66th Cong., 3d sess., p. 571–72.

²² Letter, Johnson to V. S. McClatchy, Dec. 22, 1920 (Johnson MSS, Bancroft Library.

²³ Telegram, Johnson to McClatchy, Jan. 3, 1921 (Johnson MSS).

²⁴ Letter, Johnson to Roland S. Morris, Jan. 21, 1921 (Johnson MSS).

²⁵ Letter, V. S. McClatchy to Johnson, May 6, 1921; see also letter, McClatchy to J. V. A. MacMurray (chief, Far Eastern Desk, State Department), May 3, 1921. Johnson MSS.

[26] Letter, Johnson to California delegation, April 9, 1921 (Johnson MSS).

[27] Undated memorandum, ca. April 28, 1921 (Immigration Committee folder, Johnson MSS). Senators serving included Harry F. Ashurst, William E. Borah, Thomas J. Walsh, George W. Norris, Key Pittman, and Charles L. McNary. Representatives included Carl Hayden and John Nance Garner. Years later Norris wrote: "I never trusted Japan. My record of forty years in the House of Representatives and the Senate of the United States is free from the taint of racial prejudice." George W. Norris, *Fighting Liberal* (New York, 1945), p. 208. In letters dated April 14 and 22, 1922, he assured Johnson of his complete support on the Japanese question (Johnson MSS).

[28] Letter, Chambers to Phelan, n.d. (Phelan MSS, Bancroft Library).

[29] Letter, McClatchy to Johnson, May 19, 1922 (Johnson MSS).

[30] Copy in files of California Joint Immigration Committee, Documents Division, University of California Library, Berkeley.

[31] Based on correspondence in the California Joint Immigration Committee files.

[32] *Ozawa* v. *United States,* at 260 U.S. 189.

[33] For a critical analysis of the court's thinking, see Milton R. Konvitz, *The Alien and the Asiatic in American Law* (Ithaca, N.Y., 1946), pp. 79 ff. In the same term the court also denied citizenship to Japanese veterans who had served with American forces during the First World War. On the basis of a separate statute, many of these had been granted citizenship by district courts in Hawaii and Washington. See *Toyata* v. *United States,* 260 U.S. 178. The best account is Harry Maxwell Naka, "The Naturalization of the Japanese Veterans of the American World War Forces" (Unpublished M.A. thesis, University of California, Berkeley, 1938). The following year there was some talk in Congress of passing a bill to give citizenship to Japanese veterans. Phelan dismissed it as an "uninformed and foolish sentiment" and added, rather illogically, "It is not citizenship they want—it is land." Letter, Phelan to Albert Johnson, Dec. 27, 1923 (Phelan MSS). In 1936 Congress did pass special legislation giving citizenship to a few Japanese veterans. See Naka, *op. cit.*

[34] Letter, V. S. McClatchy to Executive Committee, Jan. 23, 1923 (Phelan MSS).

[35] The most detailed account of the congressional battle over Japanese exclusion is Rodman W. Paul, *The Abrogation of the Gentlemen's Agreement* (Cambridge, Mass., 1936). Partially because of evidence unavailable to him, my conclusions are somewhat different. For an earlier, briefer, and sounder view see Earl H. Pritchard, "The Japanese Exclusion Bill of 1924," *Research Studies of the State College of Washington,* Vol. 2, No. 2 (Aug., 1930), pp. 65–76.

[36] Stanley Kunz of Chicago, Fiorello LaGuardia of New York, and Theodore Burton of Cleveland were the only members to indicate opposition; *Cong. Record,* 68th Cong., 2d sess., pp. 5681, 62. There is a lively account of the debates on immigration in the House in Arthur Mann, *LaGuardia: A Fighter Against His Time* (New York, 1959).

[37] *Cong. Record,* 68th Cong., 2d sess., p. 5681.

[38] U.S. Congress, Senate, *Japanese Immigration Hearings,* 68th Cong., 1st sess. (Washington, 1924), pp. 5–6, 34.

[39] *Cong. Record,* 68th Cong., 2d sess., p. 5415.

[40] *Ibid.,* p. 5475.

[41] *Ibid.,* p. 5741.

[42] Letter, Hughes to Sen. Louis Frotheringham, April 7, 1924. *Ibid.,* p. 5882.

[43] See U.S. Congress, House, *Restriction of Immigration,* 68th Cong., 1st sess., Report 350 (Washington, 1924), p. 7.

[44] *Cong. Record,* 68th Cong., 2d sess., p. 5829.

[45] U.S. Department of State, *Foreign Relations of the United States, 1924* (Washington, 1939), p. 338.

[46] Lodge's biographer, John A. Garraty, feels that Lodge's role was not crucial, and adduces the overwhelming vote as proof of this. He completely ignores the

possibility of a veto, which Lodge's maneuver made futile; Calvin Coolidge was no man to make a *beau geste* three months before a convention. See Garraty, *Henry Cabot Lodge* (New York, 1953), pp. 406–408.

[47] United States Department of State, *Foreign Relations of the United States, 1924,* pp. 372–373.

[48] *Cong. Record,* 68th Cong., 2d sess., pp. 6208–6209.

[49] Cf. Paul, *op. cit.,* p. 84.

[50] *Cong. Record,* 68th Cong., 2d sess., p. 6302.

[51] *Ibid.,* p. 6305.

[52] *Ibid.*

[53] *Ibid.,* p. 6315.

[54] See chap. iii.

[55] U.S. Department of State, *Papers Relating to Pacific and Far Eastern Affairs Prepared for the Use of the American Delegation to the Conference on the Limitation of Armament, Washington, 1921–1922* (Washington, 1922), p. 702.

[56] Cf. Merlo J. Pusey, *Charles Evans Hughes* (New York, 1951), II, 512–516. Pusey, a very friendly biographer, does admit that Hughes was "not willing to take responsibility" for the Hanihara letter, although clearly the responsibility was his.

[57] Letter, Phelan to Thomas B. Doyle, April 14, 1924 (Phelan MSS).

[58] See Gladys Hennig Waldron, "Antiforeign Movements in California, 1919–1929 (Unpublished dissertation, University of California, Berkeley, 1956).

A SELECT BIBLIOGRAPHY

A SELECT BIBLIOGRAPHY

MANUSCRIPTS

Hugh B. Bradford. Scrapbook pertaining to the Alien Land Law of 1913 and other matters. California State Library, Sacramento.

California Joint Immigration Committee. MSS. Documents Division, University of California Library, Berkeley.

Franklin Hichborn. MSS. Bureau of Governmental Research, University of California, Los Angeles.

Hiram Johnson. MSS. Bancroft Library, University of California, Berkeley.

Walter MacArthur. MSS. Bancroft Library.

Victor H. Metcalf. Scrapbook pertaining to discrimination against Japanese in San Francisco, 1906. Bancroft Library.

Panama-Pacific International Exposition. MSS. Bancroft Library.

James D. Phelan. MSS. Bancroft Library.

Chester H. Rowell. MSS. Bancroft Library.

THESES AND DISSERTATIONS

Chapin, Frederick L. "Homer Lea and the Chinese Revolution." Unpublished Senior thesis, Harvard University, 1950.

Hale, Robert Moffett. "The United States and Japanese Immigration." Unpublished dissertation, University of Chicago, 1945.

Hennings, Robert. "James D. Phelan and the Wilson Progressives of California." Unpublished dissertation, University of California, Berkeley, 1961.

Hertzog, Dorothy Beatrice. "The History of Japanese Exclusion from the United States." Unpublished M.A. thesis, University of Southern California, 1931.

Kachi, Teruko Okada. "The Treaty of 1911 and the Immigration and Alien Land Law Issue between the United States and Japan, 1911–1913." Unpublished dissertation, University of Chicago, 1957.

Kern, Ruth. "Political Policy and Activities of the American Legion." Unpublished M.A. thesis, University of California, Berkeley, 1926.

McLoughlin, Peter Martin. "Japanese and the Labor Movement in British Columbia." Unpublished Bachelor's Honors thesis, University of British Columbia, 1951.

Matson, Floyd William. "The Anti-Japanese Movement in California, 1890–1942." Unpublished M.A. thesis, University of California, Berkeley, 1953.

Matsui, Shichiro. "Economic Aspects of the Japanese Situation in California." Unpublished M.A. thesis, University of California, Berkeley, 1922.

Morishita, Shidzus. "The Ineligible to Citizenship Provisions of the Immigration Act of 1924 with Special Reference to Japanese." Unpublished J.D. thesis, University of California, Berkeley, 1926.

Naka, Harry Maxwell. "The Naturalization of the Japanese Veterans of the American World War Forces." Unpublished M.A. thesis, University of California, Berkeley, 1938.

Naka, Kaizo. "Social and Economic Conditions among Japanese Farmers in California." Unpublished M.A. thesis, University of California, Berkeley, 1913.

Nepomuceno, Larry Arca. "Japanese Restriction in California, 1900–1913." Unpublished M.A. thesis, University of California, Berkeley, 1934.

Niesley, Margaret. "California and the Anti-Japanese Movement." Unpublished M.A. thesis, University of Southern California, 1931.

Robbins, Albert M. "Exclusionism as a Factor in the Relations of Japan and the United States, 1913–1924." Unpublished M.A. thesis, University of Southern California, 1954.

Thompson, Richard Austin. "The Yellow Peril, 1890–1924." Unpublished dissertation, University of Wisconsin, 1957.

Weisend, William Frederick. "The Anti-Japanese Movement in California." Unpublished M.A. thesis, University of California, Berkeley, 1931.

Waldron, Gladys Hennig. "Antiforeign Movements in California, 1919–1929." Unpublished dissertation, University of California, Berkeley, 1956.

STATE AND FEDERAL GOVERNMENT PUBLICATIONS

California Legislature. *Journal of the Assembly of the State of California.* Sacramento, 1901–1923.

———. *Journal of the Senate of the State of California.* Sacramento, 1901–1923.

California State Board of Control. *California and the Oriental.* Sacramento, 1922.

California State Library, Sacramento. "Alien Ownership of Land. Select list of references to material in the California State Library." *News Notes of California Libraries,* 9 (1914), 414–420.

Consulate General of Japan, San Francisco. *Documental History of Law Cases Affecting the Japanese in the United States, 1916–1924.* 2 vols. San Francisco, 1925.

United States Bureau of the Census. *Chinese and Japanese in the United States, 1910.* Washington, 1914.

———. *Thirteenth Census of the United States, 1910.* Washington, 1910.

———. *Fourteenth Census of the United States, 1920.* Washington, 1920.

United States Commissioner of Labor. *Report of the Commissioner of Labor on Hawaii, 1901.* Washington, 1902.

United States Congress. *Congressional Record.* Washington, 1898–1924.

———. House of Representatives. Committee on Immigration and Naturalization. *Hearings on Japanese Immigration.* Washington, 1921.

———. ———. *Restriction of Immigration.* Washington, 1924.

———. Senate. *Annexation of Hawaii.* Washington, 1898.

———. ———. *Brewing and Liquor Interests and German and Bolshevik Propaganda.* 3 vols. Washington, 1919.

———. ———. *The Immigration and Naturalization Systems of the United States.* Washington, 1953.

———. ———. *Japanese in the City of San Francisco.* Washington, 1907.

———. ———. *Some Reasons for Japanese Exclusion.* Washington, 1902.

United States Department of Justice. *Annual Report of the Attorney General of the United States, 1903.* Washington, 1903.

United States Department of State. *Foreign Relations of the United States, 1911–1924.* 21 vols. Washington, 1919–1939.

———. *Papers Relating to the Foreign Relations of the United States: The Lansing Papers, 1914–1920.* 2 vols. Washington, 1939–1940.

———. *Papers Relating to the Pacific and Far Eastern Affairs Prepared for the Use of the American Delegation to the Conference on the Limitation of Armament, Washington, 1921–1922.* Washington, 1922.

United States Immigration Commission. *Reports of the Immigration Commission.* 25 vols. Washington, 1909–1911.

United States Industrial Commission. *Reports of the Industrial Commission.* 15 vols. Washington, 1901.

NEWSPAPERS

California Christian Advocate (San Francisco).

Cleveland *Plain Dealer.*

Coast Seaman's Journal (San Francisco)

Elk Grove *Citizen.*

Fresno *Republican.*

Grizzly Bear (Los Angeles).

Long Beach *Press.*

Los Angeles *Examiner.*

Los Angeles *Express.*

Los Angeles *Times.*

New York *Times.*

New York *Tribune.*

New York *World.*

Pacific Rural Press (San Francisco).

Richmond *Independent.*

Sacramento *Bee*

Sacramento *Daily Record-Tribune.*

Sacramento *Labor Tribune.*

Sacramento *Union.*

San Francisco *Alta California.*

San Francisco *Argonaut.*

San Francisco *Bulletin.*

San Francisco *Call.*

San Francisco *Chronicle.*

San Francisco *Daily News.*

San Francisco *Examiner.*

San Francisco *Labor Clarion.*

San Francisco *Morning Call.*

San Jose *News.*

San Luis Obispo *Breeze.*

Visalia *Times.*

Watsonville *Register.*

BOOKS

Bailey, Thomas A. *Theodore Roosevelt and the Japanese-American Crises.* Stanford, Calif.: Stanford University Press, 1934.

Baker, Ray Stannard. *Woodrow Wilson: Life and Letters.* 8 vols. New York: Doubleday, Doran, 1927–1938.

Baker, Roscoe. *The American Legion and American Foreign Policy.* New York: Bookman Associates, 1954.

Bancroft, Griffing. *The Interlopers.* New York: Bancroft, 1917.

Bean, Walton. *Boss Ruef's San Francisco.* Berkeley and Los Angeles: University of California Press, 1952.

Bogardus, Emory S. *Immigration and Race Attitudes.* New York: Heath, 1928.

Carr, Harry. *Riding the Tiger.* New York: Houghton Mifflin, 1934.

Chambers, Clarke A. *California Farm Organizations.* Berkeley and Los Angeles: University of California Press, 1952.

Clinnard, Outten J. *Japan's Influence on American Naval Power.* Berkeley and Los Angeles: University of California Press, 1947.

Conroy, Hilary. *The Japanese Frontier in Hawaii, 1869–1898.* Berkeley and Los Angeles: University of California Press, 1953.

Coolidge, Mary Roberts. *Chinese Immigration.* New York: Holt, 1909.

Crawford, Persia Campbell. *Chinese Coolie Emigration to Countries Within the British Empire.* London, 1923.

Curry, Roy Watson. *Woodrow Wilson and Far Eastern Policy, 1913–1921.* New York: Bookman Associates, 1957.

Curti, Merle. *The Growth of American Thought.* New York: Harper, 1951.

Daniels, Josephus. *The Wilson Era: Years of Peace, 1913–1917.* Chapel Hill, N.C.: University of North Carolina Press, 1947.

Davis, Winfield J. *History of Political Conventions in California, 1849–1892.* Sacramento, 1893.

Dunne, Finley Peter. *Mr. Dooley in Peace and War.* Boston: Small, Maynard, 1898.

Eaves, Lucille. *A History of California Labor Legislation.* Berkeley: University of California Press, 1910.

Fitzgerald, F. Scott. *This Side of Paradise.* New York: Scribner, 1920.

Flowers, Montaville. *The Japanese Conquest of American Public Opinion.* New York: Doran, 1917.

Foner, Philip S. *Jack London, American Rebel.* New York: Citadel, 1947.

Frignet, Ernest. *La Californie.* 2d ed. Paris, 1867.

Fuller, Varden L. *The Supply of Agricultural Labor as a Factor in the Evolution of Farm Organization in California.* Part 54 of *Hearings before a Subcommittee of the Committee on Education and Labor, United States Senate, Seventy-Sixth Congress, Third Session, pursuant to S. Res. 266 (74th Congress).* Washington, 1940.

Garraty, John A. *Henry Cabot Lodge.* New York: Knopf, 1953.

Glick, Carl. *Double Ten: Captain O'Bannion's Story of the Chinese Revolution.* New York: McGraw-Hill, 1945.

———. *Swords of Silence: Chinese Secret Societies Past and Present.* New York: McGraw-Hill, 1947.

Grant, Madison. *The Passing of the Great Race.* New York: Scribner, 1916.

Gulick, Sidney L. *The American Japanese Problem.* New York: Scribner, 1914.

Handlin, Oscar. *The American People in the Twentieth Century.* Cambridge, Mass.: Harvard University Press, 1954.

———. *Race and Nationality in American Life.* Boston: Little, Brown, 1950.

Heco, Joseph. *The Narrative of a Japanese: What He Has Seen and the People He Has Met in the Course of the Last Forty Years.* Tokyo, 1895.

Hendrick, Burton J. (ed.). *The Life and Letters of Walter Hines Page.* 3 vols. New York: Doubleday, Page, 1922–1925.

Hichborn, Franklin. *The Story of the Session of the California Legislature of 1909; . . . 1911; . . . 1913; . . . 1915.* San Francisco, various publishers, 1909–1916.

Higham, John. *Strangers in the Land.* New Brunswick, N.J.: Rutgers University Press, 1955.

Hofstadter, Richard. *The Age of Reform.* New York: Knopf, 1955.

———. *Social Darwinism in American Thought.* Philadelphia: University of Pennsylvania Press, 1944.

Howells, William Dean. *A Traveller from Altruria.* New York: Harper, 1894.

Ichihashi, Yamato. *Japanese in the United States.* Stanford, Calif.: Stanford University Press, 1932.

Irwin, Wallace. *Letters of a Japanese Schoolboy.* New York: Doubleday, Page, 1909.

———. *Seed of the Sun.* New York: Doran, 1921.

Jerome, Harry. *Migrations and Business Cycles.* New York: National Bureau of Economic Research, 1926.

Jessup, Philip C. *Elihu Root.* 2 vols. New York: Dodd, Mead, 1938.

Johnson, Allen, and Malone, Dumas (eds.). *Dictionary of American Biography.* 20 vols., 2 suppls. New York: 1928–1958.

Kawakami, Karl K. *The Real Japanese Question.* New York: Macmillan, 1921.

Kennan, George F. *American Diplomacy, 1900–1950.* Chicago: University of Chicago Press, 1951.

Kidd, Benjamin. *The Control of the Tropics.* New York: Macmillan, 1898.

Kipnis, Ira. *The American Socialist Movement, 1897–1912.* New York: Columbia University Press, 1952.

Kneko, Hizakazu. *Manjiro, the Man Who Discovered America.* Boston: Little, Brown, 1956.

Konvitz, Milton R. *The Alien and the Asiatic in American Law.* Ithaca, N.Y.: Cornell University Press, 1946.

Kuykendall, Ralph. *The Earliest Japanese Labor Immigration to Hawaii.* Honolulu: University of Hawaii Press, 1935.

Kyne, Peter B. *The Pride of Palomar.* New York: Cosmopolitan, 1921.

Lea, Homer. *The Day of the Saxon.* New York: Harper, 1912.

————. *The Valor of Ignorance.* New York: Harper, 1909.

————. *The Vermillion Pencil.* New York: McClure, 1908.

Link, Arthur S. *Wilson: The New Freedom.* Princeton, N.J.: Princeton University Press, 1956.

————. *Wilson: The Road to the White House.* Princeton, N.J.: Princeton University Press, 1947.

McKenzie, R. D. *Oriental Exclusion.* Chicago: University of Chicago Press, 1928.

McWilliams, Carey. *Prejudice.* Boston: Little, Brown, 1944.

Mann, Arthur. *LaGuardia: A Fighter Against His Time.* Philadelphia: Lippincott, 1959.

Masaoka, Naoichi (ed.). *Japan to America.* New York: Putnam, 1914.

May, Henry. *The End of American Innocence.* New York: Knopf, 1959.

Michener, James A. *Hawaii.* New York: Random House, 1959.

Mock, James P., and Larson, Cedric. *Words That Won the War.* Princeton, N.J.: Princeton University Press, 1939.

Morison, Elting E. (ed.). *The Letters of Theodore Roosevelt.* 8 vols. Cambridge, Mass.: Harvard University Press, 1951–1954.

Mowry, George E. *The California Progressives.* Berkeley and Los Angeles: University of California Press, 1951.

Myrdal, Gunnar. *An American Dilemma.* 2 vols. New York: Harper, 1944.

Paul, Rodman W. *The Abrogation of the Gentlemen's Agreement.* Cambridge, Mass.: Harvard University Press, 1936.

Pearson, Charles H. *National Life and Character.* London: Macmillan, 1893.

Porter, Kirk H., and Johnson, Donald B. *National Party Platforms.* Urbana, Ill.: University of Illinois Press, 1956.

Pusey, Merlo J. *Charles Evans Hughes.* 2 vols. New York: Macmillan, 1951.

Richardson, James D. (ed.). *Messages and Papers of the Presidents.* 11 vols. Washington, 1911.

Russell, Linsay (ed.). *America to Japan.* New York: Putnam, 1915.

Sandmeyer, Elmer C. *The Anti-Chinese Movement in California.* Urbana, Ill.: University of Illinois Press, 1939.

Saveth, Edward N. *American Historians and European Immigrants.* New York: Columbia University Press, 1948.

Schurz, William Lytel. *The Manila Galleon.* New York: Dutton, 1959.

Shaw, Albert (ed.). *The Messages and Papers of Woodrow Wilson.* 2 vols. New York: Review of Reviews, 1924.

Sioli, Paolo. *Historical Souvenir of El Dorado County, California.* Oakland, 1888.

Solomon, Barbara Miller. *Ancestors and Immigrants.* Cambridge, Mass.: Harvard University Press, 1956.

Stanton, William. *The Leopard's Spots.* Chicago: University of Chicago Press, 1960.

Steffens, Lincoln. *The Shame of the Cities.* New York: McClure, 1904.

Stoddard, Lothrop. *Revolt Against Civilization: The Menace of the Under Man.* New York: Scribner, 1922.

———. *The Rising Tide of Color Against White World-Supremacy.* New York: Scribner, 1920.

Strong, Edward K. *The Second Generation Japanese Problem.* Stanford, Calif.: Stanford University Press, 1934.

Swisher, Carl Brent. *Stephen J. Field.* Washington: Brookings Institution, 1930.

Taylor, Paul S. *The Sailor's Union of the Pacific.* New York: Ronald, 1923.

tenBroek, Jacobus, Barnhart, Edward N., and Matson, Floyd W. *Prejudice, War, and the Constitution.* ("Japanese American Evacuation and Resettlement," III.) Berkeley and Los Angeles: University of California Press, 1954.

Thomas, Dorothy Swaine, with the assistance of Charles Kikuchi and James Sakoda. *The Salvage.* ("Japanese American Evacuation and Resettlement," II.) Berkeley and Los Angeles: University of California Press, 1952.

Thomas, Dorothy S., and Nishimoto, Richard. *The Spoilage.* ("Japanese American Evacuation and Resettlement," I.) Berkeley and Los Angeles: University of California Press, 1946.

Tupper, Eleanor, and McReynolds, George E. *Japan in American Public Opinion* New York: Macmillan, 1937.

Vagts, Alfred. *Landing Operations.* Harrisburg, Pa.: Military Service Publishing Company, 1946.

Viereck, George Sylvester. *Spreading Germs of Hate.* New York: Liveright, 1930.

Weintraub, Hyman. *Andrew Furuseth, Emancipator of the Seaman.* Berkeley and Los Angeles: University of California Press, 1959.

Wells, Herbert G. *The War in the Air.* London, 1908.

West, H. J. *The Chinese Invasion.* San Francisco: 1873.

Wilson, F. M. Huntington. *Memoirs of an Ex-Diplomat.* Boston: Little, Brown, 1945.

Wilson, Woodrow. *A History of the American People.* 5 vols. New York: Harper, 1901.

Wolter, Robert. *A Short and Truthful History of the Taking of California and Oregon by the Chinese in the Year A.D. 1899.* San Francisco, 1882.

Woodward, C. Vann. *The Origins of the New South, 1877–1913.* Baton Rouge: Louisiana State University Press, 1951.

Young, Charles H., *et al. The Japanese Canadians.* Toronto: University of Toronto Press, 1938.

PAMPHLETS

Adams, Romanzo. *The Japanese in Hawaii.* New York: 1924.

Asiatic Exclusion League. *Proceedings.* San Francisco, 1907–1912. Issued sporadically.

Asiatic Exclusion League of North America. *Proceedings.* San Francisco, 1908.

Bigler, John. *Governor's Special Message on the Subject of Chinese Coolie Immigration.* Sacramento, 1852.

Burke, William G. *The Japanese School Segregation Case, Respondent's Brief.* [San Francisco (?), 1907 (?)].

Gompers, Samuel. *Meat vs. Rice.* Washington, 1901.

Gulick, Sidney Lewis. *Anti-Japanese War Scare Stories.* New York: 1917.

Harada, Tasuku. *The Japanese Problem in California.* San Francisco [1920 or later].

Irish, John P. *The Anti-Japanese Pogrom.* Oakland [1920].

Johnson, Herbert B. *Discrimination against Japanese in California,* Berkeley, 1907.

Kawakami, Karl K. *Senator Phelan, Dr. Gulick, and I.* San Francisco, 1920.

McClatchy, Valentine Stuart. *The Germany of Asia.* Sacramento, 1919.

Shima, George. *An Appeal to Justice.* Stockton, Calif. [1920].

Vanderbilt, Cornelius, Jr. *The Verdict of Public Opinion on the Japanese-American Question.* New York, 1920.

ARTICLES

Adams, Samuel Hopkins. "Invaded America," *Everybody's Magazine,* 37 (Dec., 1917), 9–16, 86.

Auerbach, Jerrold S. "Progressives at Sea: The La Follette Act of 1915," *Labor History,* 2 (Fall, 1961), 344–360.

Bailey, Thomas A. "California, Japan and the Alien Land Act Legislation of 1913," *Pacific Historical Review,* 1 (March, 1932), 36–59.

———. "The Root-Takahira Agreement of 1908," *Pacific Historical Review,* 9 (March, 1940), 19–36.

Bode, Carl. "Cappy Ricks and the Monk in the Garden," *Publications of the Modern Language Association,* 64 (March, 1949), 59–69.

Boothe [Luce], Clare, "Ever Hear of Homer Lea?" *Saturday Evening Post,* 214 (March 7 and 14, 1942).

Boudin, Louis B. "Immigration at Stuttgart," *The International Socialist Review,* 8 (Jan., 1908), 489–497.

Buell, Raymond Leslie. "The Development of the Anti-Japanese Agitation in the United States," *Political Science Quarterly,* 37 (Dec., 1922), 605–638, and 38 (March, 1923), 57–81.

"Captain Hobson Corrected," *Outlook,* 88 (Feb. 29, 1908), 470.

Chamberlin, Eugene Keith, "The Japanese Scare at Magdalena Bay," *Pacific Historical Review,* 34 (Nov., 1955), 345–366.

"Concerning Homer Lea," *Infantry Journal,* 9 (Nov.-Dec., 1912), 403.

Dorland, C. P. "The Chinese Massacre at Los Angeles in 1871," *Historical Society of Southern California, Proceedings,* 3 (1894), 22–30.

Flowers, Montaville. "The Third Conflict," *Grizzly Bear,* Dec., 1919, pp. 3-4.

Fujita, M. "The Japanese Associations in America," *Sociology and Social Research,* (Jan.-Feb., 1929), 211–217.

Hansen, Marcus L. "The History of American Immigration as a Field for Research," *American Historical Review,* 32 (April, 1927), 500–518.

Hearst Newspapers. Advertisement in *Business Week,* Sept. 1, 1945, pp. 34–35.

Kennan, George. "The Japanese in the San Francisco Public Schools," *Outlook,* June 1, 1907.

King, Cameron H., Jr. "Asiatic Exclusion," *The International Socialist Review,* 8 (May, 1908), 661–669.

Lincoln, A. "Theodore Roosevelt, Hiram Johnson and the Vice Presidential Nomination of 1912," *Pacific Historical Review,* 28 (Aug., 1959), 267–283.

McClatchy, Valentine Stuart. "Indisputable Facts and Figures," *Grizzly Bear,* Dec., 1919, pp. 1, 2, 10.

Mallan, John F. "Roosevelt, Brooks Adams and Lea: The Warrior Critiques of the Business Civilization," *American Quarterly,* 8 (Fall, 1956), 216–237.

Marcu, Valeriu. "American Prophet of Total War," *American Mercury*, 54 (April, 1942), 473–480.

Morton, Louis. "War Plan Orange: Evolution of a Pacific Strategy," *World Politics* (Jan., 1959), 221–250.

Neuman, William L. "Franklin D. Roosevelt and Japan, 1913–1933," *Pacific Historical Review*, 22 (May, 1953), 143–153.

Newmark, Marco R. "Homer Lea," *Historical Society of Southern California Quarterly*, 37 (June, 1955), 177–184.

North, Hart H. "Chinese and Japanese Immigration to the Pacific Coast," *California Historical Society Quarterly*, 28 (Dec., 1949), 343–350.

Nuttall, Z. "Earliest Relations Between Mexico and Japan," *University of California Publications in American Archaeology*, 4 (1906), 1–47.

Pritchard, Earl H. "The Japanese Exclusion Bill of 1924," *Research Studies of the State College of Washington*, Vol. 2, No. 2 (Aug., 1930), pp. 65–76.

Rademaker, John A. "The Japanese in the Social Organization of the Puget Sound Region," *American Journal of Sociology*, 40 (Nov., 1934), 338–343.

Reischauer, Robert Karl. "Alien Land Tenure in Japan," *Transactions of the Asiatic Society of Japan*, 2d ser., 13 (July, 1936).

Roosevelt, Franklin Delano. "Shall We Trust Japan?" *Asia*, 23 (July, 1923), 475–478, 526, 528.

Roosevelt, Theodore. "The Control of the Tropics" (book review), *Sewanee Review*, 2 (May, 1894), 365–367.

Rowland, Donald. "The United States and the Contract Labor Question in Hawaii, 1862–1900," *Pacific Historical Review*, 2 (Sept., 1933), 249–269.

Scharrenberg, Paul. "The Attitude of Organized Labor Towards the Japanese," *Annals of the American Academy of Political and Social Science*, 93 (Jan., 1921), 34–38.

"The Superhuman Japanese," *Nation*, 86 (Jan. 16, 1908), 51.

Woodbridge, Cora M. "Now's the Time to Take a Stand Against the Japs," *Grizzly Bear*, Oct., 1920, p. 3.

Yanaga, C. "The First Japanese Embassy to the United States," *Pacific Historical Review*, 9 (March, 1940), 113–138.

Yoshida, Yosaburo. "Sources and Causes of Japanese Immigration," *Annals of the American Academy of Political and Social Science*, 34 (Sept., 1909), 159–162.

Young, John P. "The Support of the Anti-Oriental Movement," *Annals of the American Academy of Political and Social Science*, 34 (Sept., 1909), 234–239.

INDEX

INDEX

Agassiz, Louis, 83
Alien Land Law (1913), 45, 58–64, 88
Alien Land Law, (1920), 87–92
Alien Regulation League, 84
Altman, Aaron, 32
American Committee of Justice, 90
American Federation of Labor, 22, 30.
  See also California State Federation
  of Labor
Americanization League, 84
American Legion, 85–88, 90–91, 105
American Peace Society, 79, 86
Anthony, Marc, 48
Anti-Chinese movement, 16–19, 20–23
Anti-Japanese League of Alameda
  County, 28
Anti-Jap Laundry League, 28, 64
Aoki, Viscount Siuzo, 37, 38, 41
Arthur, Chester Alan, 18
Asiatic Exclusion League, 27–29, 32–34,
  45, 48, 50–52, 75

Baker, A. C., 56
Barrows, David P., 90
Beard, Charles A., 80
Beck, James M., 80
Bell, Theodore A., 49, 50, 64
Berger, Victor, 30, 86
Bigler, John, 16
Bryan, William Jennings, 22, 39, 46, 47,
  58–62
Buddhism in California, 15
Building Trades Council of San Fran-
  cisco, 28, 29

California and the Oriental, 88, 89
California Delta Farms, Inc., 48
California Farm Bureau Federation, 87,
  91
California Federation of Women's Clubs,
  85, 91
California Joint Immigration Commit-
  tee, 105
California Legislature: 1905, 27; 1907,
  41–43; 1909, 47–48; 1911, 50–54;
  1913, 57–64; 1915, 79; 1919, 81–83
California Oriental Exclusion League,
  84
California State Federation of Labor,
  59, 79, 85, 87, 91, 105
California State Grange, 85, 87, 91, 105
Caminetti, Anthony, 43, 54, 59, 62
Canbu, William P., 79

Cannon, Joseph G., 29
Chaffee, Adna R., 77
Chambers, John S., 84, 92, 97
Chandler, Harry, 64
Chinda, Sutemi, 57, 58, 61
Chinese Exclusion Act, 3, 7, 8, 11, 18, 19,
  21, 22, 24, 47, 69, 92, 93
Chinese in California, 3, 8, 9, 11, 16–19,
  22–23
Chinese in Hawaii, 5
Clark, Champ, 54
Clark, John Bates, 80
Clinnard, Outten J., 74
Coast Seaman's Journal, 19
Colby, Bainbridge, 88
Colt, LeBaron, 99
Committee on American-Japanese Rela-
  tions, 79
Conroy, Hillary, 5, 6
Cook, Captain James, 5
Coolidge, Calvin, 103

Daniels, Josephus, 77
Dam, Cleveland L., 21
Davis, Cushman K., 69
Davis, James J., 100
De Young, Michel H., 25, 45
Dillingham, William P., 94, 95

Executive Committee of Western States,
  96

Federal Council of the Churches of
  Christ in America, 79, 86
Fiske, Bradley A., 77
Fitzgerald, F. Scott, 77
Flowers, Montaville, 81, 83, 86, 92
Fourteen Counties Association, 84
Fox, Edward Lyell, 75
Fresno *Republican*, 23
Furuseth, Andrew, 28

Gage, Henry T., 22
Gentlemen's Agreement, 6, 41, 44, 45, 52,
  81, 82, 85–86, 95
George, Henry, 16, 69
Gibbons, James, Cardinal, 80
Gillett, James N., 42, 43, 47, 48
Gold Hill Colony, 3
Grant, Madison, 67
Griscom, Lloyd C., 35
Grizzly Bear, 85, 86
Gulick, Sidney Lewis, 79–83, 86, 105

Roger Daniels teaches United States history at the University of California, Los Angeles. He served in the merchant marine during World War II and in the United States Army during the Korean War. He is married and the father of two children. He has published articles and book reviews in a number of historical journals including the *Journal of American History, Labor History, Pacific Historical Review, Journal of Economic History, Southern California Quarterly,* and *Pacific Northwest Quarterly.*